KEEPING THE FAITH

In the Trenches with
College Football's Worst Team

SHAWN FURY

THE LYONS PRESS
Guilford, Connecticut
An imprint of The Globe Pequot Press

To Louise, my all in one

The Lyons Press is an imprint of The Globe Pequot Press

10 9 8 7 6 5 4 3 2 1

Printed in the United States of America

ISBN 1-59228-764-6

Top photo on page 3 of photo insert courtesy of Lee Odell.
All other interior photos © John Brewer.

Library of Congress Cataloging-in-Publication Data is available on file.

Contents

Acknowledgments

This book couldn't have been written without the help of numerous people, but the cooperation of one person was absolutely vital: Rusty Bentley. Bentley enthusiastically agreed to let me hang around him and his team, on the field and off of it. For that I will always be grateful. Coaches can be a surly lot even if they're winning all the time. Not many would manage to be gracious while losing week after week. Bentley struggled to find any type of success on the field, but he was still unfailingly helpful and the doors to his office and home were always open. Bentley's wife, Sage, was also a friendly face who always had time to answer questions, even when dealing with four young children afflicted with colds.

But the Bentleys weren't alone in their graciousness. Eric Slivoskey and his wife, Essy, were perpetually friendly and forthright, whether they were suffering through another defeat on the field or relaxing at home with their two children. Eric was always thoughtful and honest with his assessments of the football program. The only troubles with talking to Eric were the feelings of envy I'd have whenever I heard another story about one of his world travels.

Brandon Strong has maybe ten minutes a day when he's not occupied with a job or schoolwork, but he always managed to find time to help me out with any inquiry.

To a man, Trinity's players were accepting of my presence and eager to help in any way possible. They want to win as much as players at a high-level program, but their frustrations never prevented them from answering my questions. They also allowed me to hang out with them in their dorms, homes, and classrooms. In particular, I'd like to thank Andy Brower, Neil Huenefeld, Lee Odell (and his wife, Jacqui), Josh McGillvrey, Sannon Norick, Matt Johanson, Lester Williams, Dustin Nichols, Will Hill, Dustin Harper, Dusty Hess, Tony Snyder, Michael Moss, Isaac Smith, Josh Thompson, Mike Martin, Nick Skief, Noah Wedan, Kevin Libby, and Nelson Felix-Tolentino. Thanks also to Trinity assistant, and former player, Tim Rasmussen.

Jerry Rush and his wife, Mona, were delightful dinner companions, and always had goodies ready for me at the concession stand.

The Trinity administration provided their full support, even though they may have always been a little leery of the entire project. They were always willing to talk about the challenges of leading a small college. They include Dennis Niles, Dan Kuno, Steve Tvedt, Michael Dusing, and Tim Grant.

Pastor John Brady, his wife, Naomi, and daughter, Aleah, opened their home and treated me with overwhelming kindness for more than a month. They welcomed me in when I was a stranger, but it's safe to say that by the time I left "the dungeon," I felt like a member of the family. Without them, my time in Ellendale would have been a lot less enjoyable and a lot less productive.

My friend John Brewer is a superb writer, but for this project I took advantage of his photography skills. His companionship during his time in Ellendale was just as appreciated.

Jeanette Robb-Ruenz, Bob Tatum, and Jesse Godding all provided invaluable insight into Ellendale and Trinity.

I have to thank my editor Tom McCarthy, for his foresight, insight, and gentle guidance. Since his first phone call to me, he's been the biggest believer in this book. But Tom wasn't a one-man show at The Lyons Press. Thanks also to Jessie Shiers, Maggie Peterson, Kaleena Cote, and Eliza Byron.

My aunt and uncle, Monica and Emilio DeGrazia, provided encouragement in the early stages of this project, and Emilio's advice, given several months before I even wrote a word, eventually helped me shape the story in ways I wouldn't have been smart enough to figure out.

My parents, Pat and Cees Fury, contributed to this effort in a very tangible way: they gave me free access to their pickup truck for six weeks. But I would have never written this book without their emotional support over the years. They'll always be my biggest fans.

Aida Reyes, Gerald Sampson, and Mike Hammer contributed to the book before it was written, while it was being written, and after it was written. Thanks, guys. My former colleagues, Terry Vandrovec and Dean Witter (yes, it's his real name), were there whenever I needed to bounce an idea off of them or simply needed to rant.

Finally, this book wouldn't have been written without the contributions of my wife, Louise, who forced me to revisit the idea of this book long after I had said it was inconceivable anyone would ever publish it. I relied on her editing skills, her marketing talents, her optimism, and her love.

Introduction

It's three days before Trinity Bible College's biggest game of the season, and practice has started.

If only they had some footballs.

"The way I understand it," says injured defensive lineman Dustin Nichols, "you need a football to play football."

While the team's twenty-five healthy players go through their stretching routines on one end of the practice field, a search party hunts for the AWOL pigskins. No one has seen the ball bag since a game three days earlier.

Assistant coaches Eric Slivoskey and Tim Rasmussen, along with Nichols, figure they are in the storage shed.

Nope.

And they weren't left back in the locker room?

Nope.

"My son has a Nerf ball," Slivoskey offers, adding, "I'm trying to laugh so I don't start to cry."

Welcome to Trinity Bible College Lions football.

The team is preparing for the penultimate game of the 2004 season. Trinity will face Principia College, which defeated Trinity in a controversial fashion one month earlier. The Lions think they have a chance to win this rematch. Some players even think it's a game they *should* win. A victory would be the program's first in three years.

Trinity made headlines and punch lines in 2003. In its first game, Rockford College defeated Trinity 105–0, setting an NCAA Division III record for most points scored in a game. The loss put Trinity on the national football map, though few fans could probably locate the school's host town on one.

Trinity Bible College is located in Ellendale, North Dakota, a tranquil community of no stoplights, eight churches, and 1,559 people. The Pentecostal school produces preachers and missionaries, teachers and business majors. The students love their Lord, and love telling others about that love. With an enrollment of 310 students, half of them male, Trinity has the fewest students of any four-year school in the nation that fields a football team.

And that team, according to some computer rankings, is the worst in the country. The much-reviled Bowl Championship Series, which is designed to pit the two best Division I-A teams against each other for the national title, uses six computer rankings, among other criteria, to create its standings. Peter Wolfe, a California doctor and instructor at UCLA, maintains one of those computer listings. Wolfe's formula rates all 697 NCAA, NAIA, and independent teams in the country. Trinity was ranked 697th in 2004.

Trinity's head coach is Russell "Rusty" Bentley, a forty-one-year-old native Texan who made his collegiate coaching debut in the 105–0 defeat. Bentley arrived in Ellendale with a booming voice, a Barney Rubble laugh, and a Scripture verse for any occasion. His career record stood at 0–17 entering the Principia game.

Bentley's coaching staff consists of three people. Offensive coordinator Eric Slivoskey earns part-time pay, but works full-time hours. Tim Rasmussen, a local youth pastor, is a former Trinity player who now serves as a volunteer coach. Brandon Strong, a twenty-one-year-old student assistant, played for Trinity in 2003. Strong would have been in pads in 2004 if not for two knees that had been ravaged the year before. Instead he helps with coaching and tapes the players' ankles. He is also the school's sports information director and a resident assistant in Kesler Hall on campus.

The season has been draining for the coaches and players, with injuries adding up as fast as the losses. Players question the direction of the program. They feel the team is disorganized and undisciplined. Bentley counters that the players need to take a longer view, see that improvements, however small, are being made.

"There's a method to my madness," Bentley says. "I cannot treat this program like it's a regular program. Because we're not a liberal arts school, we're a Bible college."

A Bible college that could use a victory on the field. A win isn't going to make the team's problems disappear. In fact, some of the players are just happy the game brings them one week closer to the end of the season. But a win would restore a bit of pride. It might even make the injuries and emotional struggles seem worth it.

Several of the team's injured players will return for the Principia game. One of them is fullback Sannon Norick, who had missed the previous game with a neck injury. Norick is in his second year with the Lions. His Trinity football career includes more concussions than victories or 100-yard rushing games.

"I never had a losing season in my career," Norick says. "Coming to where you don't win a game, that sucks. It rips you apart. I was letting it get to me way too much. The situation with coaching and losing all the time, I just couldn't take it anymore. Finally I said, 'I can't dwell on that. Let it go.'"

Maybe a victory would help with those feelings.

Now, where are those footballs?

As the players warm up to chants of "This is our bowl week, baby," Coach Slivoskey suggests searching for the footballs in the Pepsi trailer that doubles as a concession stand on game days. Jerry Rush, a Trinity student and former player, operates the stand, and lives in a trailer park next to the field. Nichols hobbles over to Rush's house and retrieves the key to the stand.

He finds the footballs. The Nerf ball stays in the closet. Practice can begin.

"I think if you evaluated all 697 football programs in America," Strong had said earlier in the week, "you wouldn't find this situation."

He wasn't just talking about the team's practices.

Chapter One

105–0

God wanted this? That's what Rusty Bentley asked himself after the fiasco. During the game he was simply too stunned to think of much of anything.

It certainly didn't look like the work of a just or merciful God.

Two college football coaches made their debuts in Rockford, Illinois, on September 6, 2003. Mike Hoskins had served as Rockford's defensive coordinator before landing the top job. His counterpart was Bentley, fresh from Texas, but new to the collegiate level. Bentley believed God wanted him at Trinity Bible College. Wanted him to move his wife, Sage, and their four young children thirteen hundred miles from Waco, Texas, to Ellendale, North Dakota. Wanted him to lead a team with fewer than thirty players on the roster. And who is Rusty to question God?

The season opener for both Upper Midwest Athletic Conference (UMAC) teams was expected to be something of a mismatch. Trinity, which was coming off a winless season, had six players on the roster who had played organized football the year before. Rockford was at home, had three times as many players, and wanted to give a good showing for its new coach.

After a 735-mile, thirteen-hour ride to Rockford, the Lions piled out of the bus.

"When I saw what we had on the field, with only approximately twenty guys, unless the teams in this conference were pretty poor, I knew we were going to struggle," said first-year Trinity offensive co-ordinator Eric Slivoskey. "When we got off the bus I started looking at the Rockford kids and it looked like a sea of black and purple that never ended and I thought, 'Whoa.'"

Funny thing was, the game started off fine for Trinity. The Lions took the opening kickoff and picked up a first down on their third play from scrimmage, a twenty-yard gain by running back Dexter Edmond. They punted three plays later, however, and from there Rockford's scoreboard operator didn't get a break until the Regents capped off a 105–0 victory, the most points ever scored in a game by a Division III team. They broke the previous record of 97, set by Minnesota's Concordia College in a 1977 contest. Rockford's statistics were absurd, really. Rockford's yardage and points looked like typos or computer mistakes. The Regents attempted only two passes in the game—and both went for first-quarter touchdowns. Running back Marcus Howard carried the ball twenty-nine times for 326 yards and a school-record five touchdowns. The Regents returned three interceptions for scores, and in the second quarter tallied five touchdowns within an eight-minute span, leading to a 63–0 halftime advantage. They matched the effort in the third quarter, scoring five more TDs in eight minutes. Trinity ran sixty-one plays in the game for a total of fourteen yards while Rockford needed only forty-four plays to accumulate 548 yards of offense.

"There's ten minutes left in halftime, and we have three offensive linemen," Slivoskey said of the injury-riddled Lions. "I'm going around to the kids trying to find two more."

Freshman Sannon Norick was one of the Lions drafted into line duty. A 230-pound running back and linebacker by trade, Norick played on an ankle that was sprained in two spots. Earlier, on the first day the Lions hit in practice, Norick suffered a sprain on the outside of the ankle. Back in the locker room, with his ankle propped up on a bench, a teammate accidentally sat down on the injured ankle, twisting it and spraining the inside. He taped it for the Rockford game. "It still hurt," Norick said. "I suited up even though I shouldn't have."

Not surprisingly, Hoskins took heat for running up the score. "The only way that game doesn't get to that point is if we call it off or we take a knee on every play, and I wasn't going to do that," he told *The Forum of Fargo-Moorhead*.

What Hoskins didn't note was star running back Howard still carrying the ball midway through the third quarter, with Rockford clinging to a 91–0 lead. But Hoskins did show some semblance of mercy. If he hadn't, the game could have, well, really gotten out of hand. Howard's fifth and final touchdown gave Rockford a 98–0 lead with six minutes, twenty-two seconds remaining in the *third* quarter. The Regents tacked on a final score in the fourth quarter.

Hoskins said, "I had no idea that it was a national record until our newspaper guy came down and said, 'How does it feel to set a national scoring record?' And right then I thought, uh-oh."

For Trinity's players and coaching staff the reaction was more "oh no." It was the first college game for Brandon Strong, who saw action in the secondary and as wide receiver for the Lions. Strong's most vivid memory is being flattened by a Rockford running back who outweighed him by a hundred pounds. Strong felt embarrassed that his parents, Bob and Connie, who made the five-hour drive from Michigan to see the contest, witnessed the carnage. His father cried after the game.

"I didn't expect college to be that fast," Brandon said. "It was surreal. Every other play, they'd score. What do you do?" Through tears, Bob Strong gave Brandon a hug and told him he was proud of his effort.

Elsewhere, awe had passed and shock set in. After coming up fifteen touchdowns short of victory, a coach doesn't spend too much time worrying about blown pass coverages or shaky run blocking. He ponders life. "I was so shell-shocked I didn't know how to respond," Bentley said. "I asked, 'God, did I miss you on this one?'"

It was a quiet ride home, save for the occasional moan from an aching Lion or the grunt of a player vomiting from exhaustion. Bentley called his wife, Sage, from a McDonald's in Wisconsin and told her the score. "You're kidding," she said. ESPN and newspapers throughout the country reported the score. Internet sites devoted to college football debated everything from whether Hoskins had run up the score (probably, most thought) to whether more prayer could have helped the guys from Trinity Bible College (probably not, most thought). Predictable jokes were tossed around, with references to a defense that parted like the Red Sea and cracks that Trinity took the nonviolence movement way, way too far. John Walters of CNNSI.com wrote a column on Bentley and the team. In his Tuesday Morning Quarterback column on ESPN.com, Gregg Easterbrook quipped, "Postgame speech of Trinity Bible coach Rusty Bentley: 'Well, boys, you held them under 110.'" The exposure proved that for attracting national attention, the only thing better than winning 105–0 is losing 105–0.

Bentley searched for any type of support in the wake of the record defeat. Even Florida State legend Bobby Bowden entered the picture. The folksy Bowden often discusses his Christian beliefs, something Bentley remembered at an opportune time. The week after the Rockford game, Bentley called Bowden's office in Tallahassee and left a message with the all-time winningest coach in Division I football. He said he needed to talk to a "Christian brother," and couldn't think of a better one to ring up. Surprisingly, Bowden returned the call. He encouraged Bentley, told him not to lose his faith, and that the team's fortunes would improve.

Bowden is a better coach than prophet.

Throughout the season, reporters from around the country called the Trinity coaches' office after home games, asking for the most recent score. There were no more triple-digit losses for the Lions, only more beatings. Opponents outscored Trinity on the season by a staggering 585–12, an average margin of defeat of 65 to 1.3. Two touchdowns in nine games. Trinity's defense snared one interception all season. The season included losses of 60–0, 61–0, 77–6, and 63–0, and the team's closest game was a 50–0 defeat against Minnesota's Northwestern.

For Bentley, it was an eye-opening, jaw-dropping experience. But maybe it shouldn't have been. His only previous head coaching experience had been at Parkview Christian Academy in Waco, Texas, where he went 3–7 in his lone season on the job.

The UMAC, a collection of small NCAA Division III, NAIA, and independent schools, had been in his sights for several years. In 1999, he attended a conference game between his wife's alma mater, Northwestern, and Martin Luther, and came away thinking about his future.

"I said then, I can coach at this level," Bentley recalls. "Little did I know, coaching at this level was not going to be just as easy as I anticipated. I thought, I'm going to come in there. I'm not going to wow 'em, but I'm going to put together something that I think, you know, will be satisfactory. And I found out real quickly after my first football game, I'm sure not."

Those words are familiar ones to Trinity athletic director Tim Grant, a wise voice who's also the men's basketball coach. Grant knows how tough it is to recruit athletes to Ellendale. He hired Bentley to replace Jeff Headrick, a former Trinity player who coached the team in 2002. That season ended with no wins and fifteen players on the roster.

"They have this perception of what they're coming into as a college football head coach. And that perception, you can't crack it for nothing," Grant says. "Once getting here and the reality sets in, there's a lot of work here."

A revolving door of quarterbacks took snaps under center for the Lions in 2003. One was thirty-year-old Anthony Werner, a native of Fairbanks, Alaska, who wandered the United States after leaving high school in 1993, still unable to read properly.

"They just kind of pushed me through the system," he told *The Forum.*

Werner, who had a newfound Christianity and aspirations to play college ball, learned about Trinity from an Internet search, and was soon packing his bags for Ellendale.

The gregarious Werner, still lean and in better shape than most thirty-year-olds, spoke of being homeless in Denver, of run-ins with the law, and of a bad marriage to an "older" stripper. Then he found Jesus, and learned how to read about eight months before coming to Trinity.

"I got a speed-reading CD on how to speed-read from a crack head," he told *The Forum*. "I went and worked on speed-reading for like six minutes a day."

Werner, who started the Rockford game, played only two games and left school by the end of the first semester. School officials raised questions about his devotion to religion, and his drinking in the dorms. No matter the age of the student, eighteen or thirty, Trinity doesn't allow alcohol.

Of the Trinity players who were with the team throughout the season, none had a better year than Neil Huenefeld, a physical, curly-haired, 5-foot, 9-inch, 175-pound defensive back who led the UMAC with 128 tackles. Surrounded by teammates with limited experience—several Lions had not even played high school football—Huenefeld was often the last, and only, line of defense. A youth pastor major, Huenefeld, himself the son of a pastor, wondered what role God played during the season. "When we're playing against some of these schools that didn't have a faith, your ego kind of gets up inside of you and you're like, 'God, these guys don't believe in you. I believe in you. Why are we losing this bad?'" he said.

Lack of numbers and talent mostly. They were pulling players out of pews to get them on the field. Following the 105–0 defeat, thirty-three-year-old Jerry Rush joined the team. The burly Rush had never played football, "except in the backyard." He moved from Idaho to Ellendale that summer with his wife, Mona, and their two children, hoping to get involved in evangelism. During a chapel service on campus, Rush said he felt "a heaviness come inside me and I couldn't get rid of it." Convinced that this meant he was supposed to go out for football, Rush approached Bentley and told him, "God put it upon my heart to come and play football for you." Just like that, the Lions had a 320-pound defensive lineman, albeit one with no experience, knee injuries, and a balky back. Still, Rush stayed on the roster throughout the season.

The Lions kept taking the field, week after week, loss after loss, believing that maybe, with a few breaks, or a dozen, the scoreboard might read in their favor. "There wasn't a week I didn't think that,"

Brandon Strong said. "If the ball bounces our way, or if I make a spectacular play, we can win."

They sacrificed their bodies for the cause. Both of Huenefeld's shoulders began popping out of their joints. Strong endured a partial tear to the anterior cruciate ligament and a tear in the meniscus cartilage in his right knee. Two months after the season ended, he had surgery on his left knee to repair a torn meniscus and to clean up scar tissue. Yet he missed only one game.

"We lived on Monday so we could die on Saturday," he said. "Guys had injuries that are going to be with them for the rest of their life. Guys that are going to remember that season, the aches and pains they had. The scars never lie. Never."

It was a season unlike anything the players or coaches had experienced. It was a season unlike anything few—if any—college players or coaches *ever* experience. Two touchdowns in nine games? But they survived. Said Norick, who battled injuries throughout his first season of college football but decided to return, "You think it's going to get better, and, hopefully, you can go out and win some."

And for the players returning in 2004, there was the expectation that nothing could be like 2003.

Chapter Two

Rusty

FALL, 2004

Winners don't get to be martyrs, but it's easy for the coach of the worst team in the country to cast himself as one.

"Everybody is not gonna like everything I do," Rusty Bentley said during his second season as head coach. "It comes out even in personal stuff. That is OK. That is OK. You get told when you go off to a Bible college, you get told when you go to work for a church or on a mission field: you're going to get mistreated by people, but remember you're doing it for the Lord. This is the first time I've ever put those principles a hundred percent into effect. I coach with conviction. God has placed me here so I will coach the way I think he'd want me to."

Maybe there was no other way for Bentley to look at his situation. When reporters contacted him during the 2003 season, they were trying to find the most palatable way to ask, "What's it like being that bad?" That can wear on a coach's self-esteem. So Bentley turned the situation around. He tried to view the season as an opportunity, not as a failure. Most coaches are as pleasant as the flu following a loss, any loss. Bentley, though, welcomed the calls with an eagerness and openness that was surprising, disarming, and sometimes even charming. Instead of wallowing in misery, Bentley said the 105–0 defeat

provided the best publicity Trinity ever received. The attention gave
him the chance to talk about what he saw as the school's true mission.
Each time a reporter asked about the team's struggles, Bentley talked
about the team's desire to "testify" its love of Jesus. Moral victories
were not the goal, he insisted, but the reality of the situation was ap-
parent: this is going to be a long rebuilding project. No matter what
kind of happy face is put on it, losing is draining for anyone.

His first season included conflicts with assistant coaches and
players, who wondered if the stocky, Bible-quoting Bentley knew
more about the Good Book than he did about a playbook. Bentley
expected the Lions to be better in 2004. Better than being outscored
585–12, which means losing by forty points instead of sixty would be
an improvement. Scoring three touchdowns in the season instead of
two would be an improvement. Collecting two interceptions instead
of one would be an improvement. The big question: could the Lions
improve enough to compete and win a game? Bentley has to convince
his players he knows what he's doing, and maybe he has to convince
himself. That's one reason he cherishes the signed, framed photo of
Bobby Bowden proudly displayed in his office in Trinity's Ray Ulmer
Field House. It's not validation from the almighty—Jesus' views on
football have never been articulated—but it is a message from a football god. Here's a coach with zero college victories receiving an "At-
taboy" from a coach with 351. It would be like Bill Gates penning a
congratulatory note to a guy who just filed for bankruptcy. The in-
scription on Bowden's photo reads:

> To coach Bently
> Keep up the good work!
> Bobby Bowden

Bowden's misspelling of Bentley's name dulls the luster of the excla-
mation point. Still, the photo, which Bentley requested from the
Florida State athletic department, is handwritten. It will always be a
keepsake. For Bentley the picture represents proof that he's doing his
job the right way. Yet, even with his convictions, he wonders sometimes. So do others.

"I think his knowledge of the game really comes through, in my perception, more from watching the game on TV," says Neil Huenefeld, the Lions' top player in 2003. "As far as the fundamentals and teaching the blocking, the tackling, the stuff you hate to do but you have to do, that's not being taught."

"I don't prepare to teach a kid how to do a G-block," Bentley says. "That's not what I need to be doing. I need to prepare the game plans, the scheme. The general comes in and says we're going to go over there and tear them up. The general says in a war, 'I want that area over there secure, and I want it done by midnight.' They give the command and the sergeants and the army men, the privates, the corporals, they do what they can to fulfill what he told them to do."

It's a good philosophy if there's a large army, or team, to command. Troubles arise when there just aren't that many underlings available. As the 2004 season approached, Eric Slivoskey was the only other paid member of the staff, and his is a part-time gig. Slivoskey pleaded with Bentley to find some more coaches before practice started.

Others involved with the program wonder if their general needs a reality check. "The whole summer long he's comparing the program to Florida State," says student assistant Brandon Strong, shaking his head. "We're not organized, we're not defined enough where he can just sit back and oversee things."

Trinity did gain one more coach when Tim Rasmussen, the youth pastor at Church of the Nazarene in Ellendale, volunteered to help. It wasn't an easy decision for the Trinity graduate. Rasmussen was an offensive lineman for the Lions in 2003. His brother Dave, also a Trinity student, was an assistant coach that season, and his younger brother, Scott, was a Lions freshman. The tumultuous season turned the big, happy family into a big, angry family. Dave Rasmussen and Bentley verbally sparred during the season, and Rasmussen eventually quit instead of prolonging the hostility. Bentley actually blamed Tim Rasmussen for the team's poor play, an odd accusation against a sole lineman on a team losing by sixty points. Tim Rasmussen, already upset over the fate of his brother and not believing he could still play for a man he no longer respected, also left the Lions. Scott

Rasmussen stayed on, but injuries curtailed his time on the field. Academic probation kept the youngest Rasmussen off the field in 2004. Tim Rasmussen, meanwhile, battled to get past his feelings about his new boss, who also attends the church where Rasmussen serves as youth pastor. "He knew he couldn't just have two coaches out there," Rasmussen says. "I've tried hard to make the relationship right with him. I believe I'm supposed to. We sat down and talked about a lot of the things that happened last year."

Bentley looked and felt like a new man at the start of the season. The round-faced forty-one-year-old shed fifty pounds off his 5-foot, 9-inch, 279-pound frame and seemed energized by his new form. Peanut Butter Cap'n Crunch replaced Snickers as the snack of choice, and he added an exercise program.

Bentley's also expecting a new addition to his family. Sage, his wife of seven years, is pregnant with the couple's fifth child. Her due date is in December, when the baby will join four siblings, all of whom are younger than six. The Bentleys already have names picked out: Molly for a girl, Austin for a boy. There to welcome the newest Bentley will be eldest son Trey (who turns six in November), four-year-old daughter, Annie, two-year-old son, Ty, affectionately known as "Scrubber," and eighteen-month old daughter, Rylee. Chaos often reigns at the Bentleys' Ellendale home, though it's the kind of chaos Rusty would now find impossible to live without. Ty, Rusty's "little linebacker," practices his tackling skills by bouncing off cushions, couches, chairs, siblings, guests, pets, and parents. Rylee is just learning to walk. Unfortunately for her, she's at the stage when she's more likely to fall on her face than complete a successful step. But she's getting there. The Bentleys feel a sense of urgency in getting Rylee moving on feet instead of knees. "We gotta get her truckin' before the new one gets here," Rusty says, "and get Ty out of Pull-Ups. That's gotta be a goal 'cause we can't have three of them in diapers." Bentley admits he's hardest on Trey and coddles Annie the most, maybe because she shares a birthday with him—August 22 (the same as Bill Parcells, Bentley proudly notes). Ty and Sage bond (though Ty's haircut mimics Rusty's: short in the back, short in the front, off the ears), but Rylee is "a Daddy's girl." The Bentleys haul the whole clan around in a pair of Suburbans, a white 1996 model and a red 1999 version, two big vehicles they landed for the price of one. Several baby-sitters take turns helping with the kids, but it's often just Sage, Rusty, and the little ones.

At the Trinity cafeteria one night, all six Bentleys enjoy a dinner of chicken nuggets and chips. Trey complains about his stomach hurting, probably because he estimates he ate "one hundred thousand chips." Annie and her curly golden locks wander around the room, working the crowd like a seasoned stage performer, trying to convince someone, anyone, to give her some ice cream. It's heartbreaking to deny Annie and her nasally requests a cool treat, but no one's willing to give her any without her parents' permission. Finally, ten minutes after starting her Please Feed Me Campaign, Annie is seen next to her father, devouring some ice cream, a faint smile on her face. The charm worked on someone.

Ten years ago Bentley could have hardly imagined this type of life. Rusty met Sage in Texas at a Halloween party in October 1995. Sage dated various men in the ensuing months but avoided Rusty. Bentley was dealing with an increased commitment to his born-again Christian beliefs while Sage was enduring a painful breakup with a man she had planned to marry. "So my frame of my mind was kill every man that I can," she says. "[Rusty] was the only one that was always there. He would call me the next day to make sure I was OK." She finally relented and went out with Bentley in June 1996. They had a short courtship: engaged in September, married on April 5, 1997. "What I put him through, anybody else would have run," Sage says. "Pretty much everybody else *did* run."

Sage teaches a statistics course during the fall semester at Trinity, giving her a chance to escape, for a few hours, the screams, scrapes, and diapers. At least until the next child comes along in December. An attractive brunette nine years Rusty's junior and two inches taller, Sage is the one person Rusty knows is always in his corner, no matter the circumstances on the field. Appropriately, Rusty calls her words of wisdom to him "Sageisms." The two adore Ellendale—"Mayberry," Bentley calls it—and their yellow, four-bedroom house, which is about a two-minute drive from the Trinity campus. Coming from larger cities in Texas, Ellendale's small-town atmosphere is appealing, even if the weather rarely is. As a couple, Sage says it's the first time they have felt at home, adding, "We're not used to all this friendliness."

Bentley grew up in Fort Worth, Texas, the oldest child of Russell and Martha Bentley, who still live in the house Russell bought in 1950. Born in 1963, Rusty was an only child for the first fifty-one weeks of his life, until a baby girl was born. She died three days after her birth, and Rusty said his parents hovered over him until his brother was born two years later. "I was babied beyond measure," he admits. "I remember being twenty-one years old and mowing the yard for my dad, and he's standing at the window watching so I don't get hurt." A self-described brat growing up, Bentley was only six years old when he confidently told a pastor of his dream of someday being a preacher. He recalls, "In grade five or six, I wanted to be a professional football player, and then it'd go back and forth. Do I want to be a preacher? Do I want to be a professional football player?" Nature provided the answer. "I was a late bloomer. Athletically, I always took the easy road. I was a fat kid, and I always took the easy road. But I loved that football, and I could have played. I would have been able to play a lot if I'd been mature enough to just put forth the extra effort out there in practice. And I wish somebody would have sat me down and said, this is where you can get, this is what you can get."

Bentley's path to the college coaching fraternity included more time in a sales office than on a football field. He has sold cars, insurance, and Yellow Pages. His football experience included serving a stint as a "mouse on the wall," at powerful Grapevine High School in Grapevine, Texas, approximately twenty miles northwest of Dallas. Bentley, who received his A.A. from Tarrant County Junior College in Fort Worth and a Biblical studies degree from Louisiana Baptist University, hung around the Grapevine varsity staff, helped out with the freshmen, and videotaped the games.

At Parkview Christian Academy in Waco, where he was also a school administrator, Bentley went 3–7 in 2001 and was an assistant coach during the 2002 season.

The light résumé didn't keep him from landing the Trinity position, even though athletic director Tim Grant was looking in another direction. After the Lions finished 2002 without a victory, Grant searched for an "older, even retired gentleman that would come in for a couple of years. When we went to Rusty, I explained to Rusty, you're young, but the administration wants to go with you. I expressed my concerns about the experience, the understanding of recruitment. I tried to make it very clear that was the hardest part, the toughest part."

And the salary for a head coach at Trinity doesn't exactly compare with that of bigger schools. Take Florida State, the program Bentley compared Trinity's to during the summer. Bowden's total salary package is reported to be worth more than $2 million, which includes his base salary, television and radio shows, and a car and housing allowance. Bentley's contract, including salary and benefits, for coaching and teaching in the school's physical education department equals $40,800. Benefits for Bentley include meal plans, retirement plans, and 50-percent health coverage. Minus the benefits, his salary would be a shade over $29,000.

Grant had interest in two older coaches, but both bowed out of contention. That left Bentley, who seemed to make up for his lack of experience with a killer sales spiel.

"Trinity gave me the opportunity," Bentley says. "Trinity was in the hole, too. They needed someone that was willing to stay, willing to take it over."

Bentley is a walking sound bite, spinning parables with thoughts on life and society. He recites Bible verses the way an English professor quotes Shakespeare. He has more opinions than a talk-radio host, and just as much certitude, on topics ranging from global economics ("I've always said, show me a country that's in poverty, and I'll link it with a spiritual problem. The Bible says we reap what we sow. In my own personal opinion, in countries that have a relationship with the Lord, there is no poverty.") to Hollywood ("They don't vote their pocketbook. They vote their morals. They want to show sex and foul language and horrendous killings.").

Even good ol' football talk is rarely straightforward—references to Jesus usually enter those conversations, too. All the stories are told with a Texas twang. He has a laugh that explodes from his gut and carries across a room. At practice he's often a hootin' and a hollerin'. His players, though, wonder if he's doing any actual coaching.

"I yell all the time," he says before pausing and adding, "No, I don't yell. What's the difference between hollering and yelling? Which one's positive?"

He ends sentences at a much higher decibel than he begins them, building to a crescendo. At the end of practices Bentley often calls the team together with a loud, "On the hop, boys. On the hop!"

While the players seem to often tune out the bombastic Bentley, gazing at the vast North Dakota prairie while he talks, they pay close attention when listening to assistant Eric Slivoskey, whose quiet nature can't conceal his deep football knowledge. When Bentley speaks, the words often sound like proclamations from a mountaintop. Big, bold ideas burst out of him, but how much reality? Slivoskey deals more in basics, listening as much as talking, instructing on tackling technique and how the receivers should run their routes. On the rare occasions he does raise his voice, he gets the players' attention. The words seem to resonate more than Bentley's do. But he's concerned when players come to him first with questions, whether it's on-field issues or off, reminding them that Bentley is the head coach and in charge. The players don't always hear him.

"Coach Slivo, he knows fundamentals, he knows the game," says sophomore Sannon Norick. "Coach Bentley, I don't know what his deal is. When we tell him, 'Hey, we need to do drills, we need to learn how to do this,' we do it for one day. He'll make us do it one day, and then we'll move on. That's the kind of stuff you should be doing in camp every day. Fundamentals are taught in the pros; they do them every day, but here we don't."

For his part Bentley tries to remind one and all that football at Trinity Bible College isn't about winning and losing. He says the program has to be built around spirituality. "I know what we can live by and what we can't live by," he says. "I know what the administration expects me to live with. That sends a message sometimes to kids or kids look for the message of not caring. Or, is this all we're going to be, are we going to be mediocre? No, we're not going to be mediocre.

But you gotta learn to be content. Paul in the Bible says, 'I'm content with what I have, I want for nothing.'"

The players and assistants wouldn't argue with that sentiment. But they also think if the school's going to have football, why not try to make it as successful as possible? It might not translate to a greater number of victories, but the games could be more competitive, there could be a clear direction to the program. They're not worried about being mired in mediocrity. Mediocrity? At this point they'd be happy just to reach that level. Mediocrity would be a step upward.

"There's a perception out there in some ways that this is kind of a Mickey Mouse operation, and that bothers me," says Slivoskey. "I don't think there's too many other schools that would be looking to copy our program."

Trinity belongs to the UMAC, but it's not in the NCAA or the NAIA. Instead the school is part of the National Christian College Athletic Association (NCCAA), an organization whose purpose, according to its Web site, is to "provide a Christian-based organization that functions uniquely as a national and international agency for the promotion of outreach and ministry, and for the maintenance, enhancement, and promotion of intercollegiate athletic competition with a Christian perspective." When Rockford crossed the century mark against the Lions in 2003, the Regents set a record for points scored by a Division III team, but Trinity itself isn't part of the division. Geographically, the UMAC is separated into North and South divisions. Competitively, the league is divided by three levels: the haves, the have-nots, and Trinity. The conference is a superb fit for the Lions as far as the competition and missions of the schools. Even in the UMAC, though, the other colleges have enrollments at least twice that of Trinity. More students, more players. More players, more depth. More depth, more talent. Trinity will always face that battle. Perpetual league heavyweights include Minnesota schools Martin Luther and Northwestern and Missouri's Westminster. Teams such as Principia College out of Illinois and Maranatha Baptist out of Wisconsin are more at Trinity's level, but even those schools have been naming the score against the Lions for a few seasons. Yet, the Lions weren't always sacrificial lambs. Under head coach Jesse Godding, a former

Trinity player, the Lions won six games between the 1999 and 2000 seasons and went 5–5 in 2001. But Godding left Trinity before the 2002 season for the head position at Southwestern Assemblies of God University in Texas. In the two years since, the Lions haven't won and enter the 2004 season with a twenty-game losing streak.

Slivoskey wonders what the other schools think about Trinity's rebuilding efforts. The college is isolated from the concentration of Minnesota schools in the UMAC and the teams from the South division. All of the other league schools have some natural rivals within reasonable driving distance, making those excursions to Ellendale feel more like treks taken via covered wagon. Opposing schools drive a long ways—twelve, thirteen hours in some cases—just to have the starters play a quarter or two. Also, the conference is on track to become eligible for the NCAA Division III playoffs, a plan that would leave Trinity on the outside of the league because it's not a division member.

"I feel there's an impression there that [Trinity should] either get with it or get out, and I don't blame them," Slivoskey notes. "Shape up or ship out. We need to upgrade. I just hope that they remember, two, three, four years ago, Trinity was beating these schools. They've shown that it's possible."

Bentley is hampered as he attempts to rehabilitate the program. Trinity's total athletic budget for the 2004–2005 school year is $223,900. For football supplies, equipment, travel expenses, uniforms, game officials, and presemester meals, the total is $23,200. Although the program is hoping to add numbers to the roster, there is only locker space for thirty-four players. Any more and they'll have to double up in the already cramped locker room. The school also lacks a full-time athletic trainer. Instead Slivoskey is left to deal with injuries, and that occasionally includes diagnosing them, something he's not an expert at or comfortable doing. "When you're playing as many kids both ways as we are, you're going to have injuries," Slivoskey says. "I really feel like down the road, if the program expands, an essential need at the school is some type of person, either a physical therapist technician or an athletic trainer. I'd feel more comfortable knowing that if something serious happens, we have someone that's really equipped to make decisions and to take care of the athletes."

So with all the obstacles, and all the losing, why even have the sport?

Several times in the past decade Trinity's board of regents has discussed dropping football. The board shelves the idea each time. One reason is simple: money. With an enrollment that hovers around three hundred each year, the school depends on the $14,790 each student brings to the college. Many of Trinity's graduates become preachers in small communities or travel overseas on mission trips. There's no rich alumni base to donate large financial gifts to Trinity; the school is tuition-dependent. With a general fund budget of $4,965,000 for 2004–2005, the $443,700 of tuition paid by thirty football players is crucial.

But the bottom line isn't the only reason the sport still exists. The Trinity administration believes learning takes place on the football field, just as it does in any classroom. Life is full of losses; everybody loses at some point in life, whether it's in love, work, or the stock market. Losing today teaches lessons that can be used tomorrow. That's the hope, anyway.

"You can be on top of the mountain or the mountain can be on top of you," says Dan Kuno, Trinity's dean of students. "It was on top of them. But what is that kind of person going to be like in twenty years? They'll never forget what carved and made them. You carve away sometimes what is good to get to that which is great. But when you carve, it hurts."

Chapter Three

Eric's Travels, Travails

A friend of Eric Slivoskey's wants to visit him in Ellendale. The friend is a liberal fellow from Arizona who majored in anthropology, the study of humankind. He's not interested in coming to southeastern North Dakota for some pheasant hunting. He's basically just interested in studying Slivoskey. He wants to discover how this thirty-three-year-old man, who has traveled to all fifty of the United States, Central America, South America, Europe, Hong Kong, China, and places between, can be content in a small town that's forty miles from the nearest McDonald's. He wants to know why someone making a six-figure income would give it up to work part-time at a Bible school.

Why Ellendale? A town of 1,559 people, Ellendale is 40 miles north of Aberdeen, South Dakota. Fargo, the nearest city with at least 50,000 people, is about 160 miles to the north. Again, why Ellendale?

"He's like, how do you exist and thrive there in a little prairie town?" Slivoskey says. "He likes a lot of the cultural things. He's like, what do you do there?"

What he's done for two years is call plays for the Trinity Bible College football team. Being on the sidelines wasn't Slivoskey's original goal. He planned to be in the blue and gold uniform of Trinity, catching passes as a thirty-something tight end with bad knees, but an experienced football mind. Strange how life works out. Slivoskey, known to the players as "Coach Slivo," jokes about stress causing hints of gray to appear in his short black hair. But a soft-spoken nature and easygoing personality belie his experiences.

Slivoskey hails from Latrobe, Pennsylvania, an industrial town of fewer than nine thousand people approximately thirty-five miles southeast of Pittsburgh. Latrobe's most famous native son is one of the most famous athletes in the world—golf legend Arnold Palmer. Fred Rogers, better known to millions as television icon Mr. Rogers, was born there too, providing the small town a double dose of star power. The town's prominent exports aren't limited to celebrities— the Latrobe Brewing Company produces Rolling Rock beer. But it was coal, not stars or beer, that made the town what it was. And coal made the people what they were. Slivoskey's grandfather was a coal miner, as were two uncles. He still remembers when they'd come home, their faces all black, cut up, and bruised. It was how people lived in Latrobe. "Most of the people are born there, raised there, and die there," Slivoskey says.

When Slivoskey was just two years old, a single death altered his entire life path. In November 1973, a month before Slivoskey's third birthday, his father, John Slivoskey, died in a motorcycle accident when a drunk driver in a coal-mining truck hit him. John had just graduated from the University of Pittsburgh with a degree in computer science, a degree that arrived in the mail a few days after he died. Slivoskey still has his father's degree, and the cracked helmet he was wearing at the time of the accident, mementos to a man he never knew. Slivoskey recalls being at his father's funeral. It's his earliest memory.

"I remember the suit my dad was wearing when he was buried," he says. "Which is actually a morbid first memory for a child. Just seeing my mom, the intensity of the situation, and understanding something very serious had happened."

Slivoskey's mom, Yvonne, was only eighteen when he was born. Her husband's death brought her even closer to her son, a bond that remains strong. At times, though, they had to survive a rough relationship, which they did. "We were so close in age, we had this dynamic; I was my mom's confidant growing up. My mom wasn't happy, she cried on my shoulder. I grew up pretty quickly."

Slivoskey had his own brush with death when he was ten and living in a trailer with his mother and her second husband. One night his young half-sister, Shaina, asked Slivoskey to sleep on the floor of her room. It was her birthday the next day; she wanted to wake up that morning and see her big brother. During the evening, an air conditioning unit caught fire in Slivoskey's bedroom, burning the trailer to the ground. The unit was in the lone window in his room, next to the door. Shaina's simple request saved her brother's life. Firemen told Slivoskey he would have had no chance to escape. "I made that decision kind of the way you'd decide if you wanted cream with your coffee," he says. "It was a life or death decision that I made, there's just no two ways about it."

His father's death and his own near-death got Slivoskey thinking about the fragility of life. The traumas didn't rob him of his faith; they made him believe God had a will for him. Had to, he figured. Why else would he have survived? By the time Slivoskey reached high school, faith was an important part of his life. Maybe even as important as football, the king of sports in Pennsylvania. Pittsburgh and the surrounding areas are famed for churning out football legends. This is where Johnny Unitas, Joe Montana, Dan Marino, Joe Namath, Jim Kelly, and others called home. As in Ohio and Texas, high school football in Pennsylvania is a religion. Residents are as passionate about their prep teams as they are about the Steelers. As a high school student in Latrobe, Slivoskey grew into his 5-foot, 11-inch frame. The hard-hitting linebacker attracted the attention of college scouts from around the country. He took a recruiting visit to Youngstown State in Ohio, where current Ohio State coach Jim Tressel was building a Division I-AA dynasty. Villanova, in his home state, expressed interest in the 1989 graduate, but Slivoskey was already showing a desire to move away from his familiar territory. Maybe most people from Latrobe lived their whole lives there. But Slivoskey had no desire to be most people. He didn't just want to get out of the town, he wanted out of the state, wanted to explore a new part of the country. San Diego State, which gained national attention when future NFL star Marshall Faulk tore up the school's rushing record book in the early 1990s, invited Slivoskey to walk-on to the team. It was a tempting offer: a

Division I-A school and a warm-weather escape. In the end, though, faith played a bigger role than average temperature in the decision. Slivoskey ultimately chose Evangel University in Springfield, Missouri, an NAIA football school.

"From a spiritual perspective, I kind of felt that was where I was supposed to go," Slivoskey says. "I can't say I was called to be a minister, but it felt like the right place for me."

Slivoskey saw action as a sure-handed tight end his freshman year, starting half of Evangel's games. He maintained a 4.0 grade point average, although college life was already losing some of its appeal. Driving across the country with his grandparents had sparked the young Slivoskey's interest in travel. And so he took to America's roads again, this time as a twenty-year-old with a sense of adventure, if not a grasp of what he wanted in life. Slivoskey knocked around the country finding work wherever he could. He worked on a farm, as a lifeguard, for the Census Bureau, and as a dishwasher. He and a friend crisscrossed the country in a Honda CRX before finally realizing the excellent adventure had to end at some point. Directionless but happy, Slivoskey says, "I realized I needed to start doing something besides washing dishes."

For a young man trying to figure out how to be all he can be, where better to go than the Army? Slivoskey enlisted and served on active duty for nearly a year and in the reserves for five years. While in the service, Slivoskey assumed the role of spiritual lay leader to approximately sixty soldiers, acting as a counselor, a preacher, a Bible studies leader. If a fellow soldier broke up with a girlfriend or needed a prayer for Grandma, Slivoskey provided counsel. Though writing has always been his passion and he once considered a career in journalism, he ended up focusing on matters of the head. Slivoskey received his Certificate in Behavioral Sciences from the U.S. Academy of Health Sciences, United States Army, and studied psychology when he returned to school at Frostburg State University in western Maryland. While at Frostburg, he returned to football, playing for a season. But the school didn't offer scholarships, and Slivoskey watched his money slip away. An offer came in to work at a Christian youth home. Slivoskey accepted the position and worked with troubled kids for three years. He loved the job. Loved the feeling of accomplishment. It was, at times, brutal work, both physically and emotionally. Unfortunately for Slivoskey, working meant abandoning football for a second, seemingly final time.

By the time he graduated from Frostburg, Slivoskey had met his wife; an English girl named Estalita, Essy for short, and had again been bitten by the traveling bug. A week after their 1995 marriage, the Slivoskeys packed up a U-Haul and moved to the ski resort town of Big Sky in western Montana, where they proceeded to live the "ski bum" life for a while. The two started a little business called Buffalo Fudge, selling buffalo jerky, huckleberry syrups, and huckleberry fudge, all made in Montana. They lived near Yellowstone, earning money as seasonal employees. Essy worked as a waitress while Eric performed odd jobs, which included cleaning condos and laying carpet. When the ski resort would shut down, Essy and Eric took their money and headed east, west, and everywhere in between. They'd backpack in Europe, take a cruise, visit friends, plant themselves for two weeks, fend off questions about what they were doing with their lives, and then head out the door. Though his family might not have known, Slivoskey knew what he wanted.

"One of my goals was to see all fifty states before I was thirty," he says. "I was twenty-eight when I stepped off the plane in Honolulu, and that was the last state."

The couple relocated to Park City, Utah, where Slivoskey worked at a resort. As part of his job, he drove rich people to the airport. This allowed him the opportunity to ferry an occasional celebrity, such as comedian Cheech Marin, post-Chong and pot-smoking fame. Essy eventually gave birth to their daughter, Kamryn, and the pair again set their sights on a new place to call home, this time landing in Phoenix. Slivoskey was now supporting two children when son Kodie joined Kamryn, and relatives back East were wondering what the Slivoskeys were planning next.

Slivoskey decided to pursue an idea he'd been kicking around in Utah—the aqua massage business, selling people the soothing comfort of pulsating waterjet streams set in a tanning bed–like coffin. Though he threw himself into the new endeavor from the outset, working seven days a week, he had no idea how the venture would turn out. He found out soon enough. He soon opened aqua massage units in Tucson, Pittsburgh, and throughout the Phoenix area, eventually earning more than $100,000 per year.

Slivoskey can testify to the benefits of aqua massage, at least the lifestyle benefits that came with success. "I had my business down to where I'm working one or two days a week," he explains. "I'm pretty much being a family guy. I play golf a little bit; I take my kids to the park. I had created my own life. I could do some writing. I had control of what I wanted to do with my life."

That control made his next move the oddest of all his travels. Established in Phoenix, living a life of relative luxury, Slivoskey was seduced by two old friends: faith and football. A schoolmate at Evangel University had mentioned Trinity Bible College to Slivoskey way back in 1989. In 1995, he planned to head to North Dakota, but the situation fell through. For years he had told Essy that they were going to end up in Ellendale. He just had a feeling. He wanted to know if she could live there. Essy said yes, and by 2003 Eric was again being pulled north. He felt happy internally, but he was complacent. "In some ways I felt like I wasn't making a difference, the way I felt I was making a difference when I was working in the Christian youth home."

Because his travels and work commitment interrupted his football career on two previous occasions, Slivoskey had two years of eligibility remaining. Two more seasons on the field. He planned to spend them at Trinity. In addition, although he didn't want to end up behind a pastor's pulpit, he did want to complete a degree in Biblical studies, maybe pick up his teaching certificate, too.

Running sprints in the Arizona heat, he got his weight down from 260 pounds to 235. He would call Trinity, trying to let them know they had a former standout player interested in the school. No one called back. "I'm thinking, is it just because I'm old?" Slivoskey says. It wasn't age discrimination; no one was around to call back. Rusty Bentley had just been hired, but he was still in Texas. He didn't arrive in Ellendale until a few months before the start of the 2003 season. Bentley eventually contacted Slivoskey, telling him he was looking for

a tight end to build his offense around. Slivoskey says he felt like he'd
won the lottery. "I didn't tell anybody," he says of his friends, who
apparently had different ideas about what it means to win the lottery.
"If I tell them I'm leaving Arizona to go to some tiny dot on the map
nobody's ever even heard of, where the wind blows twelve months a
year, and I'm going to play football and go to Bible college, well,
most people would look at me like I fell off the wagon."

In April of 2003, Essy and Eric sold their Phoenix house two days
after it was listed. The couple searched the Internet for a house in Ellendale, came across one they liked, made an offer, and bought it.
They sold the aqua massage business, loaded a camper, and took to
the country's highways. Again. The family spent the summer traveling while Slivoskey continued his training at stops along the way,
whenever he had the time. His comeback wasn't a joke, and he
didn't want it to turn into one. Slivoskey knew he had lost a step.
Well, at least a step. But he still had the good hands, still had the
knowledge of the game—more of it, actually.

Then Bentley called him again in July, this time bearing bad news.

"I just found out you're not eligible to play here," he told
Slivoskey. "The only place you could even go play now is your alma
mater because you didn't get your bachelor's here."

After giving up financial security, a two-day workweek, and
warm weather to pursue his dream, Slivoskey wasn't ready to take no
for an answer. Was there any way he could be eligible? He considered
hiring an attorney. He spoke with the UMAC commissioner. He met
with Bentley and athletic director Tim Grant to discuss his case. It
didn't matter. His playing days were, finally, officially over. Bentley
did have another offer, though. How would Slivoskey like to help out
as a coach? "It was kind of making lemonade out of lemons," he
says. "I was dealt some pretty sour news, but my commitment was to
come here, not just for football. I'm going to honor that commitment
I made. That spiritual commitment."

Slivoskey has been calling the offensive plays for the Lions ever
since, including the 105–0 loss to Rockford. "My name is now attached to the worst loss," he says with a chuckle. "What do they say?
If you can't be famous, be infamous or notorious."

At Trinity, Slivoskey has learned to subjugate his ego, something players and coaches must do when victories are as rare as points on the scoreboard. One of the coaching profession's favorite clichés is a team has to do the little things to win. For the Lions, it's often only the little things that measure victory. An improved pass rush, better run blocking, solid kickoff returns: these are the small accomplishments that can be praised no matter the score. It seems like Slivoskey, raised on the playing fields of Pennsylvania, where football was a way of life and not just a part of it, would have a difficult time adjusting to these new standards of success. He does. But whether because of his spiritual outlook or just the wisdom that comes with each new birthday, he has adapted.

"A lot of times you are looking for the smaller victories," he says. "They're harder to find sometimes when you get all the negativity that's surrounded by the losing and getting physically beaten up. A lot of our kids who come here have never played before. And then we see the improvements that they're making. But I think they struggle to see that because all they see is they're going out and doing the exact same thing they did the week before, or maybe even working a little harder, and then we get the same result."

Slivoskey chose not to take classes at Trinity, deciding the enrollment cost of just under $15,000 outweighed any future benefits. But with the financial security that came from selling the aqua massage business, the Slivoskeys made their home in Ellendale. The world traveler finds the community to his liking. He loves small towns, as long as he feels he can leave them a few times a year. The simplicity agrees with him, the "pain free" pace relaxes him.

Sure, restaurant options are limited, but the Slivoskey clan is often seen at the Nodak Café on Main Street, an establishment owned by Peggy Gilbert. Gilbert also operates the Fireside Steakhouse and Lodge in town. By the time the Nodak closes at 4:30 p.m., the Fireside has been open for thirty minutes. There is a bowling alley, Pheasant Lanes, for entertainment, and plenty of parks. Lots of parks, perfect for kids. Slivoskey says Ellendale is a great place to raise four-year-old Kamryn and two-year-old Kodie.

Living in Ellendale hasn't been a problem for the Slivoskeys, but it hasn't always been easy. Following the 2003 football season,

Slivoskey fell seriously ill for three months. He lost twenty-five pounds, couldn't get out of bed to put his shoes on, and had a fever that once reached 104 degrees. His liver swelled and bulged out of his right side; his spleen did the same on his left. Doctors suspected leukemia. It wasn't, but the mysterious illness left Slivoskey out of commission and out of touch with Trinity through the winter. Though no definitive explanation for the virus was ever found, physicians speculated that corticosteroids Slivoskey took as a youth to combat a blood disease may have made him more susceptible to the virus as an adult. Whatever the reason, Slivoskey didn't recover from it until spring. By then he was strong enough to coach the baseball team, and as the 2004 football campaign arrived, he was back to full strength, physically and mentally.

Slivoskey possesses a limitless curiosity about the world around him, the world far from Ellendale. He might be a former top jock—and even though his paunch is a bit more prominent these days, he still carries himself with the relatively effortless air of an athlete—but he is just as comfortable talking about foreign cultures as he is about football. Scotland, Germany, and the Alps are three of his favorite destinations. When he travels to Europe he visits as many World War II memorials and sites as possible, soaking in the history. He enjoys the feeling of being "a little bit intimidated" in cultures where he feels out of his element, such as in Central or South America. He learns something about himself while learning about others. When he's not visiting these places, he's reading about them. People and places, those are the things that fascinate him. He talks about possibly getting back into counseling, like the work he did in the army and at the Christian youth home. With his experiences and desires, Slivoskey comes off as someone who would be perfectly comfortable wearing a tweed jacket while he lectures as a professor at a secluded university.

He even has become a college instructor, albeit without the tweed jacket. But he doesn't teach history, sociology, anthropology, or psychology. In the fall of 2004, Slivoskey became an adjunct professor at Trinity. The coaching job remains a part-time position, at least in terms of compensation, but he is now further embedded in the Trinity community. Though his employment status means he doesn't get benefits such as health insurance, Slivoskey loves the interaction with students. He's invigorated by teaching first aid and CPR, care and prevention of athletic injuries, and psychology of physical education and athletics. He's invigorated by this latest twist in his life's tale, however improbable it all would have seemed to him three years ago. No, he wasn't called to the pulpit, but Slivoskey feels teaching and coaching at a Christian school are simply different forms of ministry.

"My life has completely gone upside down," he says. "Since I left Arizona I gave up time and money and freedom. I feel like there's a higher calling involved, that's the best way I can explain it. I came here as a student, and now I'm the offensive coordinator, I'm teaching classes, I'm the baseball coach. Doors have opened for me. That's not something I prayed for, but I feel like that came as a result of being obedient to come here. I just felt this is where God was calling me to come."

He's not so sure God wants him to stay.

Chapter Four

Strong Willed

To find the Trinity coaching offices, just enter the Ray Ulmer Field House through the main doors. Don't worry about missing it. You'll see it on the left side of the one road that leads into the center of the campus. Once in the field house, turn right and walk to the end of the hallway. Look to the right. Stroll on in through the door; it will usually be open. That's where you'll find the football coaches, gathered in an outer office that looks, in the words of Eric Slivoskey, "like Hurricane Charley veered off the coast of Florida and hit us before going back down South." Slivoskey and Brandon Strong spent a lot of time cleaning up the small area, painting the walls blue and tidying up, but the room quickly degenerated back into a garage sale–style pit. Chairs, a couch, and a desk cohabitate with football equipment, books, and other assorted junk.

Next to that outer office is the inner sanctum of Coach Bentley. It's in this office he spends much of his free time, surrounded by the standard tools of his chosen occupation: a television and VCR, dozens of videotapes of games, and a laptop. The room is also home to a passable shrine to the Dallas Cowboys. Cowboys' memorabilia junkies would pay good money for access to Bentley's collection.

He displays autographs from old Cowboys greats such as Chuck Howley, Cliff Harris, Danny White, and Captain Comeback himself,

Roger Staubach. A letter from a Tony Dorsett fan club hangs on the wall (acquired by Bentley when he was just a teenager), as does a signed photo of former fullback Daryl "Moose" Johnston. Finally, a football with Troy Aikman's signature sits near his desk.

On an upper shelf is the movie *Miracle*, the rousing story of the 1980 U.S. Olympic hockey team. A book, *Successful Coaching*, rests on his desk, along with informational material about the Fellowship of Christian Athletes.

Depending on the hour, his children's backpacks may sit discarded on the small couch.

This is where Bentley lords over the Trinity program. This is where he talks about his coaching beliefs. This is where he explains the Bentley methods.

Current topic for discussion: recruiting.

"If I call first, it sets the recruiting back," he says. "You go to a car dealership, you get the salesman. If the general manager comes right out and meets you, then you're thinking, I can deal with this guy all day long."

And that's why the only full-time coach on Trinity's football staff handed off many of the team's 2004 recruiting duties to a part-time assistant and a twenty-one-year-old student whose favorite sport is baseball.

At Trinity, Slivoskey and Strong are in charge of bringing players to Ellendale. A baseball pitcher in the spring, Strong walked with two bad knees thanks to the 2003 football season. His 2004 contributions would have to take place on the phone, not the field.

It was a remarkable turnaround for Strong, a thin, 5-foot, 10-inch junior with a wispy goatee and a body built more for soccer, which was perhaps his best sport growing up. On his first visit to the school two years ago, the Michigan native couldn't wait to get off the campus. Now he was responsible for bringing students, and their valuable tuition, to the school. During his senior year, the 2002 Waldron High School graduate took a solo car trip to the Trinity campus, which is nestled on twenty-eight acres in the southeast portion of Ellendale. There's an administration and classroom building, a student center, a field house, a library, three full-size dorms, and the Block Memorial

Chapel (home to the New Life Asssembly of God church), which doubles as Trinity's headquarters for worship. "I literally pulled up into the chapel parking lot and I said, 'What on earth am I doing out there?'" Strong says. "I was like, there's no way I'm coming to college here." Strong stayed a night, went to classes the next day, met some students, and remained convinced Trinity was not part of his future. On his drive home, though, through a "boring" stretch of road in Wisconsin, his thoughts changed. Maybe it was a bit of divine intervention or maybe it was just road fatigue. Something altered his thinking. Strong admitted to himself that he enjoyed his time on the campus, and he found the small-town atmosphere appealing. He had considered attending North Central University, an Assemblies of God university in Minneapolis, but didn't want to live in the city. So why not Trinity? "By the time I got home, I'd pretty much made up my mind I was coming here," he says. "I did a 180-degree turnaround."

In conversation, Strong often ends sentences with "sir," or "good night," an all-encompassing phrase he uses to express admiration, delight, surprise, pity, or disappointment. He exudes modesty, and only with some gentle prodding does he reveal the difficulties of his own childhood, reluctant to talk about a "big old sob story."

Strong grew up on the outskirts of Waldron, Michigan, where he endured childhood trauma to emerge as a leader. He was born with a cleft palate—"basically I didn't have the roof of my mouth"—and underwent four surgeries between the ages of eighteen months and seventeen years. As a child, he wore arm braces because he wasn't allowed to put his hands in his mouth. In and out of the hospital until the age of seven, often with pneumonia and bronchitis, Strong feels his life changed thanks to the indirect help of a blunt doctor. "He sets me up on this big old table, puts his hand on my knee," Strong recalls. "He tells my mom all these problems I'd have socially when I get older. Basically told her everything that went wrong. He said it all like I was stupid, like I couldn't hear it or I wasn't comprehending it in my brain. I wanted to jack this guy in the jaw."

Though there's still evidence of his childhood condition in the tone of his voice, Strong overcame the doctor's early predictions. He became a Michigan state officer in the Future Farmers of America, logging

30,000 miles while traveling across the state. Through his sophomore year, he was a standout soccer goalie at a private school located forty miles from Waldron. He returned to his hometown Waldron High School, though, and played football his senior season. But baseball was always his sport of choice. Even his e-mail moniker—baseball_is_nice—displays his true loyalties. Strong threw a one-hitter in high school, and he was on the mound when the Trinity baseball team snapped a nine-game losing streak in 2004. "I played eighteen games in a Trinity uniform before I finally won," he says, referring to his football and baseball campaigns. The baseball from that first victory, a 6–4 triumph, sits in his dorm room, displayed proudly like a spoil of war.

The knee injuries he suffered on the football field in the fall of 2003 nearly kept him off the baseball diamond. His mother, Connie, had warned him about that possibility, telling him he was going to ruin his opportunity to play baseball. Although he still has pain in his knees, he only missed two weeks of baseball after surgery, instead of the four to six weeks his doctor forecast.

Strong has become adept at defying doctor's prognostications.

But athletics didn't bring him to Trinity. When he was sixteen years old, Strong says he began to believe that God had a plan for his life. "I don't think any of us were put here just because," he says. "It's not how it is. I knew that he put me in this world as a leader." At Trinity that leadership involves his work as a resident advisor and as a student assistant with the football team. In addition, for his work-study Strong serves as the school's sports information director, usually a thankless job at any college. It's no different at Trinity. He keeps statistics, updates the school's Web site with game results and stories, and is at the beck and call of the coaches. It's supposed to be ten hours of work a week, but during football season it's more like twenty. In May, Strong attended a meeting of the UMAC's sports information directors in New Ulm, Minnesota. The encounter provided him a chance to mingle with peers while opening his eyes to the difficulties he'd face with his new position. "I knew right then that I had bit off more than I can chew," he acknowledges. "Seventy-five percent had full-time SIDs. Others had full-time coaches that also fulfilled SID roles. And they all had assistants. They're paying me work study money to do a job that I've never done before, that I have no experience in doing, and they've never given me a job description of this is your weekly duties."

The physical education major, who hopes eventually to become involved with short-term mission trips, also carries a full class load. Coach Bentley, while calling him the team's "football operations manager," occasionally wonders if the always on-the-go Strong takes on too much responsibility.

"He's a worker, he's a hard worker," Bentley says. "He can do anything, you name it. You name it, he can do it, but he works himself into the ground. He gets overcommitted. He gets overcommitted because if he gets doing something, he won't quit until it's done right."

Strong replies, "[Bentley] says to me stuff like 'Do you got too much to do, you got too much on your plate?' Well, yeah. Then he's like, you have too much, OK, here's some more."

With a coach who's eager to delegate, and a student who's eager to take on any and all projects, it was probably inevitable that the time would come when Strong felt overworked. With his desire never to leave a job until it was finished, there was little chance Strong would turn down Bentley's requests. Leading the school's recruiting effort was his next duty. It promised to be a daunting task. Just how daunting became evident when Bentley entrusted him with Trinity's recruiting file.

"In May [Bentley] hands me a folder for football; it says '2004 football' on it," Strong says. "It's a bunch of torn scratch paper. I'm told to start the recruiting process. I about had a heart attack that night. There's nothing on computer. If we lost some of this information, it's gone for good, we can't contact that person."

So Strong and Coach Slivoskey set about revamping Trinity's recruiting system. They don't have a choice. To avoid a repeat of the disastrous 2003 season, the Lions need more players, and more talented players. But what's the pitch to potential recruits? How do Strong and Slivoskey deal with the winless season, the 105–0 defeat, the two-touchdown campaign? Denial?

"Hi, we're calling from Trinity. A 105–0? No, that wasn't us. That was Trinity out of Texas. Really."

Instead they told the truth about the team's situation, enticing recruits with the one thing players want most. "They know they're going to be getting playing time," Strong says. Color-coded boxes help organize the list of potential players. If a recruit requests information, an index card is filled out and it goes into a green box. If Strong or Slivoskey talk to the player, that name goes into a blue box. If the player verbally commits, that name goes into a red box. Once the player mails an application, the name goes into a black box. They also kept in touch through the phone, not wanting the players to forget about the small Bible school in North Dakota. A bit rudimentary, perhaps, but the new system trumps torn scratch paper. Strong and Slivoskey would get the names of recruits' friends and try selling them on Trinity as well. "If you build a relationship with them, you can find out they've got a buddy and you can contact them," Strong explains.

That's how Kevin Kloefkorn ended up going from Missouri to Ellendale. Strong was on the phone one day with Lester Williams, a St. Louis kid looking for a return to school and football. He'd spent a year working after graduating from high school in 2003. "When they called, Kevin was sitting in the living room, and I was like, 'Kevin, we're going to Trinity.' He had no idea what I was talking about," Williams says. "I just volunteered him to come. He applied, and the next thing you know he's up here with me."

Getting players to attend Trinity involves much more than selling the football program or offering generous financial aid packages. Since each student must provide evidence of a born-again conversion experience, the coaches make it a point to inquire about the recruits' life off the football field. "A lot of the guys we brought in, we actually asked them, how is your spiritual life?" Strong says. "I don't want to know if you go to church, I wanna know about your spiritual life." Incoming students have to know about the environment they'll enter. They have to know about the town of Ellendale, but, more important, they have to know about the school. The name of the institution should provide a hint. Bentley says, "This is a Bible college, and they have to recognize the emphasis is not just being a Christian name so to speak, but it's a true emphasis on Christianity."

Not just Christianity, but evangelical Christianity. Trinity Bible College is affiliated with the Assemblies of God. As such, Trinity, as stated in the school's academic catalog, subscribes to the "Statement of Fundamental Truths," which includes the belief in speaking in tongues, divine healing, and the desire to "be an agency of God for evangelizing the world." Given these beliefs, one of the more popular questions to Trinity visitors is, "Are you a Christian?"

Rules for school and life are laid out in Trinity's student handbook: rules that aren't meant to be broken. The handbook reads, "As members of *this* community, however, we also recognize the importance of respecting the values and goals of the college and will, therefore, seek to conduct ourselves in a manner that will bring only credit to the gospel and Trinity Bible College. The college takes the position that if these basic principles are not acceptable to a student, it is expected that the student will seek education elsewhere."

Don't like the rules or can't abide by them? Find another college. Of course this means no alcohol, and tobacco is forbidden, too. To lay out the groundwork for the rules on recreation, the handbook quotes I Thessalonians 5:21–22: "Test everything. Hold on to the good. Avoid every kind of evil." Since describing every kind of evil would create a need for a handbook numbering thousands of pages, a handful of specific guidelines are set in writing. No R-rated movies are allowed on or off campus. Dorm resident directors can provide exceptions to that regulation. There's no "social dancing, clubbing, nor disturbing music in lyrics or volume." Obeying these rules is sometimes a challenge for students.

With his rugged good looks, leadership qualities (he's a football captain), and charisma, running back Sannon Norick seems like he'd be the perfect poster boy for Trinity Bible College. He is, in truth, a poster boy. His mug is one of seven adorning the cover of Trinity's 2004–2006 academic catalog. But the no-dancing rule is a tough one to take for the Montana native, the oldest of Shawn and Ruthann Norick's eight children. Growing up with a mother who is an avid swing dancer, Norick was exposed to the joys of dancing, not any of its "evils." "She just said don't be bumping and grinding on a girl. Be smart," he says. "I just love to dance. I don't care what's going on, I'll break out and dance in the middle of nowhere."

Men cannot have tattoos or body piercings, although they are allowed "one modest earring." Defining *modest* is the next task. Men and women live in separate residence halls, and the opposite sex is not allowed in the other's dorms. Dating couples are expected to maintain discretion in public. "Anything other than holding of hands and gentlemen's escort, or a goodnight kiss is unacceptable," reads the handbook. Relationship policy also extends to behind closed doors. When listing what it deems acceptable, the school doesn't differentiate between legal acts and illegal acts. Trinity requires that all students "refrain from any form of sexual immorality, including promiscuity, homosexuality, sexual violence and abuse, adultery, date rape, premarital sex, pornography, phone pornography, and pornography on the Internet."

Rules are easy to write; hormones are hard to control.

"A Christian guy is not exempt from all those urges that everyone else has," says Neil Huenefeld, a Trinity senior, but a grown man. The twenty-four-year-old campus leader works in the admissions office and as a resident assistant in Kesler Hall. Huenefeld's girlfriend is Charissa Bennett, a Trinity student and daughter of David Bennett, Trinity's student ministries director. Huenefeld and Bennett would probably be winners if the college ever held a cutest couple contest. But the youth pastor major talks about his belief in the importance of living pure, of needing discipline to survive the ministry. He wants to live that life even before he gets involved with his own congregation. If the couple plans on being alone, Huenefeld will tell some of his friends what the plans are and what time they'll return. Bennett does the same with her friends. "There's many people you hear of on campus that have their private time and will compromise something in their life sexually," Huenefeld says. "We've set up boundaries and neither of us has ever crossed that boundary because we just know where we need to stop, what we need to do. I do tell you, though, there's times I sat in the car with her, we talked. We're just hugging each other and I say, 'Well, it's now time to go.' She said the same thing, 'I think it's time to go.'"

Students are required to attend daily chapel service on campus. At 10 in the morning, classrooms, offices, and halls clear out, and the doors to Graham Library are locked as students and professors stream into the thirty-year-old chapel. When walking through the administration building at this time—usually a hub of activity—it looks like someone called in a bomb threat; a few stray papers on the floor are the only items left behind.

Services are a passionate affair, filled with music provided by students on vocals, drums, and guitars. The musicians serve as the warm-up act to the real stars of the service: the speakers. Faculty members, guests, and student ministers all preach. Chapel attendees aren't embarrassed about public displays of affection for Jesus. They sing. They vocalize their prayers. They open their hands and raise their arms. They sway. They kneel in the pews and the aisles.

"The chapel is at the center of our schedule, it's at the center of our college," says Dean Dan Kuno, a former student. "It's the greatest classroom we have. The greatest speaker there is the Holy Spirit because he speaks to us all about our own issues." Students are allowed ten chapel absences each semester. If a paper needs to be finished or a morning nap is required, students are allowed a few passes. But Trinity's students aren't being dragged against their will to the chapel. As Kuno said, the lessons learned there are why they are in Ellendale.

"I go because I like it. It refreshes me when I'm struggling," says sophomore linebacker Dustin Harper, who joins his teammate Norick on the catalog cover. "There's days I show up I don't want to be there, but I hear the praise and worship and it gets me going."

If a student flouts one of Trinity's rules, fines of up to $50 speak louder than any lecture. But the students know the expectations when they arrive in Ellendale; many are seeking the type of structure Trinity provides. This isn't *Footloose*. Norick is not Kevin Bacon, inspiring rebellious students to put on their dancing shoes and stick it to school elders. Although it sometimes seems as if an invisible force field surrounds the campus, isolating it from the outside world, Trinity isn't trapped in a time warp. Its leaders aren't naïve. The rules evolve through the years. Blue jeans used to be barred, as was handholding. "I was forever defining what jeans were," says Trinity's vice president of college relations, Steve Tvedt. "We had to really define it by material and color. It just got ridiculous."

The rules are meant to separate Trinity from other colleges, while the changes are implemented to keep the school, and the church, relevant. In the 1980s, Trinity's enrollment shot up to more than 500. By 2002, enrollment had sunk to 286. It rose to 307 in 2003, and 310 for the 2004–2005 school year.

"I think the school was behind, and the administration has honestly realized that we're behind," Strong says. "We gotta get caught up. We gotta effectively witness to society, where society's at. Honestly, I don't want to be involved in a church where it's shirt and tie every Sunday. I won't go to church in my shorts, but if somebody else does I don't care. When the church finally decides to go out and reach out, instead of wanting to just hope people will show up at the doors, that's when the church will be effective."

The school added a physical education major, which is expected to help bring in prospective students. But it's Trinity's spiritual environment that Kuno believes sets the school apart. "If six out of ten girls, before they're eighteen years old, are going to be abused one way or another, whether verbally or sexually or physically in some way, and four out of ten young men, we've got a problem coming to every one of our universities," he says. "And a kegger doesn't solve that. Being part of the Greek society or whatever doesn't solve those issues. One of the goals is to help make a man or woman of God here. Are we always successful? No. But I hope they can handle the challenges better because Trinity has touched their life."

As a resident assistant on the first floor of Kesler Hall, Strong is responsible for helping enforce the school's policies. He says many of the other colleges that he considered attending had tougher rules than Trinity, and "nine out of ten" minor infractions are immediately rectified. Playing hall monitor and conducting room checks are just small parts of Strong's job. He rules the floor with a benevolent touch, welcoming students into his tiny room whether it's eight at night or four in the morning.

Under Strong's desk sit gallons and gallons of water; he has more water than a militiaman stocking up for Y2K. And with *Sports Illustrated* and *ESPN The Magazine* covers lining his wall, the décor is not that of a typical therapist's office. But any shrink would be familiar with the problems Strong confronts. Residents knock on his door seeking advice on situations big and small, and visits can easily get emotional. Matters of the heart are the most common concerns. "These freshmen, I'm telling you, it's a different girl every night," Strong says. "The love of their life, it's a new one each week. I honestly want to tell them, go be a monk. Go to a monastery, be a eunuch." Often, though, they don't need advice, simply someone to listen. "That's what I've learned as an RA," he says. "Just shut your mouth and listen."

Many of the students on Kesler's first floor are first-year football players. Though Strong is a good listener, many of those students are at Trinity because of his ability to talk. All told, Slivoskey and Strong brought in more than twenty new players to the roster. Time will tell if the incoming recruits have the skills to lift Trinity on the field and the discipline to follow the school's regulations off the field.

There is talent coming in. Quarterback Dusty Hess spent the previous season playing for a semi-pro team in his native Indiana. Lee Odell was a standout high school center in Kansas, and had been a team member at Highland Community College and Independence Community College. The 290-pounder brings experience and skill to an offensive unit lacking both. Fiery safety Josh McGillvrey came up from South Dakota, packing a punch and plenty of self-confidence in his 5-foot, 7-inch frame. Andy Brower, a lanky receiver from South Dakota, was expected to boost the offense. Unfortunately for the Lions, Huenefeld, their defensive stalwart in 2003, would not play in 2004 because of his shoulder troubles. Still, the team looked to be much better.

"Brandon and Eric have done the work of six men," Bentley says. While happy with the number of new players, Bentley wonders whether he should have done more, this despite his car dealership analogy. "It's my nature to talk and visit with kids. Now I feel lazy because I have those other guys doing it first. Not that I want to do everything; I just don't want to feel like I'm doing nothing."

That's all right, Strong says, even though the recruiting process added on to his already overloaded schedule. "Honestly, we didn't want him to have an active role in it," he says. "He had enough of an active role just having his name on the bottom of the letter. I'm not a big fan of the way he gets players, saying it's God's will for you to play football. Come play for your college, come play for your school, you know. I can't sit here and tell you it's God's will for you."

But it is time for kickoff.

Chapter Five

The Newcomers

Lee Odell has waited five years for this game. Five long, difficult years, filled with more heartbreak than hope.

There have been stops at four colleges, a roommate who wiped out Odell's bank account and fled town, and a fiancée who cheated on him. Finally, there was a marriage to the new love of his life. It's all led the 290-pounder to Trinity, and it's all led to his first game as a collegiate starter.

Technically, Trinity's season opener against Haskell Indian Nations University won't be his first college game. Up to this point, though, Odell's college playing experience has most closely resembled the baseball career of Archibald "Moonlight" Graham, whose story was dramatized in the movie *Field of Dreams*. Graham was the baseball player turned doctor who played one inning of one major league game with the old New York Giants and never got the chance to come to the plate for an at-bat. Aided by a sentimental music score and Burt Lancaster's acting chops, Graham's portrayal on the silver screen brought tears to many eyes. Odell's "Moonlight" moment wasn't quite as, well, dignified.

Before coming to Trinity, Odell had been on the football teams at Highland Community College and Independence Community College, both in his home state of Kansas. At Independence, Odell was the backup center to someone he calls a "Saturday hero," a player with a bad knee who didn't practice during the week but got the snaps on game day. During a game against a junior varsity NAIA squad, the coach put Odell in with less than a minute left and his team up by more than thirty points. One play later, he was again off the field, the victim of his own frustration.

"We were whipping them the whole game and he didn't let any of the backup linemen go in," Odell says. "I finally got to go in, and I just took it out on some poor guy and got thrown out."

At least Odell left a mark on the game while he had the chance. It was his only play in his only game of the season. For a time he thought it would be the final performance of his football career, an ignominious ending in the sport he loves. But as he had several previous times in his life, Odell ended up turning a negative into a positive.

He learned that skill from his mom, Lea Anne. Divorced from Phillip Odell by the time Lee was seven years old, Lea Anne raised her son and daughter, Ashely, by herself. Lea Anne used welfare to return to college, attending nursing school. The same year Lee graduated from the eighth grade, Lea Anne graduated and received her nursing degree. Mom, son, and daughter eventually settled in Thayer, Kansas, a town of five hundred near the Oklahoma border. Shy as a child, Odell's insecurities grew when a stick struck him in the right eye and left him legally blind in that eye. Odell wore an eye patch for a spell, which caused him embarrassment. "It's hard being a kid having everyone staring at you and pointing at you," he says. But by the time Odell became an upperclassman, he had earned the respect of his classmates and was popular in school. He lettered three years in football as a standout lineman and was also on the small school's basketball and baseball teams. Vice president of his senior class, Odell was an A-student. He credits Lea Anne's efforts when he was young for his classroom achievements. Before he even started school, she taught him how to read and worked with him on math problems. The lessons lasted. To this day, he talks just as passionately about his exploits on Thayer's Scholars Bowl team as he does about his football successes.

"I was putting myself out there and I was getting such good grades," Odell says of his transformation from class loner to leader.

"By the time I was a senior people respected me. I'd walk down the hall, freshmen would move aside so I could get by. I was pretty much one of the only seniors on the team that didn't pick on the freshmen because I knew what that was like."

After excelling in eight-man football at Thayer, Odell attended Highland Community College, where he received a scholarship, but never got an opportunity to play. He left Highland, and his fiancée, after three semesters to play at Independence. Although his football career at Independence consisted solely of that embarrassing ejection, Odell remains grateful for his time at the school. In addition to receiving his associate's degree, Odell says he learned the proper technique needed to succeed on the line. It appeared he wouldn't need any of those skills, however, when he left the world of junior colleges for Kansas State University in Manhattan. Rather than football, the English major concentrated on academics and finding treasured parking spots on the 20,000-student campus. He balanced his schoolwork with a fifty-hour workweek, toiling at Arby's at night and stocking shelves at a grocery store on the overnight shift. The hours took their toll on his studies and he struggled to stay afloat. An introduction to literary studies, which required one or two papers per day, proved taxing.

"That was a rude awakening for me," he says. "She went to Berkeley that teacher. I think she was a flower child or something. She'd come up with these weird meanings for these poems, and I was like, OK, sounds like a lady washing clothes to me."

Then there was the roommate from hell. College wouldn't be college without a roomie experience that conjures up homicidal fantasies, but Odell's travails went beyond living with someone who refuses to wash the dishes or throw away sour milk. Working two jobs allowed Odell to save $1,000. The roommate and the money disappeared when his roommate gained access to Odell's account information. He had cleaned Odell out and fled Manhattan. Odell's landlord then told him the rent hadn't been paid, nor, Odell learned, had the roommate been paying the cable or phone bills. Odell moved out and rented a room in a woman's house on a month-to-month basis.

All was not lost for Odell, just most of his money. While at Kansas State he started dating his future wife, Jacqui, who attended school at

Haskell Indian Nations University in Lawrence, Kansas, ninety minutes from Manhattan. They saw each other on weekends, and by this
time Odell had started thinking about getting back into football.
Haskell, Trinity's opening-game opponent, seemed like the ideal place
to get back on the field. Not only would he be going to school with
his girlfriend, but he also thought he met the key qualification for admission. To attend the school, a student must provide a certificate degree of Indian blood, proving his or her Native American heritage.
Jacqui is Cherokee. Much of Odell's immediate family thought his
great-great-grandfather was Apache. But finding proof of that heritage was difficult; a fire destroyed key census records, and Odell's
family speculated that his great-great-grandfather might not have even
registered. Odell did a bit of his own research, and concluded the
whole thing might just be something of a "family myth." He couldn't
prove his ancestor was an Apache. He couldn't prove he wasn't.

Haskell was out.

Workouts intensified after Christmas of 2003 as Odell increased
his bench press from 210 pounds to 310. Several UMAC schools contacted Odell, but by then he was interested in Trinity. He enjoyed his
visit to the campus and his talks with Coach Bentley.

"I finally made the decision that I wanted to come here," Odell
says. "I said I'm ready to make a commitment to Trinity. [Bentley]
said, 'Praise the Lord' right there on the phone. When he said that, I
just felt the spirit on my body like I'd never felt before. I was letting
God work in my life and it felt good because I'd made too many mistakes in my life at K-State. I was going to bars, partying and stuff. It
wasn't how I wanted to be, but I was letting myself fall into it."

Before packing their bags, Jacqui and Lee were married on May
29, 2004, even though they were "flat broke." They held the ceremony in his mom's yard. Lea Anne, who remarried Carl Johnson,
made the cake and arranged the flowers. Odell's uncle is a pastor and
performed the ceremony at no cost. Jacqui found a free wedding
dress, thanks to a friend of her father's. The couple only paid for the
marriage license and Lee's clothes.

"We were really blessed with our wedding and getting up here,"
Jacqui says.

In Ellendale, Jacqui and Lee live in an off-campus one-bedroom apartment, whose availability they heard about from Coach Slivoskey. Several Trinity students live in the complex and pay only $25 per month, including utilities, because it is low-income housing. For the newlyweds, the apartment provides plenty of space and the kinds of amenities not available in a confined dorm room. The building is as quiet as a nursing home. They also don't have to worry about bed checks. They don't worry about sharing a bathroom with fifteen other people. And Lee enjoys the accommodations, which border on the luxurious compared with those of some of his teammates. During a lull in practice one day, fellow offensive lineman Michael Moss said he looked forward to getting back to his room in Kesler Hall. He planned on cooking up some meat on a hot plate.

"A hot plate?" Odell replied with a laugh. "I'm going back to my apartment, to my nice kitchen and making a real meal."

Life at Trinity has been good so far for the Odells. Raised in small towns, they enjoy the environment and the hospitality of Ellendale, though it was difficult to leave their home state of Kansas. Jacqui is like a mother to her five-year-old niece, Aspen, and now they have to stay connected just through the phone. For Lee, leaving Kansas meant leaving the other important woman in his life.

"It was really hard to leave my mom because she misses me a lot," he says. "I'll admit it; I'm a mama's boy. I respect her a lot for all the sacrifices she had to go through to make sure we had what we needed."

That respect Odell has for his mother does not extend to his birth father, Phillip. Usually easy to smile and quick with a laugh, Odell talks about his father with a clinical detachment, explaining their relationship in quiet sentences that sound like they're being read from a cue card. Phillip's in Leavenworth State Prison now, incarcerated for driving stolen cars from Indianapolis to Kansas City. But even when he was on the outside he wasn't a significant influence on Lee's life. While Odell was attending Highland Community College, William Jewel College near Kansas City recruited him. Lee and Phillip met the coach, went to the football games, and ate out together, typical father-son activities.

"I thought we were building a relationship," Odell says. "Then the next thing I know, I haven't heard from him in a year again, don't know if he's alive, dead, or in jail."

Phillip missed his son's wedding because he was in prison and missed his junior college graduation because, well, Lee is not really sure why. Odell's sister Ashely still writes to Phillip, something Lee finds himself unwilling to do. At least for now. At least for the foreseeable future.

"People tell me I should try to forgive him because I guess that's the Christian thing to do," he says. "I've tried to forgive him so many times it's hard. I probably will write him eventually, but I have to voice my concerns to him. I have to set myself in my mind not to care anymore because when I do care that's when I get burned."

According to what he tells Ashely, Phillip rarely contacts his children because he's broke and he knows they need money. Phillip, Odell says, "is the kind of guy who loves money and will do anything to get money and he puts money above all things.

"It's always someone else's fault," he continues. "He says he got in with the wrong people. If that's what happened, it wouldn't happen this many times. I don't want to turn out the way he did. I want to show him: I made it without you."

Jacqui and Lee have quickly become recognizable faces in Ellendale, around town and on the campus. Professors know the couple because they're in all but two classes together and sit in the front row. When she's not working as a waitress at the Fireside Steakhouse and Lodge, Jacqui is a member of the squadron of babysitters for Coach Bentley's four children. And they both work in the school cafeteria.

Although disappointed he wasn't named a team captain, Odell nonetheless wants to be a leader for the new-look Lions. He knew all about Trinity's 2003 troubles. To learn more all he had to do was watch some game film, which showed scene after scene of opposing defensive players flying past Trinity's linemen. Pop in a tape; see a quarterback sack. Throw in another; see a running back get crushed. "I watched a couple of films from last year when I first got here, and the offensive line looked like bullfighters," Odell says. "I saw an offensive tackle do a swim move on a defensive lineman; I don't think I've ever seen that before."

Odell's goal is to make the UMAC all-conference squad, a task that will be difficult given his dual roles of anonymity: he plays at Trinity, and he's one of the grunts who usually only gets noticed after a screw-up. Odell is an offensive lineman through and through, eager to discuss the intricacies of blocking and snapping the ball from a shotgun set.

Short, sturdy, and built like a bowling ball with auburn hair on top, the 5-foot, 8-inch Odell looks like he was created to burrow off the line toward a defender. He takes pride in his chosen craft. A lot of pride. How many other people carry a poem written about offensive linemen? Though odes to the hogs in the trenches remain on the fringe of the poetry world—it's doubtful Odell's former professor at Kansas State will have them on her syllabus any time soon—Odell's favorite piece on the boys up front isn't too bad. Especially since an Indiana middle school student named Josh Sabinas penned the missive. Odell found it on a Web site dedicated to eight-man football.

It reads:

Halfbacks dance and halfbacks flirt, while linemen crawl and eat dirt
When game time comes, backs run the ball.
When glory comes, they get it all.
But if 100 yards they gain, it's through the linemen's sweat and pain.
While halfbacks cry when they see blood, linemen hide it under mud.
Some backs have moves and others speed, but spirit's all a lineman needs.
Backs are good and some are fine, but they'd be nothing without the line.
A halfback loves and then he weds, but linemen only love their sleds.
The fans all see halfbacks run, but few see what the line has done.
And that's why those who know agree,
There's half a game the fans don't see.

Somewhere, a lineman weeps.

Odell's cohorts on the Trinity line include Tom Chaplin, the lone senior on the team who's often known simply as Big Tom. At 6-feet, 5-inches and 323 pounds, it's not an ironic nickname. Michael Moss, he of the hot plate exploits, came to Trinity from Arkansas, complete with an accent that leads to ribbing from teammates for his pronunciation of *bench* (sounds like a female dog out of Moss's mouth), and legendary Notre Dame coach Knute Rockne, known by Michael as "Ka-nute." The good-natured Moss takes the jabs in stride, an aw-shucks grin denting the impact of any barb. Moss played flag football as a youngster, but that's his only gridiron experience; he didn't play in high school, and planned on only trying out for the basketball team at Trinity. Moss isn't the only neophyte lineman for the Lions. Matt Johanson has experience, although it's as a running back and he hasn't played since graduating from high school in 2002. Isaac Smith was a good athlete growing up, but he spent his school years involved with the fine arts, not athletics. He last played football in eighth grade.

Offensive coordinator Eric Slivoskey likes the enthusiasm of the offensive line. But whether they're effective enough to help the team improve on its two-touchdown campaign from 2003 is in question.

"I said to Rusty, well, I think we're better this year, but we're still missing a line," Slivoskey says. "Our line, they give you everything that they have, but we're inexperienced there. We just don't have the physical size and strength that you see across the board on these other teams. Our strength is probably our running backs and a couple of our skills people."

Andy Brower is one of those skill-position players the Lions are counting on. The 6-foot, 3-inch receiver from Canton, South Dakota, is long and lean, with good size and good hands. Friendly and perpetually laid-back, Brower is often seen in the Kesler Hall lounge or his dorm room stringing a guitar. Seated on the lounge's couch, with a mop of shaggy brown hair hanging down near his eyes, Brower looks like he should be performing an acoustic set in some hip coffeehouse.

His living quarters look like those of any college student free from the pressures of keeping a room tidy for Mom and Dad. A Christian lives here, but a pig would be reluctant to enter. There's a microwave, mini-fridge, open drawers, loose change on the bed, and a Dallas Cowboys garbage bin overflowing with paper. Shoes and clothes—some dirty, some not—mingle on the floor with DVDs of *Charlie's Angels* and *Blue Streak*.

But the wall's a little different. Where many students might hang a poster of Eminem or one espousing the top fifty virtues of beer, Brower has printouts of various Bible verses. One paraphrases Proverbs 20:19: "A gossip tells secrets, so don't hang around with someone who talks too much." Another recites 2 Corinthians 6:3: "We try to live in such a way that no one will be hindered from finding the Lord by the way we act, and so no one can find fault with our ministry."

Along those lines, Brower also posts an essay he wrote. It was for a girl, not a class. In an online chat, a girl told Brower that she didn't know what to say to one of her friends who swears. Inspired to act, Brower wrote the paper, sent it to her, and also showed his father, Stan. Brower liked it so much it went up on his wall. In it he explains why he believes swearing is unacceptable for Christians. After citing some more Bible lines, Brower concludes with his own thoughts. He writes, "Now, if I am not mistaken, blasphemy is an unforgivable sin. Now don't get me wrong, I don't think swearing sends you to hell, but why would you even want to come close to being associated with blasphemy?"

Though only nineteen years old, Brower holds strict religious views that fit right in at Trinity. On Wednesday nights, Brower goes to the Church of the Nazarene in Ellendale. "I'm kind of iffy on that church," he says. "They don't believe in speaking in tongue. It's just weird because they say they want the Holy Spirit to move their serv-ice, but then they deny the power of speaking in tongues. You can't only believe in some things about God and shut out other things."

Religion's a family affair for Brower—religion and auto mechan-ics. His grandpa, Wesley Iverson, has been a pastor for fifty years, and Brower's father had a pastoral license through the Assemblies of God. Grandpa Wesley also opened Iverson's Body Shop in Canton,

South Dakota, which Brower's uncle now owns. When Iverson wasn't preaching, he was under a car hood. He could piece together a sermon or vehicle with equal aplomb. Still can. Even today, as he closes in on his eighty-third birthday, Iverson comes into the shop each day to get down and dirty with the vehicles. Brower started helping out around the shop when he was just five years old and began working there every day after school when he turned fourteen. He still knows his way around the shop; this past summer Brower completed the restoration of a 1957 Chevy for his uncle.

Brower's mom, Barb, attended Trinity for one semester after high school before getting married. While contemplating whether to come to Ellendale, Brower asked his grandparents for advice, and requested prayers from his grandpa and father. Barb suggested he think about Trinity since it offered degrees in business and Biblical studies. That fit with Brower's desire to be a pastor, and, as important, would give him the opportunity to play college football.

And this is college football, though Brower wasn't so sure once he started practicing with the Lions. He prepared hard for the season, thinking it would be tough to break into the lineup. Some teammates' conversations convinced him otherwise. "People are saying, 'Oh, I never played football in my life before,'" Brower says. "You don't come to college and play football if you've never played in high school. It's justifiable to me if your school was too small to have a football team, but you still wanted to play. I say if you had a high school team but you just decided not to go out for some reason, don't come out for college football."

Of course, there might not be a Trinity team without those players.

Brower grew up in a country home with three older brothers and a younger sister. The family dynamic left Brower wondering where he fit. Living in the country meant his social life consisted of family time. He played with his brothers, fought with his brothers, measured himself against his brothers. And, like pretty much all little brothers, Brower felt slighted that his older siblings ruled the roost. And with younger sister Beth being the only girl, and getting the attention that comes with being the baby of the family, Brower occasionally felt like an outsider. Birth order experts would have loved analyzing his childhood.

An accident that nearly killed him added to those feelings.

When he was nine years old, Brower was riding to school in a truck driven by his brother Kenny. On a country road, they collided with a grain truck, sending both Brower brothers into the windshield and shattering their faces. Andy broke his jaw on the right side and spent two weeks in the hospital; Kenny was hospitalized for nearly a month. Doctors wired shut Andy's jaw, and growing up he had difficulty opening his mouth. His jaw didn't grow as long as it should have. He had chubby cheeks, messed up teeth, and the pain was intense and constant. It was basically a recipe for ridicule.

"I used to be really mad all the time," Brower says. "Why do I always have to get the crap end of the deal? No one else has to deal with this kind of jaw or this kind of pain in their face all the time. I don't necessarily look like any of my family members because my face will never be square. I'm kind of glad God allowed me to go through it because I understand what it feels like for people to look at you differently or not understand you."

Even today, Brower lives with the ramifications of the decade-old accident.

Three years ago Brower underwent a surgery that made his jaw longer. In January of 2004, surgeons put a metal socket in the right side of his mouth. It left the right side numb for nearly three months. Fortunately, it alleviated the pain and doctors believe it will last the rest of Brower's life. The surgeon told Brower he could play football in a year; eight months later, he'll make his college debut.

An emotional transformation accompanied Brower's physical healing. Around his seventeenth birthday, Brower says he rededicated himself to God. The anger and bitterness he felt about his injuries, his place in life, dissipated. Serenity set in. Brower now glides through life with a "What, me worry?" attitude. The fights with his older brothers became a thing of the past. Brower even started seeing his sister in a different light.

"I didn't get along with my sister very well when I was little," he says. "She'd always be around me and annoy me. Once I rededicated myself to God, we became really close. For once she was actually a person, you know, instead of this stupid little sister." A birthday card from

Beth now hangs on Brower's wall, next to the selected Bible verses. Brower's parents were strict. No cards, no movies, no dances. Brower once ran into trouble when his parents discovered a ticket for the Tom Cruise movie *Minority Report*. The film's forays into the future, and the alteration of the future, bothered them. Now that he's away from home, Brower does attend the occasional R-rated movie, reasoning that they usually have that rating because of "war scene" violence. "There's a lot of movies that I just won't watch," he says. "Like *Gothika*, it's just like demonic garbage. There's no need to be watching that." He's not the first person to label the Halle Berry supernatural thriller garbage, though detractors focused more on plot problems and inane dialogue than religious implications.

Brower is breezing through his classes, making sure to read all required texts and assignments, not because he's after a high grade point average, but out of concern for his future profession. "If I'm a pastor someday I want somebody to be able to come up to me and ask me a question, and I don't want to tell them I don't know the answer," he says. "People are expecting me to learn this stuff."

Life in the classroom is going much better than on the practice field. Brower wishes the Lions worked more on individual receiving drills, which would help him develop more confidence in his hands. With a limited number of coaches, that proves impossible. Thirty-one players are on the Trinity roster. It's a geographically diverse group—the players hail from twenty states. There's only one player from North Dakota on the team, and more from Texas (four) than from Minnesota and South Dakota combined (three). Brandon Strong, who was responsible for bringing in many of the players, would like that changed in the coming years, believing small high schools in the upper Midwest could be fertile recruiting ground for Trinity. "We can start tapping into those schools," he says, "and not necessarily the Christian schools either. Because there's Christian guys at public schools."

Those are future plans. Today's Lions have their own challenges. Injuries have already hit the team before the first game. Defensive lineman Dustin Nichols, a twenty-eight-year-old freshman, known by one and all around campus as "Heavy," tore his knee in a preseason practice, ending his season before it even started. Heavy admirably uses his quick wit and outgoing personality to become a team motivational speaker, cheerleader, and frequent sideline critic of referees, but the Lions would rather have had his physical skills. Players express frustration that Bentley, who runs the defense, has not given them a defensive playbook, something Slivoskey provided for the team's offensive unit. Players request a defensive meeting, but one is never held. A lack of communications among the coaching staff leaves Slivoskey feeling a bit uneasy, even before the team has suited up for a game.

He frets, "Kids come to me, and say, 'What do I do on this defense?' Sometimes I just don't know because it really hasn't been communicated to me, and I look like a fool. And that bothers me, kind of makes me mad sometimes, just because it's a reflection onto me whether I want it or not."

SEPTEMBER 4, 2004

Although Trinity's first contest is a nonconference game, it's against a familiar foe. Haskell belongs to the NAIA, and it is unique among the country's colleges. It's the only tribal college that accepts students from all federally recognized tribes. Today there are one thousand students enrolled from nearly 150 tribes. Trinity has become a regular fixture on the Haskell schedule, which is anything but a football power. For ailing programs, the Lions are like penicillin in shoulder pads. In 2002, the Fightin' Indians defeated Trinity 68–0 in their seventh game of the season, snapping a twenty-three-game losing streak that extended back to the 2000 campaign. A 60–0 pasting of the Lions followed in 2003. That game was in Ellendale. This year Trinity makes the 620-mile trip to Lawrence, Kansas. The Lions take their road trips on a dilapidated, late-1970s model bus that looks like it last offered a comfortable ride around 1980. It's a tin tube on wheels. Players joke that the MTV show *Pimp My Ride* should take on the bus for a future project. But the ol' girl gets the job done; the Lions make it to Lawrence.

Game day doesn't start on a promising note. Strong stayed back on the Trinity campus at the request of his boss, Dan Kuno, to get to know the students on his dorm floor who aren't football players. The night before the team left for Kansas, Strong packed the team's medical tape. But just hours before the 1:00 p.m. kickoff Saturday, the kit is nowhere to be seen. Strong also tapes the players' ankles. Trinity needs equipment, and a replacement. In a bit of disarray, the Lions turn to their opponents for a helping hand.

"We're in the locker room before the game, and their trainers have to wrap us," says Trinity quarterback Dusty Hess. "We were using their tape, their pre-wrap, and Coach Bentley's watching."

On the field, it's the first chance for the Lions to see if they've improved. They have. By three points. Maybe Haskell's trainers taped Trinity's ankles too tightly. The Fightin' Indians jump to a 30–0 lead at halftime, highlighted by running back Marcus Benally, who slices through the Lions for 100 yards in the opening half. Any hope the Lions have that the second half will be different ends ten seconds into the third quarter, when Haskell's Cory Murphy returns the opening kickoff for a touchdown.

Final score: Haskell 57, Trinity 0.

Hess makes his first collegiate start after spending two years playing semi-pro ball in Indiana in the Cross Roads Football League. The league boasted some big names—Hess was a teammate of former NFL running back Curtis Enis. But many players in the league, including Enis, were past their prime and in their late thirties or early forties, old enough to be Dusty's dad, if not reliable receiving targets. Even at the small-college level, the competition is higher. A fact Hess's body quickly learned.

"College, everything happens so fast," he says. "My first scramble, I got hit, and that was the first time in my life I had seen stars. I realized, this could be a long year." Hess also suffered a burst blood vessel in his right hand, but hopes ice will be enough to heal the injury.

Following the defeat, his tenth in a row as a college coach, Bentley calls home, a tradition after road games. His four kids usually boost his spirits with their presence and nonstop energy. This time, his eldest son, Trey, offers verbal encouragement, using the same words Rusty told him after a youth soccer game the previous spring.

"He said, 'How'd you do, dad?' I said we lost. He goes, 'That's OK, daddy. Just remember, when they're bigger and they're stronger, you gotta run faster.' That's what I told him. When they're bigger and they're stronger, you just gotta run faster."

It's a difficult homecoming for Lee Odell, whose mom, stepdad, and several cousins attended the game. Work kept Jacqui back in Ellendale, unable to return home or see her husband's first college start. Back spasms plague the anchor of Trinity's offensive line, but he plays through them. Odell hoped for a good showing against his wife's former school and the college he once hoped to attend. Now all he wants to do is get home.

Unfortunately, a marathon bus trip waits. Torturous bus journeys are a way of life for the Lions, who spend more time on the road than rock bands. The U.S. Navy has shorter road trips. Though Haskell was a nonconference game, Trinity's travel for conference games is not any better. Following defeats, the Lions climb aboard, knowing they are still hours and hours away from being back in the comforts of their homes (or dorms). On the team bus, where every bump is felt, the team usually relaxes with a movie—as long as the flick meets the school's moral guidelines. That can mean some censorship that frustrates the players, who just want a little distraction after a long day on the field. Anyone in authority can be a critic, from the bus driver to Bentley. They have the power to dole out the ultimate thumbsdown to any picture deemed too racy for the players.

During one trip, the team began watching *The Replacements*, a seemingly harmless choice since it involves a ragtag bunch of football players achieving an upset victory. But, Odell says, "They said the S-word twice and Coach Bentley shut it off. But then we watched *Major League 2* and it said, like, everything, eight times. We're like, 'Why can't we watch *The Replacements?*'"

Still, viewing pleasures are secondary to the desire to get home. Odell, in particular, doesn't want to waste time anywhere on the road. Not even when nature calls. "We'll be on there for seventeen hours, and people want to stop," he says. "I'm like, 'No, keep going. Just use the bathroom on the bus. Don't stop.'"

After the Haskell game, Odell only thought about Ellendale. Tiny Ellendale, 730 miles from his tiny hometown of Thayer. Despite being surrounded by loved ones, Odell didn't want to be in Kansas anymore. As he dragged his aching body on to the team bus, he reflected on where he's been, where he is, and where he wants to be.

"I was thinking, I want to get home. Not, I'm in Kansas, I am home. It was like a whole different mindset for me," he says. "That home is a different place. I'm married now, home is with my wife. Yeah, I want to go home and visit my parents and all that, but I have no intention of leaving and moving back before I graduate. I want to finish at Trinity."

Trinity is home. Ellendale is home. Ask folks at Trinity, and they'll say it only took a miracle to bring town and school together.

Chapter Six

Small Places

U.S. Highway 281 runs from the Canadian border to the Mexican border, stretching nearly two thousand miles, winding through North Dakota, South Dakota, Kansas, Nebraska, Oklahoma, and Texas. Along the way drivers can stop and view the Alamo in San Antonio or the world's largest buffalo (a twenty-six-foot high, sixty-ton statue of it, anyway) in Jamestown, North Dakota. But of all the big cities and small villages along the road, there's probably not a college town quite like Ellendale, North Dakota.

Maybe "college town" is the wrong label. College town evokes images of cultural and recreational institutions, of campuses teeming with thousands of young people, of bars and clubs bustling with action, filled with those looking for action. So maybe Ellendale's not a college town, but more like a town that happens to have a college. Travelers on Highway 281 don't even have to stop while driving through the flat, fertile farmland surrounding Ellendale. There's a flashing yellow light where the road intersects with Main Street, but only vehicles going east or west stop, thanks to a flashing red light. Passersby probably never realize that Ellendale is the seat of Dickey County, even though the imposing and impressive courthouse stands just across the street from Ellendale High School. And unless they catch the sign on the side of the road, outsiders won't know this is home to Trinity Bible College. The school is easy to miss, tucked away from the town's throughways.

They're linked now and seem like they were made for each other, the small town with 1,559 people and the small school with 310 students. Ellendale's had some kind of college since 1899, only seventeen years after the town was founded. The names of the school changed, as did the missions, but the pride residents felt in having an institute of higher learning remained. From its nearly forty-year stint as the State Normal Industrial College, to its days as the University of North Dakota–Ellendale Branch, folks in town have always been able to puff their chests out a bit when it came to the college.

But in the fall of 1972, people in Ellendale wondered how long they could live with the town's newest residents. That's the year Trinity Bible College arrived to take over the campus. It took only a dollar to bring the school to Ellendale. It took only a few proclamations of eternal damnation to nearly tear the two apart.

In its first twenty-four years, Trinity had more homes than a military family as the school wandered the Dakotas, searching for a permanent residence. In 1948, classes began at the school in Devils Lake, North Dakota, although the school was originally named Lakewood Park Bible School. Eighteen students attended classes that first year in Devils Lake. Enrollment increased each year until, finally, in 1960, the school was forced to move, not because of the host town's name, but because of a lack of facilities. Aberdeen, South Dakota, was the next stop for the school—which, as an ode to its new home, became known as Hub City Bible Institute. In 1967 it relocated again, this time to Jamestown, drawn by the vacancy at the Trinity Hospital building, not by the famed statue of an oversized buffalo.

By the 1970s, Trinity was again scouring the land for a new home. At the same time, Ellendale was losing its beloved University of North Dakota campus, doomed by flames and politics. A fire in January 1970 ravaged the college, destroying Carnegie Hall, the school's signature facility, which contained classrooms and an auditorium for assemblies. It also leveled the home economics building. Townspeople suspected arson. A student at the school, "a known fire bug," according to one local, was believed to be the culprit. But authorities could prove nothing.

Unfortunately for the people of Ellendale, the fire nudged along a fate that was probably inevitable.

For years the state of North Dakota had threatened to shut down the University of North Dakota–Ellendale Branch, citing declining enrollment, along with other financial, geographical and structural reasons. The college remained open thanks to the determination of the townsfolk, who often provided money for improvements, such as men's dormitories. The flames made it even easier for the state to get its wish, and it shuttered the campus.

The state legislature conducted a nationwide search to find new tenants, advertising in a wide array of publications throughout the country. Dozens of proposals were submitted; lawmakers considered everything from a police training school to a residential school for the mentally challenged. Universities also expressed interest in purchasing the equipment left over at the Ellendale school. The collection at the campus's library, which contained more than fifty thousand volumes, was thought to be on the selling block. It looked like the school might be sold off piece by piece, its valuables farmed out to bidders and buyers.

Into the situation strolled Trinity president Roy Wead, who became the school's first president in 1968. Wead, a former pastor whose students were crammed into a single building, the converted hospital in Jamestown, put in his own bid for the campus: one dollar. A buck for the whole works. Instead of laughing at the audacity of Wead's proposal, the legislative committee was intrigued.

"There were legislators who were saying, if the proposals we're getting for it aren't very good, if we're going to give it away, let's give it to someone who's going to be helpful to North Dakota," recalls Doug Wead, Roy's son. "This one would educate students in the state and help keep young students in the state."

Improbably, Trinity acquired the campus, starting classes in the fall of 1972. The twenty-eight acres, the classrooms, the library, the print shop, the dorms, the sports complex—everything belonged to Trinity. And all for a single dollar. As land grabs go, it didn't exactly rival the Louisiana Purchase in terms of historical significance, but it might have been a better deal.

Doug Wead told the entire story of his father's quest to land the new campus in his 1975 book, *The Great Multimillion Dollar Miracle*. In the thirty years since the book's publication, Doug Wead has become one of the leading evangelical figures in the country, especially active in political circles. He also became a best-selling author with the historical books *All the Presidents' Children* and *The Raising of a President*. He's written nearly thirty books and given speeches on four continents.

He was special assistant to the first President Bush, and was considered a friend of the second. At least until he created a minor furor in February 2005 when he allowed a *New York Times* reporter to listen to a series of recordings he had made of George W. Bush before his ascendancy to the White House. In the recordings, the then governor of Texas discussed political rivals such as John McCain and Al Gore, saying McCain would "wear thin" with voters and mocking Gore for admitting marijuana use. Bush also said he would refuse to answer questions from the press about any past indiscretions, telling Wead, "I wouldn't answer the marijuana questions. You know why? Because I don't want some little kid doing what I tried." The recordings inflicted minimal political damage on the president—some pundits said the tapes actually helped him because they showed him speaking in private the same way he spoke in public. Still, the author expected fallout. Wead told the *New York Times* he knew Bush might feel betrayed by the release of the recordings, an assumption that sounded accurate when a White House spokesman announced, "The governor was having casual conversations with someone he believed was his friend."

Wead no longer has any contact or relationship with Trinity, but his fondness for the institution is still evident in conversation. When asked about the school, he turns a bit wistful, as if he's just been asked about an old high school sweetheart.

The author never has to worry about the Trinity population turning against his work. Despite all he's accomplished since, the slim, ninety-four-page book he wrote three decades ago remains his most admired accomplishment on the Trinity campus, though he might like to forget the book's black-and-white photos of him sporting a mustache and mini-Afro. For several years students were required to read the book; now it serves as an uplifting reminder to students and staff of how the school found a home in Ellendale.

While happy that a fresh batch of students now occupied the campus—business leaders especially were anxious for the college to find new occupants—a few Ellendale residents were perplexed and upset at the price of the transaction. Four quarters buy you a college campus? They directed much of the anger at the state.

Those feelings were exacerbated by the exuberance of the new students. Buoyed by what they saw as a financial miracle—and it's hard to call the title of Wead's book an exaggeration—Trinity's students set about trying to spread the word of Jesus, living by the message, "It's easy to believe in miracles when you live on one." They wanted to save their new neighbors. Oh, how they wanted to save them. Students marched up and down Main Street and door to door, proclaiming their beliefs, preaching to anyone who wanted to listen and even those who didn't. A shocking lack of tact matched the over-the-top enthusiasm. Turn or burn, they warned, not so subtly. The message didn't take with the longtime inhabitants, already wary of the outsiders who had taken over the pride of their town.

"They came across as if we were all heathens and they were going to save everybody," says Jeanette Robb-Ruenz, who moved to Ellendale when she was two years old in 1941 and has lived in a country home since 1971. "They came on a little strong, and it's too bad. They stepped on a lot of toes."

It's not as if Trinity had relocated to Sodom or Gomorrah. Religion runs deep in Ellendale, with an even longer history than the town's college. Robb-Ruenz, the sixty-five-year-old former teacher who's also the town's resident historian, says there were church services within the first year of the town's creation. "It was held in a saloon, but it was a church service." Today there are eight churches in town, including a Catholic, Lutheran, Assemblies of God, and First Baptist. In 1972, those parishioners, and those who never stepped foot into a church, really weren't interested in hearing that they were headed to hell. Especially from a bunch of fresh-faced youngsters barely out of high school, students some in town viewed almost as intruders.

Dan Kuno was a seventeen-year-old Trinity freshman in 1972, too intimidated, he says, to be a part of the rabble-rousers or to intimidate anyone else. Thirty years later, as the school's dean, he often has to play the campus heavy, enforcing Trinity's myriad rules and keeping tabs on the student body; the dreaded dean, who's really not that frightening as long as you don't screw up. And even when that happens, the brawny Kuno says he is more interested in helping solve a problem than punishing one.

But he's also part of a continuing effort to bring town and school closer together. Time healed many of the old wounds; students toned down the public zealotry and residents grew more comfortable with the newcomers. A generation that was around in 1972 is gone now. Another has never known a time when Trinity wasn't a part of the community. For their part, Trinity students likely have no idea how that first class acted upon entry into the town. The school also took active steps to smooth over the relationship's rough start, not wanting to ruin life at their new home after so many years searching for a place to call their own.

"I think in their exuberance they lacked the knowledge," Kuno says of the first Trinity class in Ellendale. "I watched some of those people, and I watched some of those not make it in ministry because you have to deal with people. We made some mistakes; let's not repeat history. Let's make a new history."

That new history includes a day each September when students go around town painting, mowing, and cleaning up wherever they're needed. Trinity's leaders have also ingrained themselves in the community. Steve Tvedt isn't just the vice president of college relations; he's the pastor in Ellendale's First Baptist Church. Trinity President Dennis Niles, whom Robb-Ruenz and many others credit for working to bring school and community together, has been involved with Ellendale's civic association and job development authority. The college bookstore, the Carpenter's Shop, is now located on Main Street. Trinity is also one of the largest employers in the town, providing jobs for fifty full-time workers and twenty-four part-time workers. Neither party can afford to exist as separate entities. Not with a school this size in a town this size.

"We just don't have the resources that we can just sort of independently operate and ignore one another," Niles says.

There are those in Ellendale who still grumble that the Trinity community does ignore the town, at least its businesses. They prefer taking Highway 281 to Aberdeen, a city perhaps best known for rather ghoulish reasons: In 1999, the plane of golfer Payne Stewart crashed in a field outside of town, killing him and the others on board.

When Trinity first arrived in town, some residents felt they saw—or at least heard—too much from the students. Now they feel they don't see enough of the college population. But Trinity students and professors wouldn't be the only ones skipping the charms and stores of downtown for the variety and pricing of Aberdeen, which will never be confused with a metropolis, but does at least have a Wal-Mart.

"When I was a kid Aberdeen was a place you went to once a year," says Dickey County recorder Tom Strand, a 1966 Ellendale High School graduate. "Now people are going there if they want a drink of pop."

Dying small towns would almost be cliché if they weren't so prevalent, deserted downtowns and closed schools serving as testaments to better days. Ellendale isn't near death, but it has seen more prosperous times. The railroad, which brought Ellendale to life in the 1880s, stopped coming through town around 1980. Back in the day, Ellendale had two car dealerships, three grocery stores, a couple of clothing stores, and a movie theater. Townsfolk were just minutes away from nearly every service they needed. Now there's one dealership, and Char's Food Pride is the only grocery store. The clothing store went out of business. So did the theater. But the town of fifteen hundred does manage to support two funeral homes.

There's also no cell phone service available in Ellendale, meaning users have to drive a few miles outside of town to get a signal. An Ellendale resident even spotted one desperate citizen sitting atop a park slide attempting to complete a call. That's not the type of service that makes for a good billboard campaign on the edge of town.

ELLENDALE: Come for the friendliness, leave for a phone call
Getting a tower up is one of the city's primary goals.

Both Trinity and Ellendale are taking aggressive measures to energize themselves. The school started work in 2005 on a $2.2 million student life center, which will house offices, a computer lab, science lab, and classrooms. The facility will be attached to the cafeteria and will have an enclosed walkway between it and the campus chapel. It will also have a snack shop and lounging areas. With a nod to its past, Trinity calls the campaign "Building on a miracle."

Ellendale's not after a miracle with its projects, just a few visitors. Architectural students from North Dakota State University in Fargo spent the fall months presenting plans for a new-look Ellendale. Proposals focused on downtown, where the students advocated a historical look for storefronts. More important, they offered plans for ways to get traffic to slow down, giving those behind the wheel a chance to take in the view. Instead of speeding through, oblivious to the surroundings and slowing down only out of fear of being clocked by a radar gun, maybe travelers would snoop around a bit more, perhaps even spend a night in a local motel.

Ellendale, North Dakota: Tourist trap.

A group is also attempting to restore a bit of culture to downtown. The Opera House on Main Street opened for business in 1909. Over the next several decades, plays, debates, dances, basketball games, and various other events were held there. In addition to housing several businesses, it was the regional center for performing arts. In the 1970s, though, the auditorium in the Opera House was no longer in use. According to Robb-Ruenz, that section was likely shut down because it was no longer safe for crowds. By 1996 the building, which the city owned, began to suffer from a leaky roof. Businesses moved out, and the city shut down the three-story edifice. Robb-Ruenz, whose obsession with the town's past is matched by her passion for its future, is president of the team trying to restore the building.

O.P.E.R.A. (Organization of People in Ellendale for the Restoration of the Arts) has raised money and received a grant from the North Dakota Historical Society. They're hoping to complete the restoration by 2007, which will be Ellendale's 125th anniversary. It will cost approximately $2.5 million, although that number is expected to rise, and when it's done O.P.E.R.A. hopes the Opera House will again host dinner theaters, musical productions, conferences, and businesses.

Robb-Ruenz is a one-woman, bespectacled Google search when it comes to information about Ellendale and Dickey County. Ask her a question; get an answer, usually within seconds. She balances her time with O.P.E.R.A. with work as secretary of the Ellendale Historical Society. She's also chairperson for Preservation North Dakota, president of the American Legion Auxiliary, and vice president of the Whitestone Hill Battlefield Historical Society (in 1863 a brutal fight between white troops and American Indians on the battlefield, twenty-eight miles northwest of Ellendale, left an estimated three hundred Indians and twenty soldiers dead).

And that's not even the whole list. Robb-Ruenz also finds time to work as a features reporter and proofreader for the weekly *Dickey County Leader*, whose offices are in Ellendale. She's found in the Leader one day poring over the newspaper's archives from the 1980s, searching for information that a caller requested on a murder-suicide that occurred in the area. It's a rare piece of local history that's not simply cataloged in her mind and at her fingertips. When she's not playing historical detective or advocate for all things in Ellendale, Robb-Ruenz also finds time to substitute teach. All this after a thirty-year career as a junior high teacher in nearby Hecla, South Dakota. "My obituary's going to look really nice," she jokes, but she's got much to accomplish before those lines are ever written.

"There's not a lot to do in the community, unfortunately, and we'd like to change that," she says. "I love Ellendale, and I want to see it grow. I want to see it become something more than it's leading toward. There's potential here. It could become bigger and better, and it has a lot to offer."

Ellendale's not alone on the Great Plains when it comes to questions about the future. The state has been facing the problem of population loss for some time. According to U.S. Census numbers, North Dakota's population grew by one percent in the 1990s, the lowest growth of any state in the country. And that one-percent growth occurs in the bigger cities such as Fargo, not in the rural towns. Robb-Ruenz knows firsthand the desire many young people feel to leave Ellendale once they've grown up. Of her three boys, one now lives in California, another in Minneapolis, and a third is a career Navy man living in Washington State.

Passionate people like Robb-Ruenz, who says that her husband tells her she's trying to "save Ellendale one building at a time," provide the town hope that it's not going to be a footnote in fifty years, that it won't be a place that's simply remembered for what it once was. But it'd be a stretch to think Ellendale's ever going to experience a large-scale transformation. It is what it is, says county recorder Strand, who has lived in Denver and Phoenix, but prefers his current home. He came back to run for office in 1982 and has no regrets.

"If you like hunting, fishing, outdoor stuff, it's a good place to be," he says. "You can have your privacy if you want to, and if you've got a family it's a good place to raise them."

Indeed, orange-clad pheasant and deer hunters invade the area each autumn, filling the lodges and local watering holes, where they regale each other with tales—some true, most probably not—from the day's activities.

It's not just an outdoorsman's paradise. With a virtually nonexistent crime rate and cheap housing—Rusty Bentley paid about $29,000 for the family's 2,100-square foot home—Ellendale is great for families, especially those with small children. It's when those kids get older that the town might lose some of its attractiveness.

"The educational system seems good," Eric Slivoskey says. "I think as my kids would get older, the cultural things would probably be more of an issue. When they're four and they're two, it's like, 'Man, there's a lot of playgrounds in town, this is a great place, dad.' But when they're twelve and ten, 'Where's the mall at, dad? That's not a mall in Aberdeen. That's a ShopKo.'"

Life certainly moves slower here, perfect for anyone looking for some peace. Residents must make sacrifices. "I get the USA Today," Slivoskey says, "but here you get it a day late. So it's more like the USA Yesterday."

But is it a good place for the college crowd? Well, there are only three places to get a drink in town—the Corner Corral, the American

Legion, and the Fireside Steakhouse—so most college students wouldn't describe it as energetic nightlife. For Trinity students, of course, the establishments might as well put moats in front of the doors because any consumption of alcohol would be against school rules. And there are eyes on the students. One year a thirsty, daring student bought some alcohol and returned to the dorms. Vice President Tvedt, tipped off by the business owner, greeted the potential imbiber, and confiscated the loot. Can't fool The Man at a college the size of a small high school, in a town where everyone knows your face, if not your name.

There's also the weather. Anyone from North Dakota can tell you the winter really isn't that bad and doesn't last ten months (maybe nine, but not ten), but adjusting to the cold, wind, and snow is tough for students who have spent their whole lives in warm climates. During practices, Trinity's players from warm-weather states are often seen bundled up, huddled together like refugees, comforting each other with the phrase, "Ooh, it's cold." And that's when the temperatures are in the forties, balmy fall weather for the natives. For the football program, it's just one more hurdle in the never-ending recruiting battle, and one reason why Strong's desire to attract more players from the Midwest might be smart. It's hard enough being homesick, which is inevitable for the students from places like California, Texas, and Washington. Being homesick and cold? That's too cruel. Bentley, for one, doesn't mind the climate, even after a lifetime in Texas. A four-legged member of his family has different feelings. Chico, the family's Chihuahua, doesn't take to the cold.

"Chico is the one Bentley that hates this town, hates this climate," he says. "When he goes and wee-wees, it freezes."

Trinity does diversify the Ellendale population. The town, which has many residents with German and Norwegian backgrounds, is overwhelmingly white—97.3 percent of the population, according to the Census, with 1.3 percent being Native American—but Trinity attracts students of all races from across the country. Twenty percent of the Lions' thirty-man roster is black. One of those six players, Lester "Train" Williams, came up from St. Louis. Williams grew up in a black neighborhood, but went to a school that was primarily white, making the transition to Ellendale fairly smooth. He says his parents brought him up to not see a person's race.

Adjusting to the look and pace of North Dakota was a bigger challenge.

"Coming up here I was like, wow, look at all this land," he says. "And all the cows. We see cows once in a while, but not as many as I've seen up here.

"Back in St. Louis there's a lot to do, it's right out in front of you. Here it's like I gotta go find entertainment."

Entertainment might consist of a long walk around town or a trip to the bowling alley. Students also get creative. For instance, when the snow falls, Lions linebacker Dustin Harper straps a plastic snowboard to a rope behind his 1992 Honda Accord, providing a land-based version of water skiing for anyone daring enough to climb aboard. Riders don't wear helmets—"We're stupid like that," the usually smart and sane Harper says—but it's an exciting adventure that at least shows imagination on the part of Trinity's students. The leaders of the campus dorms often organize group activities, including late-night games of dodgeball in the campus gymnasium, where as always the strong prey on the weak. Still, a good time is had by all, except those who get their glasses shattered. The boys in Kesler created an alternate, slightly more brutal version of the game that involves tennis balls, but no shirts. It's against the unwritten rules to hide behind the hall breaks on each floor for more than five seconds. Only cowards do that; if you do, the opponents get a free shot. Welts are commonplace and, for a generation raised on the antics of the *Jackass* crew, a source of pride.

But the students' feelings on the town itself?

"This town is just pretty hard-core dead," says Sannon Norick, Trinity's standout sophomore fullback.

Norick is always blunt and straightforward when he speaks, whether it's about the football team's future or the school's newest students ("This freshmen class brought in a lot of nerds"). In many ways Norick embodies everything Trinity feels is good about its students—he's deeply faithful, articulate and charismatic. But he often wonders what he's doing in Ellendale, whether he should already be experiencing more of the world. His ambitions include those of many an All-American boy—wanting to become a fireman, perhaps on the East Coast—and the goals of many a Trinity student—going on a mission trip overseas, perhaps to Australia or New Zealand. And he's got the dreams of many a, well, English soccer hooligan—"I wanna go down to South America, start a riot," he says. "Go to a soccer game and be part of the mob. I just think that'd be something huge."

Although he's outgoing and enjoys mingling with anyone on campus—nerd or no nerd—it feels like Norick might be misplaced in this North Dakota village. Many Trinity students have pasts that are the stuff of after-school specials or an *Oprah* episode. They've often been wounded, occasionally physically, but usually emotionally and spiritually. They were picked on as kids; they battled a deadly disease, fought drug addiction or alcohol abuse. They didn't always live by the words they preach so feverishly today. They come to Ellendale to find acceptance, to find a place where they can turn their life around and find out what Jesus has in plan for them. That's the school's mission, at least.

Norick, on the other hand, has been an alpha male for years, an independent kid with no popularity problems. It's been that way most of his life, dating back to his days growing up in Montana. His seven siblings, two brothers and five sisters, worship him; one of them—Shyann Norick—followed him to Trinity, where she's in her first year (presumably, Shyann is not one of Sannon's aforementioned geeks). The first-born son loves the large family. He can't imagine growing up any other way. Can't imagine not having a bunch of kids to someday call his own. "When you can split into teams and play games as a family, that's pretty cool." Norick excelled at running back and linebacker for Chester High School in north central Montana, where as a senior he led the perennial playoff contender in tackles and averaged more than one hundred yards rushing per game, a figure he hasn't come close to approaching at Trinity.

The Noricks moved into Chester when Sannon was fifteen. Until then the family lived in the country, at the base of a mountain, surrounded by rolling hills, thirty miles from the nearest town and two miles from its closest neighbor. Shawn Norick, the head of the household, was the epitome of a mountain man, Sannon says, able to "kill anything with his bare hands." Shawn worked on a ranch and, along with his wife Ruthann, taught the Norick children how to enjoy their environment. The Norick brood rarely watched television, instead using their surroundings as amusement. In an activity that would make People for the Ethical Treatment of Animals weep, Norick and his friends would hop on their four-wheelers and "play polo with rabbits," belting the cute, hopping, furry creatures. The Norick kids also enjoyed jumping off a barn and onto their trampoline, propelling themselves onto a nearby haystack. It was X Games for the rural set. At Trinity, Norick is part of the group riding the snowboard behind Harper's Accord.

"I've never broken any major bones," Norick says. "I've got my guardian angel. He's getting his money's worth."

Even after the family left the wilderness for Chester, the Norick household remained the center of activity. Sannon's friends hung out there, his sisters' friends hung out there, and they all looked up to him. He's grown comfortable in the leadership role, though it took some time. Norick says he's never drank alcohol or smoked, activities he says were common in small-town Montana, especially among high schoolers. But Norick felt he needed to be a role model for his friends and siblings. It could be tough, especially when his little brothers would make sure to be seen when Sannon had a girl over, but Norick appreciates his responsibility. He once saw his own prep football idol at a party, "slobberknockered and passed out," and resolved to be "a hero that's worth looking up to, especially to my little brothers. To them I'm the king."

Growing up in Montana prepared him for the cultural life in Ellendale, but the football team's struggles in his freshman year were something that caught him off guard. He suffered a severe concussion in the second game of the season that affected his entire first-year campaign. "The definition of a true power fullback," according to Slivoskey, the 6-foot, 1-inch, 230-pound Norick, who was named the most dedicated player on his Chester High School team, is a key to

Trinity's offensive plans. Along with speedy first-year tailback Stephen Poyser, the Lions hope to feed Norick the ball, using him to eat up a bit of the clock, shorten their games, giving them a better chance to maybe win a game, or at least stay close.

The muscular sophomore's in for a beating.

On any team and at any level, fullbacks always take more punishment than nearly all other players. They're the crash test dummies of the offense, sacrificing their bodies for the betterment of all. At Trinity there's just a bit more punishment. Norick is a bit taller than the average, squat, no-necked fullback, but his role's the same. When not blocking, challenging linebackers head-on, he's carrying the ball, often for minimal yardage. The Lions' struggles at offensive line mean defenders usually hit Norick a second after he gets the ball tucked in his arms. Instead of three yards and a cloud of dust, Norick is lucky to get one yard before being nearly pounded into dust.

Norick spent most of his freshman season disappointed on the football field. Finally he did manage to find a bit of inspiration between the sidelines, just not during a game, and not during the season. One night in February, with frustrations piling up in his life, Norick wandered over to Trinity's football field, which is no more than a five-minute walk from the men's dorm. "That's where I feel at home. It's the place that I'm most comfortable," he says. Norick went looking for a sign that Trinity was the place for him. He rested on the field, looking up at the dark sky.

"Foolishly, I was like, 'I'm calling you out, God,'" Norick says. "'I want to see that you're here.' We're taught that you're not supposed to do that, you're supposed to have that faith. I told him, 'I want a shooting star.'"

Nothing happened. No star. No sign. But as he started walking off the field, "something lit up the sky. It was huge. Right there I sort of broke inside, because at that moment I knew God was real. To me it felt like he was standing right there beside me saying, 'I'm here, you're just not looking.'"

Whether the work of a deity or just a random celestial occurrence with impeccable timing, the star made Sannon's life at Trinity easier. It acted like a tranquilizer, but without the side effects. He felt more at peace, with himself and the school. Before his sophomore season, Norick flirted with the idea of transferring to play football at Bethel University, a strong Division III program in Minnesota. He chose to stay at Trinity, a decision he calls a blessing since it gives him a chance to attend the same school as his sister. Not that he'll be sticking around for the long term. There are goals to fulfill, like working as a firefighter, like going on a mission for the church, like, well, maybe not that whole riot plan, but who knows?

"People back home said I was a dreamer, but I made it out of Montana," Norick says. "Not too far, but I'm not going to stop here."

When he graduates he'll leave Ellendale, like many young people before him, only a little less nostalgic than those who grew up here.

And surely the town will live on; probably looking much like it does today, with perhaps a few fewer people, with perhaps a few fewer businesses. It'll still be the small town with the small college and some big dreams. And some good hunting.

Chapter Seven

A Game of Inches

There aren't many games on Trinity's schedule that the Lions look at and think, "Now this is a team we can handle." There's only one opponent that fits that description: the Principia College Panthers.

Trinity's 2004 home opener on a sunny, seventy-degree Saturday afternoon presents the Lions with a great opportunity for victory, their best opportunity all season. Tiny Principia College out of Elsah, Illinois, forty miles from St. Louis, has an enrollment of fewer than six hundred and a football roster of twenty-five. The small roster is not for a lack of effort from Principia coach Mike Barthelmess, a positive, high-energy guy facing challenges that even Trinity can't quite relate to.

Only Christian Scientists attend Principia, which was established in 1912 and is part of a school system founded by a St. Louis woman concerned about the moral and spiritual lessons her children were learning in school. Enrollment has been dropping at the school for a few years, from a high of about 900 to its current 542. That the school is home solely to Christian Scientists severely limits the team's pool of potential players. How shallow is that pool? For 2004 Barthelmess had fifty kids in the country he could recruit. Fifty. Fifty Christian Scientists he hopes can play college football at the Division III level. At a meeting of UMAC coaches, Barthelmess listened patiently to his coaching peers bemoan various problems. Finally he interrupted and explained a bit about his situation. Each year, he told them, he'd have to land a fifth of his recruiting class just to bring ten fresh players to the program. But even that kind of success on a yearly basis would ultimately land him only a forty-man roster, a size any team in the league outside of Trinity would be terrified to play with. Suddenly the other UMAC coaches felt better about their own difficulties.

Barthelmess attacks the recruiting challenges. When the season ends in November, he hits the road, personally visiting each player he's pursuing. With only fifty recruits, he can't afford to conduct his campaign solely via mail or phone calls; it requires face-to-face interactions with each name on his list. He takes some time off in December to spend with his family, but when school begins in January he's back at it. And in February he's again on the recruiting path for several more weeks. He also keeps watch on high school juniors, potential players he can't yet contact, but can watch. The recruiting pool for the 2005 season will shrink even more, all the way down to only thirty-five potential Panthers.

Barthelmess faces other obstacles. The price tag for a Principia education is $26,000 per year (like all Division III schools, Principia cannot offer athletic scholarships). Coupled with the school's rigorous moral guidelines, Barthelmess could be excused if he engaged in a little self-pity.

But he doesn't. He loves his job, primarily because he loves the school. It's where he received his own college education as a two-sport stud in the early 1980s. In addition to his exploits on the football field, the 1983 graduate still holds the school record for lowest ERA by a pitcher for a single season. Although he scrapes and claws for players today, Barthelmess does know how the other half lives. In 1989, he worked as a graduate assistant at the University of Houston, helping coach the Cougars' wide receivers and quarterbacks. That year Houston quarterback Andre Ware directed an aerial show that netted him college football's highest honor—the Heisman Trophy. Barthelmess enjoyed the game of football, but not the lifestyle of Division I-A football. He saw the hours coaches put in and witnessed the turmoil that resulted from the pressures. He saw what it did to the coaches' families; many of the coaches only saw their kids when their wives would stop by the offices. He knew he wasn't long for that world.

Barthelmess brought his love of the passing game to Principia as its head coach in the early 1990s, directing a high-flying attack that cracked the record books. One of his quarterbacks, Jordan Poznick, set a Division III record with eighty-one pass attempts in a single game, and twice led the nation in total offense. Barthelmess left the school in 1996 to start up the South Carolina Sports Academy, saying he was "still trying to figure out what I want to be when I grow up." But he returned to Illinois a few years later. He began his second stint as football coach in 2002, fully aware of the challenges.

"It's David and Goliath all of the time here," Barthelmess says. "The fact that we have a football program at all in my mind is a miracle. There just seem to be so many things going against it."

Goliath is nowhere to be seen when the Panthers face Trinity. This is David versus David, and they're both still using slingshots while the rest of the conference has moved up to machine guns. Principia's not a sister school of Trinity's, but it's the closest thing to a soul mate the Lions have in the UMAC. Their sizes and struggles bond them, as do their strict guidelines off the field and their disappointments on it. Principia does have one thing going for it against the Lions. While the Lions are a hodgepodge of experienced players and those suiting up for the first time in their lives, the Panthers have seasoned football players throughout the roster. These guys can play. There's just not very many of them.

"We have thirty ballplayers, but we may have twenty football players," Rusty Bentley says of his Lions. "They have twenty-eight football players, but no non-football players. That makes a difference."

This should be a close game. But Trinity thought its 2003 game against Principia would be close, too. That one was basically over at halftime and ended 55–0, the final game in Trinity's winless, twelve-point campaign.

The week prior to their contest in Ellendale is a mixture of apprehension and optimism for both teams. Both teams are fairly confident about winning the game (Principia more so than Trinity), but they're also reflecting on lopsided losses from the opening week. While Haskell dismantled Trinity to start the season, Principia took its lumps against Southwestern Assemblies of God University, losing to the Texas school, 55–7. Both Principia and Trinity have numerous key players who play on both sides of the ball the majority of the game, a common occurrence back in, oh, the 1950s, but nearly unheard of at the college level in 2004. And it's not just players who offset their wide-receiving duties with an occasional appearance in the defensive backfield. Offensive linemen play on the defensive line. Linebackers double as running backs. If nothing else, Trinity and Principia players get plenty of exercise on game days.

That first loss of the season left Barthelmess wondering about the future of the miraculous program, and whether the safety of his players might be compromised. Christian Scientists occasionally make the news for their reliance on prayer in healing. Principia follows its church's guidelines. The team does have a trainer on hand and the school doesn't ignore medicine. It simply puts more emphasis on faith when it comes to injuries. But Barthelmess's concern comes from a simple lack of bodies, not any lack of science. He wonders if his small corps can withstand a nine-game schedule. The determination of the players might actually hurt them, their desire to perform perhaps overwhelming common sense. Part of him wishes they weren't so eager, weren't so willing to play through pain. As a coach he admires the attitude. As a humanitarian it's tougher to watch.

"I got a bunch of go-getters, which isn't much help," Barthelmess says. "These guys would have wanted to keep the team intact if we had eleven guys."

In a story for the definitive small-college Web site D3football.com, he discussed the upcoming Trinity game, telling writer Pat Coleman, "If we go up there this weekend and find out we are at their level, then we may have to rethink this thing."

Bentley doesn't have those concerns about his team—though Trinity's often dealt with questions about the solvency of the program—but he did worry about finding enough players to practice. Depending on the day, the Lions' practices include anywhere from thirty to twenty players, sometimes fewer. Many who sit out are nursing injuries and need the time to rest, especially if they're going to play nearly all of the sixty minutes. Others just sort of show up on a random schedule; their attitude seems to resemble that of NBA star Allen Iverson, who in 2002 famously riffed, to the horror of some and comedic delight of others, "If I can't practice, I can't practice. If I'm hurt, I'm hurt. . . . I know it's important, but we're talking about practice. How the hell can I make my teammates better by practicing?"

Injured players often have to step in to help out with either the scout offensive or defensive units, gingerly going through the paces in their civilian clothes just so the team can have twenty-two players on the field to run the plays. Assistant coach Tim Rasmussen is occasionally called upon to step under center, calmly and fairly efficiently flinging passes as, perhaps, the world's first 300-pound quarterback.

Bentley knows how one of his coaching heroes—old-school tough guy and occasional jerk, Bill Parcells—would handle the situation: bench 'em, take a no-nonsense approach, teach the players a lesson or two. But he doesn't feel that's the right thing to do at a Bible college. Besides, he feels fairly powerless, believing the players are in control of the situation. If there's power in numbers, Bentley believes the players have it because there are so few of them.

"You can't even fool 'em," he says. "I mean, what are you going to do? They've got you over a barrel; can't sit them and they know that."

Many players, such as Lee Odell, wish Bentley would do exactly that: sit some of the offenders, no matter how little depth the team already has, no matter how thin they'd be with the loss of any player. They're craving that kind of discipline.

"That kind of stuff doesn't happen in programs that I've been," says the team's center. "With the programs I've been in in the past, one time you're late and that was it. You never did it again because you paid for it. 'See me after practice,' that's all they said. The way I think about it, nobody's going to take us seriously until we start to take ourselves seriously."

Principia arrives in Ellendale in style. Well, they arrive on a bus like always, but it's a much shorter ride than the usual seventeen-hour haul. A Principia alumnus learned about the arduous journey and arranged a flight for the team to Fargo, cutting the team's bus trip by fifteen hours. Any hope the Lions had of facing a fatigued Panthers squad flew out the window with that flight. Trinity can only dream about and envy those kinds of accommodations. Principia's advantages don't stop there. Six assistant coaches aid Barthelmess, three for offense, three for defense, numbers that double Bentley's staff.

Trinity plays its games at Bob Tatum Field, named after the first football coach in the school's history, who started the program in 1984 and still attends many of the team's contests. Tatum Field is located directly next to the team's practice field, which is across the street from the school's gymnasium and administration building, accessible after a short walk across the campus parking lot. There are plenty of good spots available.

Brandon Strong spends the pregame juggling multiple tasks, helping ensure that both team and field are ready. His duties actually begin the night before, when he puts the players' jerseys and pants into their lockers. After an early breakfast, he sets up the team's medical kit and gets the computer program ready for the stat crew, finally hauling the machine up to the booth above the game field. Then it's back to the locker room, where he tapes ankles and other limbs as needed. Strong also leads the team in stretching, though the other assistants step in if needed. After meeting with the opposing team's sports information director and letting them know when the statistics will be ready after the game, he works with the receivers and defensive backs as they go through drills. As the game begins, he joins Bentley and Rasmussen on the sideline while Slivoskey calls the plays from the booth. Strong is part manager, part trainer, part SID, part coach.

Otherwise, game days unfold slowly at Trinity, with little urgency or stress. Players from both squads meander from the small locker rooms to the field in groups of three or four, going through the early portions of their warm-ups in front of a handful of fans. A lone worker sits at a small wooden table, collecting admission money and handing out game rosters. Arrive early enough and it's easy to avoid paying the admission fee, as long as your conscience is OK with the small act of financial disobedience. Tailgating consists of some visiting fans snacking on potato chips and soda while stretching their legs after a marathon drive.

A single set of metallic bleachers stand behind the Lions' bench, the crow's nest rising above. The visiting sidelines don't have any bleachers—trees and bushes border the bench—but fans from the opposition make themselves comfortable on the home team's side, sitting on blankets or in the stands. Fans for both schools leisurely settle in, viewing with polite, curious interest, like the dignitaries who sat on the hills eating picnic lunches and watching the Civil War's Battle of Bull Run.

Just outside the south end zone rests a statue of a proud, dignified lion, watching over the action. Outside the north end zone sits a cluster of mobile homes—where many of Trinity's married students live. Give 'em this: the homes provide a unique, if not intimidating, background. They don't have the majesty of Notre Dame's Touchdown Jesus, for instance, but at least it's a short commute to the field for the students who live in the units.

The Lions draw decent crowd support from the student body. "Decent" in this case meaning several dozen of the school's three hundred students attend the game. In school, Strong says he occasionally hears a snide remark from a fellow student about the football team, but the ones at Tatum Field are only there to offer encouragement, not to heckle. Female students usually line the first row of bleachers, standing and cheering for most of the four quarters, regardless of Trinity's deficit.

But it's difficult to get an accurate attendance count. Trinity played five home games in 2004, and according to the box scores, the crowds ranged from a homecoming high of 350 for the Principia game to a mere 150 for the team's final contest against Maranatha Baptist. The accuracy of those estimates is about as dubious as Nostradamus's predictions; the common denominators for the crowd tallies for the five home games are they're all three digits and multiples of five. The homecoming count is probably the closest to the truth; the beautiful early fall weather proves to be a siren call. An enthusiastic group of students will flock to the sidelines by game's end.

Nearly all of Trinity's fans have some connection to the school, whether as students, professors, administrators, janitors, or librarians. Because most of the Lions are from states far from North Dakota, only a small number of players' parents ever make it to see their sons play college ball. Few Ellendale residents not associated with the school watch the local college's gridiron product, a fact that frustrates and confuses some of the Lions' players.

"It really blows my mind," Sannon Norick says. "We may not be winning games, but at least come to watch the other teams. College football is college football."

And the school's proud to have football, feeling it's a worthy endeavor. Everyone associated with Trinity knows the team's recent record—they've lived it—but the mere presence of the team, along with the effort, provides a sense of satisfaction. That pride is even evident in the team's gold-colored game programs, where a message on the inside page reads, "Mr. Bob Tatum, to whom our field is dedicated to, started the football program here back in 1984. We have never flourished in the game, but we have stood strong through the years. Don't expect them to back down now!"

Especially not today, not with the Panthers standing on the opposite sideline. A first-time visitor to the field might think a mistake has been made when Principia and Trinity go through their pregame paces. Where are the rest of the players? Were they told the wrong starting time for the game? Barely fifty players stand on the field. This is small college football at its smallest. By comparison, defending Division III national champion St. John's, which in recent years has played UMAC teams Crown and Northwestern, routinely suits up between 175 and 200 players for its home games.

The pregame features a short remembrance on this, the third anniversary of the September 11 attacks.

Once the noon contest begins, it takes the Lions twenty seconds to claim their first lead since the 2001 season. On the opening play from scrimmage, Hess hands off to Norick. The Panthers converge quickly, stacking him up at the line of scrimmage. But the Trinity fullback manages to stay on his feet a few extra seconds, allowing him time to flip the ball to running back Stephen Poyser. Up to that point

Poyser was just an innocent bystander on the play, watching a few yards behind the action. No one on the field really notices Norick's maneuver until Poyser is ten yards down the field. Shedding a Principia defender, Poyser sprints for a sixty-five-yard TD, stunning the fans, the Panthers, and the Lions. As the play develops, a Principia player on the sidelines raises his arms, the universal signal for touchdown or, in this case, what in the hell is happening? Poyser's still 50 yards from the end zone when a Panthers coach begins to chew out an official. Noah Wedan's extra point conversion puts Trinity up 7–0—the first lead for the Lions in twenty games.

Was it a legal play? Questionable. OK, highly questionable. Depending on the angle, the play could be interpreted as an illegal forward lateral. On the game tape, it looks like Poyser hauled in the ball around the thirty-five-yard line, the original line of scrimmage, but that the Panthers had knocked Norick back a bit with their initial surge. If this happened in the NFL and instant replay was available, the call would probably stand, not necessarily because it's absolutely correct, but for a lack of conclusive video evidence. But when you're on a three-year losing streak, you need whatever breaks you can get. Maybe a little hometown cookin' from the officials is just what's needed. Or maybe Trinity finally has some good karma going.

Principia responds with an easy, six-play, fifty-nine-yard drive that features four completions from quarterback Kyle Gillum, the leader of Barthelmess's air attack. The drive culminates with a twenty-yard touchdown reception by Tucker Savoye in the left corner of the end zone. The extra point kick fails, though, and Trinity leads 7–6 at the end of the first quarter.

Yet, the Lions are squandering too many scoring opportunities. They march sixty-three yards on their second possession, only to miss a field goal. Their third possession ends with an interception at the Principia twelve-yard line. The Panthers finally make Trinity pay for their generosity when Michael Statos runs in a four-yard TD, giving Principia a 12–7 halftime advantage.

Despite the deficit, this is a new experience for Trinity. For two years the Lions have spent halftime assessing damage, both physical and emotional, not offensive or defensive schemes. Finding healthy bodies is usually the goal, not finding flaws in the opponent.

"At halftime it was definitely a different feel to it, it had a different vibe," Slivoskey says. "The kids, they'd never really experienced that before so it was exciting to see their confidence grow. They were really excited about the prospects of, 'Wow, if I do my assignments, if I play hard, this is what could come of it.'"

The consensus is that the Lions need to keep the ball on the ground. They're finding success—Poyser and Norick are eating up yardage behind Odell and the line—and the passing game is struggling; Dusty Hess throws three interceptions in the first half, including one near the end zone after Trinity took over at the Principia twenty. Hess somewhat makes up for the errors by furiously pursuing the defender after each pick. The self-deprecating quarterback is officially credited with two tackles in the game.

"When I throw the interception, I'm mad so I like to get the tackle. It gets me in the box score."

Trinity limits Principia to twelve first-half points mostly thanks to the big-play abilities of safety Josh McGillvrey, who ended two Panther drives with interceptions and picked off another pass on a two-point conversion attempt. In a little more than an hour, he doubles Trinity's interception total from 2003.

McGillvrey comes to Trinity from South Dakota, having spent the previous year at Northern State University in Aberdeen. He's something of a pigskin mercenary; he knows he's not going to be in Ellendale past this season. McGillvrey plans on studying international business, a major Trinity doesn't offer. For the fall semester he'll take a few business classes and hope the credits transfer. But he missed football—he last played in 2001—and had friends at Trinity encouraging him to head north and play. Although aware of the environment when he enrolled, as a Catholic at the Pentecostal school, he admits he feels a little uncomfortable at times, particularly when one of his professors made what he construed as a disparaging remark about Catholicism.

And he chafes at some of Trinity's more stringent rules. He calls it "just mind-boggling" that the school forbids students to watch R-rated movies, lamenting the cinematic classics Trinity students are sheltered from. "I could see them not watching a porno or something, but some of the greatest movies are R-rated."

Although he says he'll join the cast of teetotalers at Trinity and avoid alcohol during the season, he believes the overall strictness goes a bit overboard.

"I'm twenty years old. If I haven't been taught right or wrong by now, I'll never learn."

But overall he's mixing in fine, perhaps because he knows it's a one-year stint. He's quickly acclimated himself with his teammates and earned their respect, emerging as a leader for the Lions—of the team's four captains, McGillvrey is the only one who wasn't with the team in 2003. On the field he's feisty, a hard hitter with strong instincts for the ball. McGillvrey also isn't above engaging in some chatter with his foes. The discussions don't center on NAFTA or the value of the dollar compared to the euro. Throughout the year more than one opponent will mutter about "number 34," often with an expletive attached. To the opposition, he's perpetually annoying and causes more than a little pain, sort of like a wooden sliver stuck in the bottom of their feet.

He's also a hell of a football player. In addition to his interceptions against the Panthers, McGillvrey adds two pass deflections. When not swooping in to nail a receiver, he's coming up to help stop the run. The revamped Trinity secondary holds its own against the Panthers' aerial efforts. Gillum often lines up in the shotgun formation with three or four receivers, but Trinity gets good pressure up front and good coverage in the secondary, keeping Principia frustrated.

As the second half progresses it becomes obvious this game isn't going to degenerate into a blowout, which has to be something of a surprise to Principia. The Panthers defeated the Lions by fifty-five points in the final game of 2003. They weren't expecting circumstances to be much different just two games into the new season.

"The fact that we were flying, they were kind of looking at it as a vacation," Barthelmess says of his players. "They went up thinking this was going to be a nice break. For Trinity, this was their game. If they're going to beat anybody, it's going to be us."

In every upset, no matter the sport, there comes a point when the underdog begins to sense victory is possible and the favorite starts to sweat. They realize something bad is happening to them. They also recognize it might be too late to do anything about it. In this game that moment probably occurs midway through the third quarter, on Principia's second possession of the half. Having been stymied at the Trinity twenty-yard line the first time they got the ball in the third quarter, the Panthers again threaten to break the game open when they pick off Hess for a fourth time and set up shop at the Trinity twenty. But the Lions hold again, allowing only four yards before Principia fails on a fourth-down play.

Another Panthers drive, this one in the fourth quarter, reaches Trinity's sixteen before stalling. By now the teams have combined to blow more than a half dozen scoring chances, partly due to good defense and partly due to poor offense. Trinity's offense finally gets going in the fourth quarter. Receiver Tony Snyder executes a perfect out-and-up pattern, fooling the Principia defensive back and breaking out into the open in front of the Trinity bench and down the left sideline. Hess, still confident despite the picks, lofts the pass and hits Snyder for a thirty-two-yard gain. It's the second time in the game Trinity's top receiver has burned Principia. A similar route produced a big gain in the first half. Although Snyder's reception turns into the final first down of the drive, the Lions have found a play that works.

The game comes down to the final three minutes, when Trinity forces a Panthers punt, just their second of the game. Trinity takes over at its own thirty-six-yard line with 2:36 remaining, still trailing 12-7. On the line for the Lions: the game and a three-year losing skid.

After Norick bulls his way for three yards, Hess and Snyder again hook up. This time there's nothing tricky about Snyder's route. He simply runs straight down the left side of the field. But while Snyder's running vertically, Principia defensive back Graham Wightman is inexplicably turning toward the line of scrimmage, perhaps expecting help from a Principia safety. Instead, Snyder's in the clear. Hess finds him at the Principia thirty-five. Wightman makes up for his blunder by hustling downfield and snaring Snyder, who was temporarily slowed by another Panther. Wightman clings to Snyder's right leg, finally pulling him down at the twenty with 2:03 left on the clock, plenty of time for the Lions.

Norick then carries for five yards, pushing the ball to the Principia fifteen. Poyser, who has found success throughout the day on the outside of the Principia defense and finishes with 175 yards rushing, breaks through the left side of the line and nearly scores, falling at the three. A killer false start penalty sends the Lions back five yards. With forty-one seconds remaining Poyser rushes to the four-yard line, where Trinity calls time-out. After a short Norick gain, a slight bit of confusion hits Trinity in the frenzied final seconds. Norick jogs off the field and Lester Williams, who hasn't had a carry all day, replaces him. With the clock ticking and less than twenty seconds remaining, Hess, slightly surprised that Norick isn't in the game, turns and hands to a hard-charging Williams.

"When I handed the ball off, Sannon had turned black and a little chunkier," Hess says.

It looks like Williams will score right up the middle, but Principia knocks him down just inside the one-yard line. An anxious Bentley takes a few steps onto the field before walking back. He alternates between watching the action and glancing at the scoreboard. But it's out of the coaches' hands now. On fourth down, with the rest of the team frantically trying to get into position and with the clock about to hit zero, Hess coolly organizes the team at the line of scrimmage. He tells Odell it's going to be a QB sneak on a silent count. Trinity spreads the Principia defense with three receivers to the left side and only Williams in the backfield.

Odell snaps the ball and surges forward. Hess follows his center, veering slightly to the left, searching for the two feet that will give Trinity the victory. It looks like he's got it, like he's cracked the goal line. It's tough to tell for certain, though, because Hess quickly disappears, consumed by both friend and foe. Each team's linemen pile onto one another and on the 175-pound Hess, who's stuck at the bottom among a mass of flesh and pads, fighting for air and the ball.

"And that's when death began for me," he says later.

Twice Principia defenders manage to wrestle the ball from Hess in the scrum, but he gets it back each time.

The referees stroll toward the pile, leisurely unearthing players from the heap, looking like playground supervisors breaking up a scrap between a group of fourth-graders. Hey, guys: show a little more enthusiasm; no one would have complained if the zebras had been in a bit more of a rush to get to the bottom of the pile. Their ruling is only going to decide the game.

"Sometimes I think our refs need to be on the Atkins diet," Hess cracks. "It shows when they're in bad position for a lot of plays."

It's bedlam on the Trinity sideline. Players leap in celebration, certain Hess scored. After all, in the history of football, when a team needs less than a yard for a first down or touchdown, quarterback sneaks have probably succeeded 95 percent of the time. The confidence slowly dissipates as the officials continue their search. Are they looking for buried treasure?

It shouldn't be taking this long; the longer the wait, the worse it looks for the Lions. A couple of players kneel, waiting for a call. Finally one of the officials signals, methodically waving his arms side to side. In football the motion usually signifies an incomplete pass. Today it means defeat for Trinity; Hess has come up an inch or two short, at least according to the men whose opinions matter most.

After scoring on the first play of the game, the Lions nearly win on the final play. Principia's players rip off their helmets and storm off the field in celebration. Enraged Trinity offensive lineman Matt Johanson tears off his helmet and slams it to the turf, practically in one motion. Many of his teammates are too shocked to perform similar acts.

"I've never been so mad in my life," Trinity's left guard says. "[Dusty] was on my leg because I could feel him. I'm laying stretched out in the end zone. It felt like no matter what, that even if we do play good, we're not going to be able to win. Any other team would have gotten the benefit of the doubt."

Andy Brower had a grand view of the action. He blocked for Hess from his tight end position. From his angle, there wasn't much doubt what happened.

"He was three feet into the end zone."

"He exaggerates sometimes," Hess says, though not arguing with Brower's basic premise.

Bentley's ten yards on the field, incredulous, a feeling shared on the sideline by Rasmussen and Strong. Up in the coaches' booth, Slivoskey struggles to comprehend what he's just seen down below.

So much for homer refs. So much for good karma.

Of all the losses over the past three seasons—the 105–0 defeat, the 60–0 losses, and the 77–6 routs—none of them could compare with this one, which is a hundred times less embarrassing, and a hundred times more painful. It's an old question in sports: Would you rather lose by a lot or a little, by 20 points or 1 point? Or, in this case, would you rather lose by 105 points or 5 points?

"This one was harder," Slivoskey says.

While it might be easier to get over a lopsided defeat, the consensus for the Lions is they'd rather lose like this. A loss like this shows they have pride. A loss like this shows they have more talent than last year. But several Lions can't even consider the question; they feel Trinity *did* win.

"I'm working, I'm driving, and I'm pushing guys forward," Odell says about the final play. "I'm laying in the end zone from my knees up, and Dusty came right behind me."

On the Principia sideline, Barthelmess feels a bit queasy about the whole affair. Although he believes Poyser's original touchdown should have been ruled an illegal lateral, he still feels Trinity deserved to win. Not because he's certain Hess scored—Barthelmess couldn't tell from his angle on the sideline—but because of the respective games each team played.

"Walking off the field I felt dirty," he says. "We couldn't get anything right. I felt that our players were saying, 'This is Trinity. This is going to be a piece of cake.' It's not like we're a team that can afford to do that."

It's a game of firsts for the Lions. For the first time in three years, the Lions accumulated more total yards than an opponent—341 to 251. Two hundred twenty-nine of Trinity's yards came on the ground, where Norick complemented Poyser's monster game with seventy-three yards. For the first time in three years, Trinity led in a game. For the first time in three years, Trinity held an opponent under twenty points. For the twenty-second-straight game, though, Trinity lost.

Slivoskey laments all the drives before the final one, the ones that ended with Trinity failing to convert on several key chances; pick up a score or two there and the Lions don't need to rely on a late drive. They wouldn't have been at the mercy of the officials.

"We had many opportunities to win that game aside from that call," Slivoskey says, though he's also certain Hess sneaked into the end zone. "We should have taken care of business before that."

A few of the players are in tears after the game, still unable to accept the result. Knowing that this will be Trinity's best chance at a victory adds to the searing disappointment. There are a couple of other teams in the UMAC Trinity can, perhaps, match up with on a good day, but the players also know they'll be overmatched in many of their remaining eight games. It's like Barthelmess said, if Trinity is going to beat someone, it would probably be his Panthers. Now that chance is gone. And it could be a long, long wait before an opportunity such as this one comes along again. It's like a six-year-old kid waking up on Christmas morning and finding his parents setting fire to the collection of gifts under the tree.

The Lions can at least comfort themselves with the knowledge that they'll likely see Principia again this year. Late in the season, the conference takes over the Metrodome in Minneapolis on a Friday for five games between the league's ten teams. The games match the top teams from the North and South against each other, as well as the lower-tier teams. But that's two months down the road. On this day, all the Lions have are the images of Hess plowing toward the goal line and the officials waving their arms. They'll see that play on film in the coming days; they'll see it in their sleep for weeks.

As the team returns to the locker room, the players' agony is compounded by the sounds of the loud celebration going on next door in the nearby visitors' locker room; Principia's jubilation is warranted, but it's a victory the Lions felt was wrongly taken from them.

The loss lingers through the night.

"He was really disappointed," Jacqui Odell says of her newlywed husband. "He didn't even really want to talk about it."

Bentley too is deflated and defeated. This wouldn't have been just a major victory for the direction of the program. It would have been a personal milestone as well: his first college victory. Would have been something to tell the kids about, something to tell his folks back in Texas about.

"We didn't win on the scoreboard, but we did win in our hearts," he says.

Unfortunately, the only thing that kind of victory provides the Lions is a different kind of heartbreak, a worse kind of heartbreak.

Chapter Eight

God Talk

Does God care? About winning, that is. Does he—or she—care who wins, who loses, who scores, who fails? Is God the ultimate game fixer, manipulating individuals and teams on a whim, doling out triumphs and defeats based on some subjective criteria that only a deity can understand? Can a simple prayer lead to a victory? What if you pray really, really hard? Does God favor those who do pray? And if he—or she—does, then how do you explain Trinity Bible College's three-year losing streak?

God talk is ubiquitous on the Trinity campus. Phone conversations end with "God bless" and e-mails conclude with Scripture verses. Dinner parties finish with group prayers as participants join in a circle and hold hands. Only after they've thanked Jesus will they say good-bye to each other. In this environment, it's seemingly impossible to separate anything from religious connotations, including athletics.

Sharing the gospel is one of the primary goals of the school. The words are right there in the academic catalog, at the top of page eleven, where the beliefs of the Assemblies of God church are laid out, along with the church's relationship with Trinity. The church's mission is, "To be an agency of God for evangelizing the world."

The world plays football. So, the school's football coach figures, why not extend those goals onto the field?

Rusty Bentley says the goals of the team aren't necessarily touchdowns, but are to testify. Those were the words he used after the team's 105–0 defeat. It's not the sort of quote you usually see in a newspaper's game story. Bentley wants the players to employ a similar attitude. But he's not sure this year's team does.

"A year ago I had a bunch of kids that loved Jesus, but were very short on the football end," he says. "This year I have a bunch of kids that weren't short on the football end, they were short on the . . . I don't mean spiritual end, but they made them equals. They didn't say football was more than the Lord, but I think we had a lot where they were equal."

That broad characterization irks some of the players, particularly receiver Andy Brower. To Brower, it's not a matter of picking and choosing either football or God. That doesn't mean he makes them equals. Far from it. Ten years from now he plans on being a pastor, and his football days will be long over. Forty years from now he plans on being a pastor, and his football days will be just distant memories. His life will be about God.

But now? Now he wishes football could be football. No, he doesn't put it above God and he doesn't make them equals. But couldn't they be separated?

"God, yes, he cares about everything big and small," he says. "It's good if you're a Christian in football. But you don't have to make—it's terrible to say you don't have to make it all about God. Have that in your own life, have that as like an overall thing.

"But don't include God in your game plan as a way to help you out. God's not going to intervene and let you catch an eighty-yard pass and take it to the end zone."

And this comes from a player who says he does get frustrated when he sees players laughing during prayers. Swearing on the field bothers him, too. These things bother him as a Christian, not as a football player. He has no trouble separating the two.

"Let's just be a football team," he says. "You don't pick them up in the middle of the game and tell them you love them. Once the game is over, that's when you tell them you love them. He just makes it cheesy. And Christianity's not cheesy. It's a whole-hearted love. I can still love you and hit you at the same time. It's not like I'm actually mad at you, or have anything against you. You're on the opposite team of me. Football is not cheesy and God is not cheesy. That's not sacrilegious."

Unfortunately for the football Lions, they lost a key part of the team just three weeks into the season. A player brought to the school by his love of God.

SEPTEMBER 18, 2004

The game program lists Dusty Hess as being 176 pounds, and there's no reason to think that's a lie. Well, maybe it's high by about ten pounds or so. If it is a true 176, it's a skinny 176. It looks like a good North Dakota wind gust could topple Trinity's six-foot-tall starting quarterback, even when his football pads weigh him down.

Hess is no physical specimen; he acknowledges as much. Hess doesn't have the strongest arm; he admits it. And he's not a running quarterback. He does, though, bring something to the quarterback position that Trinity lacked all of 2003, when the team trotted out player after player after player to take snaps: experience. Street smarts, if you will. Or, in this case, field smarts.

He knows his way around the huddle, just not a college one. Before coming to Trinity, Hess played two years of semi-pro football for the Randolph County Rage in Union City, Indiana. He didn't make any money, just memories. Spent the first year as a backup, the second as the starter. Despite being fifteen years younger than some of his teammates, Hess had no problem assuming a leadership role as the quarterback, unafraid to tell someone to shut up in the huddle.

"You have to let your team know that you're in charge and you have confidence in the play that's being called," he says.

The league gave players an opportunity to hold on to past glory, such as running back Curtis Enis, the former first-round draft pick out of Penn State who had little left in the tank when he joined the Rage. People still sought his autograph, but because of what he used to be able to do on a football field, not what he can do now. "Legs like tree trunks," Hess says, but they had little speed left in them.

Hess had fun in the league. He loves the sport, and football is one reason Hess came to Trinity.

Ministry is the other. Hess has always enjoyed football, but he credits his older brother Kevin with sparking his interest in the church, with inspiring him to want to follow in his sibling's footsteps. Hess saw his brother preach one night at a church in Muncie, Indiana, and felt himself being called to the ministry. While playing for the Rage, Hess got a jump-start on a career in the ministry, leading the team in prayers. His teammates joined in, let him lead the prayers, despite his youth. In addition, he served as a sort of spiritual sounding board for the team's head coach, Keith Maloy. They talked marriage, life, and religion—on the road and at the coach's house. The conversations continue to this day, "I'm still kind of witnessing to him," Hess says.

With his Indiana drawl and dry wit, delivered with decent timing at key moments, Hess sounds sort of like a poor man's Jeff Foxworthy. But his one-liners can't disguise the intense nature of his commitment to his faith, a commitment he hopes will one day lead to a career as a youth minister, preferably in partnership with his brother. The Hess brothers sharing a pulpit—that's Dusty's dream.

That's why he came to Trinity. For the spiritual education. He has no complaints about that aspect of his time in Ellendale. He marvels at his professors, the degrees they've attained, the experiences they've had.

"And they're here in Ellendale, teaching a bunch of doorknobs like me. At chapel, it seems like all the men and women have pastored in churches before. We're never going to have someone with that much knowledge preaching to us again."

A different story has been told on the football field, where Hess, like his teammates, wonders what direction the program is headed. People don't come to practices, they don't come to film sessions, and there are no consequences.

"The one positive I could say is that Coach Bentley is the first Christian coach I played for," Hess says. "But there's just not much discipline. And the organization factor. There's just not much of that."

Hess knew all about Trinity's football struggles during the 2003 season; he played e-mail tag with Bentley during the season. When he arrived on campus before the 2004 school year, he didn't know what to expect out of the football season. He did know, though, he had arrived at the right destination.

"Right when I saw the Trinity Bible sign, I felt a warmness inside my heart," he says. "Maybe it was God giving me a hug."

The entire Trinity team could have used a big hug after the heartbreaking defeat against Principia. A big hug, from God or anyone else. Instead they had to hit the road a week later, traveling to Carlinville, Illinois, to face Blackburn. It promised to be a good day for Hess, regardless of the outcome on the scoreboard: his parents, Nick and Lisa, along with his brother, came to the game, making the five-hour drive from Winchester, Indiana.

Well, it would have been a good game for Hess regardless of the outcome. If he would have finished the game. Or even the first quarter.

On Trinity's seventh play of the game, Hess hit Tony Snyder with the combo's favorite pattern—an "I Right Roy Z Go," where Snyder lines up isolated on one side of the field, fakes an out pattern, and runs upfield. The play worked several times in the Principia loss, and works again against Blackburn. Snyder catches the pass for a twelve-yard gain. Back behind the line of scrimmage, though, a defender knocked Hess down. In an attempt to brace his fall, the Trinity QB put his right arm down, placing all the pressure on his right wrist. Hess instantly felt pain, knowing it wasn't a normal jolt. It would be his last play of the game. His game ends with one completion for twelve yards and one severely injured wrist.

"Wonder what my quarterback rating was for that?"

Following Hess's injury, the Lions can't get any offense generated, losing 35–0 after trailing 28–0 at halftime. The loss on the scoreboard proves secondary to the loss of their quarterback.

While Hess nursed his injury, Brower was having his face rearranged. Literally. Brower can't say he wasn't warned. Surgeons told him to wait a whole year before playing football with his surgically repaired jaw, which has been pieced together like a broken sculpture in the years following his car accident. Maybe he should have listened. But if he had, he wouldn't be out on the field this year. Against Blackburn, though, Brower took a hit and felt his jaw, held together with screws, come loose. He staggered to the sideline to assess the damage. He found his jaw now had some newfound capabilities.

"I could open it a lot further than I could before," he says. "I kept messing with my jaw, trying to put it back in place."

He eventually did. Hess wasn't so lucky. Not only did he fail to finish the Blackburn game, but his quarterbacking days were done for the season. He just didn't know it at the time.

On the 890-mile ride home, each time the team bus hit a bump (and it found a lot of them) pain shot through the wrist and Hess wanted to scream. The pain didn't keep him from leading Sunday school, though he conducted the class while sporting that cure all of any ailment—an Ace bandage. When he finally received a diagnosis, on the Monday following the Blackburn game, it confirmed what Hess already knew in his heart—"I told Coach Bentley this wasn't a sprain. I couldn't even brush my teeth." No sprain. A break of his right wrist. He can return to the field in several weeks, but not as a quarterback. He is finished in that role.

Hess's favorite target, Snyder, takes over at quarterback. The Lions thought Hess could provide some stability behind center. Maybe he will. Just not this year.

Pastor John Brady doesn't have any official title with Trinity Bible College. They don't pay him a dollar. His office is in the New Life Assembly Church in the middle of the campus, but that's because he's the pastor, not a part of the college. No title, no official responsibilities, no salary from Trinity.

But he just might be the soul of the school.

Brady and his wife, Naomi, are like spiritual advisors and surrogate parents to three hundred students. Students, teachers, administrators, office staff, townsfolk, strangers—they all find comfort in Brady's office. They hear a soothing voice that comes only after he's listened, and listened for a long time. His eyes are like a hypnotist's when he talks with someone—they never leave the subject. And if people don't find consolation or wisdom in his office, they find it in the Bradys' comfy home, which is only about a decent seven-iron away from the small campus. The Bradys welcome visitors for official functions and casual dinners, for serious talks and light ones. They also get more phone calls than a 911-dispatch center. People ring day and night, six a.m. to midnight. People call with good news and bad, mundane and tragic, prayer requests and complaints. Sometimes they want to talk to John, sometimes to Naomi, and sometimes to Aleah, their seventeen-year-old daughter, the youngest of three girls and the only one still at home.

In many ways, Brady is the glue of the campus, binding together one and all, even factions that might not agree on much of anything.

And Brady does actually have one title at Trinity: football water boy.

Since 2001, Brady has been on the sidelines for the Lions, filling the role usually reserved for eager elementary kids or college-aged volunteers. He does it for one reason: as a service. It's what he does every day of his life, whether as a pastor or an everyday person. He serves.

"I'm not the coach: I'm the water boy," he says. "When I go there and give them a bottle of water, when I touch somebody on the shoulder and say, 'Good job, buddy,' it's just Pastor Brady coming over. And hopefully that means something to them. When I offer the coach a drink of water, I'm saying, 'Coach, I'm here for you.' The water is just kind of the means to do it. Sometimes I give the guys a touch, a nod, a wink, a word of encouragement. Sometimes if they're hurt, I can pray with them."

Rarely is Brady stationary on the sideline; he's a man on the move, filling water jugs, handing out snacks, encouraging for three hours. He eagerly throws himself into every task, acting like a man auditioning for a job that has two hundred other candidates.

He sees the players' struggles up close. Hears them, too, though he says his presence might keep the players from letting loose with some of the four-letter words they'd like to release.

"I take all the fun out of it," he says with a laugh. "I can't wait for them to win. A victory for us is if we just score. It's like we won the Super Bowl. So my main thing is I really want to try to encourage the guys to stay true to their Christian character. I know it's emotional, I know they're passionate, and they're giving their all so they're going to blow some steam. But that's my desire for them."

Brady knows Ellendale well. He graduated from Trinity in 1980, but he only attended the school after serving as a jet mechanic in the U.S. Navy. He married Naomi, a fellow Trinity student, in 1977. After leaving Ellendale twenty-five years ago, Brady served at churches in North Dakota, South Dakota, and Michigan, never thinking he would end up back where it started—in Ellendale, on the Trinity campus. In 2001, he got the chance to return, moving back to North Dakota from Ishpeming, Michigan.

"They'd had ministers, but what they needed was a pastor," he says of the New Life church. "A pastor is what their lives are. The gift of a pastor is to love people, encourage, serve."

Family photos provide visual evidence of the stress inherent in Brady's work (as a pastor, not a water boy). The black hair has gone gray, spiky on top, but thinning; he looks five or six years older than his forty-nine years. The aging process seems to be transpiring at a slightly faster rate than for a layman.

That's what comes from being there for people when they're at their lowest moments. Those moments can come at anytime. In the late fall, in a matter of days, Brady went from celebrating with a Trinity student headed to a mission trip in Africa to attending the funeral of the young sister of a New Life Assembly member, who died in a workplace accident.

"I think the greatest privilege as a pastor is to be in the highs and the lows of the people. That they allow you into their most intimate pain. If I can't weep with them, then I need to be doing something else."

Though John calls the perky, effervescent Naomi the "perfect pastor's wife, way smarter than I am," she's not just a spouse standing by her man. She's also a partner in the church. Naomi works right outside John's office at the chapel, visiting with guests, and occasionally screening them when she feels her husband is being stretched too thin.

In November, the members of New Life Assembly paid the Bradys back for some of their service to the church, giving the family a giant Brinkmann Pro Series grill that's the size of a small coffin. It's the kind of grill that makes grown men swoon or grunt their approval, and it is big enough to prepare food for a Royal Family reunion. When John and Naomi finally got the contraption wheeled into their single-car garage, they gazed at the grill with bemused, slightly awed grins, the kind they might wear if they discovered a small asteroid on their front yard. John and Naomi can't wait to use it, but they discussed maybe donating it to a worthy cause. The gift might be a bit over the top. But then, New Life's members feel the Bradys' service is probably over the top, too.

Brady's basically a free agent in the Assemblies of God. Any church in the country can contact him about an opening, and he can inquire about any openings. But Brady says he's not looking for the next assignment, isn't looking to move up the career ladder. Any move would happen only if he feels his work in Ellendale is done. And only if he feels some other parish needs his service. It won't be about what the church can give him, but about what he can give the church.

"It seems to me most of our churches have been rebuilding of congregations," he says. "It seems that's what the Lord uses me for. I think part of what we do is go in where nobody else wants to go. I'd rather rebuild than just keep on going."

Rather rebuild? He's not just the perfect pastor for the college. He's the perfect water boy for the Lions.

Chapter Nine

No Mercy

Kansas called it the "mercy rule," a gentle phrase with a decidedly blunt message for weak high school football teams: it's time to go home. In Kansas eight-man football—which Lee Odell played at Thayer High School—officials call off a game if one team goes ahead by forty-five or more points after halftime. A team can score as many points as it wants in the first two quarters, but if the lead gets over forty-five points after that the game ends, keeping games from reaching, say, 105–0.

Odell's teams occasionally won games in that manner, putting seventy points up against an opponent before the mercy rule went into effect, limiting the damage on the scoreboard, if not on the field. He just never thought he'd be thinking about the benefits of the mercy rule while playing in college. But Odell quickly learned what those teams he played against in high school were going through: it ain't much fun being at the mercy of your opponents.

"Sometimes we're getting beat by more than that," he says of the Lions, "and back in high school if you're getting beat like that we would have quit the game. But that'd be even more embarrassing, to have to go home early, even though sometimes you might want to."

He might have wanted to leave during a stretch of games from late September through early October that tested his resolve and that of all the Lions.

Starting with a 79–6 loss against the University of Minnesota–Morris on September 25, a trio of opponents outscored Trinity 194–26, a series of defeats that dazed the Lions and threatened to divide them. The routs conjured up memories of the 2003 season, images the Lions thought were a thing of the past, especially after the heartbreaking, but close loss against Principia. And maybe the whole season would have been different if the officials had ruled in favor of Dusty Hess on that quarterback sneak against Principia. Results might not have changed—all three opponents had vast more talent and experience than the Lions—but the players' reaction to the losses might have differed. Instead, players who were on the team in 2003 saw history repeating itself while the newcomers wondered what they'd gotten themselves into. It's one thing to hear about the team's difficulties while being recruited, it's another to experience the suffering firsthand.

"We're not being trained or put in a situation to win a football game," Andy Brower says. "In high school practice, if we didn't get a play right, we ran it until we got it right. Here, if less than three things go wrong we're done. And Coach Bentley is like, 'Great, great, great practice.' I'm like, coach, that was pathetic."

Morris started the carnage with its 73-point victory, which was even more lopsided than the final score indicated—the Cougars led Trinity 69–6 after three quarters before easing off. They still set a school record for most points in a game. Just a few years ago the thought of Morris scoring 79 points—or even 39—was laughable. In the 1990s, the Cougars set an NCAA Division II record with forty-six consecutive losses. When they finally snapped that losing streak, it wasn't even as a Division II school—Morris left that level in 2003. Their victim in the game that halted that skid? Principia College, which Morris defeated 61–28 on September 20, 2003. That was Morris's first victory since 1998, but joining the UMAC turned the team's fortunes. Since dropping out of Division II, Morris has been like the kid who gets held back a year in school and finds himself bigger than everyone else and now able to dominate dodgeball games. Though Morris doesn't dominate in the UMAC, the Cougars do get to flex their muscles a bit, taking out years of frustrations on teams with inferior firepower.

Teams like Trinity, which is like the little brother of the ten-team UMAC, forever being picked on and knocked on the head by the older siblings. Picked on even by the ones that usually struggle to find victory, like Principia, like Morris, like Crown.

Crown entered its October 2 game against Trinity winless, but finished the game 74–20 victors, outscoring the Lions 47–6 in the first half. Brower provided one of the few highlights for the Lions, returning a third-quarter kickoff 90 yards for a touchdown. Unfortunately for the Lions, the score was 60–12 at the time of Brower's exploits. Crown has a Trinity connection on its staff—its offensive coordinator, Matt Brakefield, played quarterback for the Lions in the 1990s. Against his alma mater, Brakefield's offense found its groove for the first time all season, accumulating 527 total yards.

While the Morris defeat came as little surprise to the Lions, the Crown setback proved more confounding. Trinity feels Crown is one of the UMAC teams it should be able to compete against on a yearly basis. Although the team's twenty-point output was the most points scored by the Lions since the 2001 season, and was eight points more than the squad scored in all of 2003, the fifty-four-point defeat was a crushing blow to the players' confidence. In themselves and, more crucially, their head coach. Halfway through the season, Bentley appeared to be losing his team.

For the players, the frustration was compounded by their belief that someone on the staff could be the ideal head coach for the team: Eric Slivoskey. Slivoskey, though, was in an unenviable position. Loyalty matters, he says, but so does standing up for what you believe. Take the players' side and it could be construed as being disloyal. Take Bentley's side and he would be going against what he thought was right. Slivoskey has concerns with how Bentley deals with some of the team's injuries, believing there's an occasional callousness toward the players. Other issues include the players' number one complaint: practices.

"He says he has fifteen years experience, but I watch him try to organize and run a practice, and I just don't understand how you can be around any kind of high-level program and not be able to run one."

The team will go from doing no tackling for weeks to repetition after repetition of hard-hitting drills. Then nothing.

The coaching staff splintered as the season wore on. Slivoskey came down from the booth during the Blackburn game and began calling the plays from the sideline. He did it partly for practical reasons. He'd love to have someone up in the booth watching coverages, but that's impossible with only three other coaches. He needs to be near the action, where he can keep tabs on the ever-changing personnel situation the Lions go through on a weekly basis, depending on injury. He admits it: he could use some help, some eyes in the sky while he's on the ground.

"Maybe some coaches can do it, but I'm too young, I'm not one of 'em. I'm just gonna admit it. I'm not that experienced. I wish I was; I wish I had that kind of vision. I'm trying to think ahead for play calls, one or two plays ahead. And watch the linemen a little bit. And do the personnel thing. I can't follow, where is the safety, where is the corner? OK, is the nose lining up in the A gap? So I came down largely because of those reasons, to be able to do things on the fly. I can get those things a lot easier on the sideline, instead of relaying it down and then they have to relay it to the players."

But he also came down to ensure that the offensive players had someone sticking up for them if need be. In the first couple games of the season, Bentley told offensive players that they were "killing the defense."

It's common for coaches to stir up an "us against the world" mentality among players, but an "us against us" model is not real conducive to team harmony. It would also be hard to pull off at Trinity, where many of those offensive players "killing" the defense also play on the opposite side of the ball.

Bentley further tweaked the offense by talking about the team's number-five ranking in pass defense in the UMAC. Slivoskey calls it a misleading statistic. Frankly, teams don't have to pass against the Lions to beat them. All they really have to do is hand the ball off forty times and usually that's good for at least thirty-five points. Also, when teams get up by large margins, they will almost never throw the ball. Helps with Trinity's pass rankings, but means little in the big picture.

The irony, assistant Tim Rasmussen says, is that the defensive players often ignore Bentley's plans, changing the calls in the huddle—such as switching to a zone coverage instead of man-to-man—while the head coach remains oblivious to the happenings. Safety Josh McGillvrey switched some of the defensive calls, admitting his role with a bit of a chuckle and a "Well, you know," as if the players were trying to cover for a flighty bank manager who keeps leaving sacks of money out in the open. It happened in the first Principia game, when the Lions held the Panthers to two touchdowns, far and away the team's best defensive effort of the season.

"He didn't even know," Rasmussen says of Bentley. "And at the end he was like, 'Man, I did a good job preparing that defense.'"

Whichever side of the ball is enjoying success, Slivoskey just doesn't think the teams' two squads should be put in situations where they're competing against each other, instead of the opposition.

"My point is, why do you even have to pull attention to that?" he says. "The only team that has to pass against us to beat us is Principia, because that's their game. The other teams that we play, they know they can run against us and beat us. All they gotta do is run right up the gut and they're going to wear us out. So saying those kinds of things, I feel like, it's just not really beneficial."

All in all, there are times when Slivoskey looks like he would just like to pack up the family and head to yet another far-flung destination. Fortunately for him, this year he can fall back on his teaching. Teaching relaxes him, even with his heavy class load. As in his coaching situation, Slivoskey attempts to overcome his inexperience with hours of preparation, not wanting to squander an opportunity he never thought would come.

Slivoskey's office is located on the second floor of the administration building. It's a cubbyhole across the hall from the men's bathroom. There's a counter attached to his door, lending a concession stand feel to Slivoskey's place of business. Inside he shares the space with only the creepy, lifelike mannequins that are staples of every CPR class, their half-open mouths just waiting for a student's lips. It's there in the office Slivoskey labors and prepares in relative anonymity, a hard task to pull off on a campus of three hundred students, but one he manages to achieve. A visitor to the campus asked another Trinity professor if a particular office was indeed Slivoskey's.

"That's not a faculty office," the professor replied, unaware of the colleague hidden behind the door.

Slivoskey doesn't mind the obscurity; it gives him the chance to work a bit on the outskirts. In some regards, he is a bit of an outsider at Trinity. He doesn't follow any type of herd mentality, even with matters of religion, which at Trinity are the most important matters in life. His mom taught him always to think for himself, Slivoskey says. Stand up for what you believe in. He does, including his faith.

He's not Catholic, Lutheran, or Pentecostal. He attends a nondenominational church in Aberdeen.

"I consider myself a follower, a believer of Christ," he says. "I feel pretty well-accepted. I feel pretty comfortable being honest with my beliefs, or with my convictions. A lot of people have the belief that if you're not Assembly of God, you're not on the right track. I just don't feel that way. I have friends, we talk for two, three hours, and I miss that in a lot of ways. It's very stimulating conversation. I like having my mind stretched, I like to be challenged sometimes. And you can debate all night. Here, I don't know if I'd be able to get into a lot of those conversations."

He'll keep looking for them.

The three consecutive lopsided defeats triggered the question: What does the Trinity administration think about the football team's struggles? There really isn't pressure to win. Never has been, never will. If there ever would be pressure to win, it would only mean expecting two or three victories—at most—a season. But there are expectations.

"Everyone wants to win, but it's not the ultimate goal," says Trinity administrator Steve Tvedt, who snaps photographs from the sidelines at Trinity's home games. "It's a little better this year than it was last year, and certainly better than the year before. The ultimate score is not the real determiner on how you've done. Although you like to see improvement, you like to see growth. The team obviously has to recruit more players and retain players from this year, both

academically as well as motivationally into next year in order to
build. And I think that's the expectation."

Odell's expectations for the season included at least getting one or
two victories. He had to tone down the team expectations, and instead focus more on individual goals. That's not the way it should be,
he admits, but he's determined to enjoy a successful season. That's
not going to be happen in the win-loss department. He knows that
now. But there are other ways to win.

Much of Odell's internal drive seems to stem from a desire to
prove worthy of the respect and admiration of others. From showing
his father he can make it in life without him, to displaying his skills
to UMAC opponents, most of whom only regard Trinity as a blip on
the schedule, Odell doesn't want to be trapped by his past or his environment. Particularly in football.

"There's a lot of guys on this team that probably couldn't play
football anywhere else, and I want to show that I'm not one of those
guys, that I could play for any team in the conference," he says. "You
might beat us, but I came to play, and you're going to respect me because I'm going to do my job regardless of whether or not we lose. D-
linemen come up and told me good game. Even players that I didn't
block came up and said good game. And that's rewarding in itself."

On October 9, Northwestern trounced Trinity in a fairly bloodless
41–0 contest, a victory that leveled Northwestern's record at 3–3
and left Trinity at 0–6. In many ways it was a painful game for Trinity. The first home game in a month, the contest quickly got away
from the Lions. It was also a painful experience for offensive lineman Isaac Smith.

Smith came to Ellendale from Missouri. A "pretty good athlete"
all the way through eighth grade, Smith eventually gave up sports to
concentrate on the fine arts. Someday he hopes to work in inner-city
missions. But he's enjoying this athletics thing while he has the chance.

"I've made friends, we build each other up," he says. "Our relationship is stronger. A lot of it doesn't make sense, but the bottom
line for me is I'm just here to praise God anyway."

In a practice the week of the Northwestern game, Smith hurt his left shoulder, an injury eventually diagnosed as tendonitis that ran from his shoulder blade to his forearm with a hint of bursitis in the shoulder joint. It basically made him a one-armed lineman, forced to fight off defenders with his good arm. When that one arm wasn't good enough, he adapted. His efforts caught the attention of the mother of a Northwestern opponent, who wasn't real enamored with Smith's line improvisations.

"She came up and yelled at me for holding her boy all game long. I was like, well, that's how they do it on the line."

Give Smith credit: he might be inexperienced, but he's a quick learner.

Chapter Ten

Builders

Losing is nothing new for the Trinity football program. Losing big is nothing new, either. Since the program's inception in 1984, Trinity has often thought of itself as the little team that could, even when it couldn't.

In twenty-one years, Trinity has enjoyed one winning season and one .500 season. More than half of Trinity's seasons—eleven—have ended without a victory. A listing of Trinity's year-by-year scores and records contains a seemingly never-ending string of zeroes. Zero points, zero victories, season after season.

Many people are surprised when they hear Trinity even has a football program. When author Doug Wead was told of the fact, while discussing his thirty-year-old book about the school's early history, he responded with the one word that's most often uttered when folks hear of the program's existence: "Really?"

Through the years, though, one thing has been as consistent as the program's struggles: a belief among coaches and players that it's a worthwhile fight. And there's another belief, too, which isn't discussed as frequently or by as many people, but is still prevalent: the idea that, in some way, God was behind the creation of the program and its continued survival.

Two men—Bob Tatum and Jesse Godding—have been the key figures in Trinity's gridiron history. Today the two men are separated

by more than a thousand miles, but linked by a common desire to see
the football team back on its feet. Both believe it's possible because
both have proven it's possible. They've done it, and know the trials
that Rusty Bentley goes through. Still, they feel the future can be
much brighter than the present is for the Lions.

Tatum is the father of the program, the man who started it from
scratch, with a mixture of will, experience, and faith. Even today his
contributions live on—his name adorns the Trinity scoreboard, welcoming players and fans to "Bob Tatum Field." Unfortunately for the
Lions, there haven't been many victories on the field dedicated to the
program's creator. Godding, meanwhile, resurrected the program
from the ashes in the 1990s and made Trinity a respectable member
of the UMAC.

Today Tatum is creeping up on his seventies, the inexorable
march of time showing in many ways: the thinning hair, the slower
walk, the scars from the double-bypass heart surgery that saved his
life in 2003, they're all present. But inside Tatum hasn't aged much
at all. In nearly every aspect of his life, Tatum remains as active as
ever, both in his professional and personal ventures.

Fifteen years removed from the coaching sidelines, Tatum still
lives in Ellendale. He now spends his time operating the Oxenrider
Motel. The Oxenrider, which Tatum purchased in 1988, is a cozy
lodge with fewer than twenty rooms. It's on the north edge of town,
right off Highway 281. Business booms during the fall months, when
hunters flock to the area, but the rooms are often quiet the remainder of the year. Tatum's a one-man show at the Oxenrider, answering
the phones, handling check-ins, and training the small cleaning crew.
That's when he's not washing the linens himself.

The Oxenrider's not just his business—it's his home. Tatum lives
there with his wife, Gwen, who retired from the Dickey County
Courthouse in December 2004. They rent out the house they previously lived in.

Tatum spends much of his free time working on his favorite political causes; namely, doing everything he can to get as many Repub-
licans elected as possible. He has more bumper stickers than an
interstate truck stop. Stickers and posters for various politicians

running for state and national offices plaster the Oxenrider's entry-way. There are advertisements for the big guys—Bush/Cheney—and the unknowns such as U.S. Senate candidate Mike Liffrig. If there's a North Dakota candidate with any type of conservative credentials, there's a sticker with his or her name on it posted in the Oxenrider. Tatum loves his favorite candidates. Loves telling others about them, too. In a September letter to the editor in the *Dickey County Leader*, Tatum implored people to vote Republican in the upcoming elections, writing, "The real hurt to America and North Dakota comes when elected politicians do not have spiritual insight and are not connected to the love and power of Jesus Christ. . . . The reelection of George W. Bush and Dick Cheney is the only hope for winning the war on moral values for the next four years."

God and politics, politics and God. They're the two issues that dominate Tatum's life, even when he's taking a few minutes of rest from the inn. His television's often tuned to Fox News and its "fair and balanced" political coverage—he's particularly fond of conserva-tive Fox talking head Sean Hannity, whom Tatum calls a "good Catholic," compared with the Kennedys, Ted, John, Robert, et cetera, whom Tatum offhandedly refers to as "immoral Catholics." On a table in the living room is the book *The Purpose Driven Life*, Rick Warren's best-seller, whose publishing popularity practically makes the tome a twenty-first-century Bible.

His activism doesn't just include notes to newspapers; Tatum helped organize a dinner at the Fireside Steakhouse where various Republican candidates spoke. But as passionately as Tatum speaks about politics, he's equally excited when talking about his coaching past, a career that spanned four decades and included terrific suc-cesses and tremendous struggles, often during the same seasons.

Tatum came to the prairie from the West—where he coached high school ball in Wyoming and assisted at the University of Wyoming in Laramie.

Early coaching experiences prepared him well for what life would be like at Trinity twenty years later. Tatum started his coaching career in 1959 in tiny Burlington, Wyoming, which had a mere twenty-two boys in the entire school, a fact that didn't keep the school from playing

eleven-man football. That didn't mean Tatum always had eleven players available. There were fewer, until school would start and all the players were attending classes. He coached in Burlington for two years,
finishing his first season with twelve players available for the final game:
eleven on the field and one lonely soul next to Tatum on the sideline.
That team lost all its games except one, which it tied. The next year,
though, Tatum convinced all but one of the boys in school to go out for
football and the team finished with a .500 record. Tatum then went to
the University of Wyoming in Laramie to work on his master's degree.
During his time there, he worked with the college's football team,
coached at the time by Bob Devaney, who would go on to the University of Nebraska and win two national championships. After his stint in
Laramie, Tatum knocked around schools in two other small Wyoming
towns, though not quite as small as Burlington. First in Shoshoni, which
had just over one hundred students, and then in Kemmerer.

In 1967, the Tatums left Wyoming for the desert in Trona, California, where Bob was head coach for two years at a school that had
a somewhat odd home-field advantage: an all sand field. No grass,
just sand, which the school sprinkled on and packed with a roller before games. Opposing teams hated playing there. The sand penetrated their helmets, and players were always, as Tatum recalls,
"spitting it out of their mouths. We found it kind of humorous."

Trona is where Tatum says he became a Christian, but it's not
where he found the most contentment. That came at Santa Fe Christian School in Solana Beach, California, a school that hired Tatum as
athletic director and football coach, positions he was the first to fill
because the school had just opened. It wouldn't be the last time he'd
build programs from scratch. While at Sante Fe, Tatum began advo-
cating a program called "total release," a philosophy developed by
former weightlifter Wes Neal, who wrote that winning is "the total
release of all that you are toward becoming like Jesus Christ in each
situation," while "losing is not releasing your entire self toward becoming like Jesus Christ in each situation."

For Tatum, the longtime coach and relatively new Christian,
learning about the program was an awakening, an experience that
completely altered how he went about his job.

"The methods I had used to coach before, hollering and screaming, basically ridiculing and insulting, was no longer attractive to my personality," he says. "I began to feel bad, and that wasn't right to deal with people and kids that way."

Coincidentally, or not, Santa Fe quickly became an athletics power under Tatum and his total release beliefs. But he wanted to test his methods at a different level, feeling "God had something for me in a college." So in 1983, Tatum sent letters to six colleges throughout the country, inquiring about any possible openings. He sent one to Trinity, not even knowing if the Bible college had a football team. It didn't. But it did have an opening for a basketball coach and athletic director.

The school flew Tatum and his wife in for an interview, a gesture Tatum didn't want to be a waste of the school's time. Before flying out of California, Bob and Gwen gathered their two kids who were still at home—the couple has five children—and asked them what they thought of leaving their home on the sunny West Coast for the unknown of North Dakota. The girl, Jill, who was going to be a sophomore, said she thought God wanted the family to move. The boy, Todd, thought God wanted that for the family, too. He had another reason. A more practical reason. A more earthly reason.

"He'd get to play tackle football in the eighth grade," Bob Tatum says, "and we didn't have tackle football at the junior high level."

Gwen was more on the fence; she struggled mightily with the decision. California had been home for nearly twenty years. Should they abandon all they had built for a tiny spot on the map in the middle of the country? But Bob knew what he wanted even before getting on the plane.

"I had read a Scripture, and I felt that God's going to take us away. It was going to be hard, but we're attached to God, and not to a place."

So he interviewed in May 1983. May 20, to be exact. Even today, Tatum still remembers dates and records from his entire coaching career, even though it began five decades ago.

After talking with school administrators during the day, he met them for dinner, telling them, "I didn't come over here to waste your college's money. I know that's the Lord's money. I just want to tell you that I've decided it's God's will for me to be here. If you offer me the job, I'm going to take it."

So much for playing hard to get. But Trinity shared Tatum's feelings and offered him the job. The Tatums packed a U-Haul two weeks later, took a month-long vacation and eventually settled down in Ellendale, where Bob and Gwen have lived ever since. It didn't take long for Bob, who figured his football coaching days were over, to again start prowling the sidelines. In his first year at Trinity, a student, whose name has been lost to the history books, asked Tatum why the school didn't have a football team. Tatum didn't know. And, honestly, didn't really care to know. He felt that God had sent him to Ellendale to remove him from football. Also, as athletic director, he didn't feel he should be getting involved since it could give the impression he wasn't content with just the basketball position.

Tatum told the young gridiron activist to talk with some higher-ups, which the eager student did, an effort that wasn't quashed by the administration. The school's leaders asked Tatum what it would cost to field a football team. After a few calculations, he gave them a figure: $10,000. The team, Tatum told his bosses, wouldn't need much money for travel expenses because the players wouldn't stay in hotels. They'd lodge in churches, ministering wherever they stayed. The school gave Tatum the go-ahead. Now all he had had to do was build the program from nothing. Nothing. The school had no uniforms, no helmets, no footballs. And, of course, no players. Tatum rounded up some helmets—and some old blocking sleds—from an NAIA school in New York that was dropping the sport. By chance, the New York school's colors were blue and gold, the same as Trinity's. The school then bought footballs and jerseys. To find bodies to wear those jerseys, Tatum got on his phone and started "recruiting like crazy."

A few months later, in the fall of 1984, the Trinity Bible College Lions made their football debut. Let the record show Bismarck Junior College's junior varsity team defeated Trinity 40–0 in that first game. Seven more defeats followed that season; the closest game was a 12–8 loss. The next season brought nine more losses in nine games. Trin-

ABOVE, TOP Ellendale is a welcoming rural community in North Dakota with an estimated population of 1,550 people.

ABOVE, MIDDLE Quiet downtown Ellendale on a Saturday afternoon.

ABOVE, BOTTOM Founded in 1948 as Lakewood Park Bible School, Trinity Bible College is located on 28 acres in Ellendale, which has been home to the school since 1972. Having only 310 students, Trinity is the smallest four-year school in the nation with a football team.

ABOVE, TOP Rusty Bentley came to Ellendale from Texas, sporting a Bible phrase for any occasion. "There is a method to my madness," he said of his coaching techniques.

ABOVE, MIDDLE Brandon Strong, a twenty-one-year-old student assistant, played for Trinity in 2003.

ABOVE, BOTTOM With a roster of only thirty, Trinity's players, including Kevin Kloefkorn (far left), savor any moment of rest.

TOP, LEFT Trinity center Lee Odell earned all-conference honors his first year, though he struggled to adjust to the difficulties the team experienced on the field.

MIDDLE, LEFT The team huddles for a post-game prayer.

BOTTOM, RIGHT Andy Brower practices his kickoffs. Brower scored three touchdowns in 2004, one more than the entire Trinity team scored in 2003.

ABOVE, TOP Trinity offensive coordinator Eric Slivoskey (far right) talks with Andy Brower and Tim Rasmussen after another difficult Trinity defeat.

ABOVE, MIDDLE Running back Stephen Poyser provided Trinity with a new backfield threat, but endured a lot of punishment during the season.

ABOVE, BOTTOM Running back Sannon Norick (left) came to Trinity after a successful prep career in Montana. He led Trinity in rushing, despite missing time with a neck injury.

ABOVE, TOP Receiver Andy Brower (right) and fellow teammates listen to the coach.

ABOVE, MIDDLE Eric Slivoskey (left) and Tim Rasmussen discuss strategy.

ABOVE, BOTTOM The Trinity Lions get pumped up for a big game.

ABOVE, TOP In 2003, Jerry Rush was a 33-year-old defensive line-man who had never played football until arriving at Trinity. In 2004, injuries kept him off the field, but he ran the concession stand at home games.

ABOVE, MIDDLE John Brady serves as a pastor in Ellendale, but he is also enthusiastic about his job with Trinity: team water boy.

ABOVE, BOTTOM Trinity doesn't draw many fans to its games, but the true fans do their best to keep enthusiasm high.

ABOVE, TOP The Trinity Lions face off against the Martin Luther College Knights.

ABOVE, MIDDLE Andy Brower gets checked by an athletic trainer after suffering an injury.

ABOVE, BOTTOM This statue of a lion sits near the Trinity football field. Over the years it has witnessed very few victories.

ABOVE, TOP **The Trinity Lions getting ready for their next game.**

ABOVE, BOTTOM **Shaking hands after the game.**

ity broke into the win column with a 26–0 victory over St. Paul Bible in its 1986 season opener.

Tatum wasn't used to losing, at least not during his years at Santa Fe. The competitor in him struggled with the lack of wins, but he says the Christian in him believed the team was achieving victory, simply by having a team. He says he completely devoted himself to Wes Neal's philosophy on athletics, which includes the view "If you give a total release of yourself toward becoming like Jesus in your athletic performance, you will never look on a defeat from an opponent as a loss."

Trinity's players lived, or tried to live, anyway, by those words in the football program's infancy. Their coach did, too. He didn't have a choice.

"I had settled in my heart that I was not going to be considered a loser just because I couldn't win, and I believed every inch of it," Tatum says. "I really tried to get my kids to believe that all we had to do was do the best we can in all phases, to release our talents and worship God playing football. You can lose twenty-five games in a row, and still win in God's eyes."

According to Tatum, most coaches use the basic concepts of total release—the idea of improving every week; concentrating on the team getting better each outing, regardless of the opponent; working hard, whether the opponent's strong or weak—but "they just leave Jesus out of it." Tatum says he does wonder what those coaches, and their players, fall back on when the victories don't come, when the losses pile up and the frustration grows. He had his belief in Jesus. How do they do it, he wonders.

Through the years discussions occasionally occurred that centered on whether Trinity should continue to support the football program, discussions that always ended the same way, with school leaders choosing to forge ahead. Tatum never believed there would be any other outcome. He saw how the program came together, the events that needed to take place for the school to have football—his decision to send those letters from Santa Fe, Trinity's desire to hire him, the school finding helmets from another school with colors that matched its own—as acts of a power above even the board of regents.

"I could see that God was in this, and I wasn't," he says. "I could honestly see that I was not in the program, it was God. Because from a worldly standpoint, we were never ever going to be able to win many games. Trinity would have faded years ago if God would not have had his hand on it."

Early in Tatum's time at Trinity, a young Jesse Godding toiled for the Lions on the line, playing from 1985 through 1987, three years that saw the program win five games, though the losses were usually respectable with only the occasional rout. For instance, in '85 the Lions didn't win a game, but were only outscored by a 275–114 margin. But the schedule wasn't nearly as difficult as the one Trinity plays now.

Back then, junior varsity teams and fellow small Bible colleges dotted Trinity's schedule. Four of Trinity's victories during Godding's years came against St. Paul Bible, a school that was often the Lions' patsy during the 1980s, consistently getting sand kicked in their faces by the team that was usually the one being bullied.

Godding completed his education at Crown College in Minnesota, but returned to North Dakota in 1992, this time as Trinity's head coach, three years after Tatum retired as the Lions' leader. Tatum purchased the Oxenrider in 1988, but his daughter Becky operated the motel when it first opened. Bob took over after leaving coaching, an occupational switch that gave him the opportunity to follow his son Todd's college career at Northern State in Aberdeen. He did enjoy one winning season with the Lions, the 1988 campaign, which saw the Lions compile a 6–2–1 mark, the best in school history. The good times didn't last. Trinity went 0–9 the next season and was outscored 454–48.

Godding, meanwhile, spent his first five years back in Ellendale wondering what he'd gotten himself into. He looked for a way out. Any way out. It took him three years to win his first game, and in his first seven years at the helm Godding won a total of two games. A series of circumstances conspired against Godding those years. For one, the team's schedule underwent a makeover—junior varsity opponents became rarer and the level of difficulty rose (for instance, Trinity stopped playing St. Paul Bible in 1991). Recruiting proved to be a struggle as well. Some of the reasons were the same as they are today—location of the school, mission of the school—but Godding was handicapped even more by the majors Trinity offered at the time. More accurately, the number of majors hindered him.

There were three: elementary education, pastoral, and missions. Despite those limitations, many of Godding's Trinity teams were competitive, even when they ended up on the wrong end of the scoreboard. Which was basically every week. In 1995, the team went winless in nine games, but lost by five, fifteen, eighteen, and twenty points. In 1998, the Lions went 1–8, but lost by one, three, and thirteen points, and held leads in five of the games.

But they were still losses. Losses that made Godding question the very existence of the program. What was the program accomplishing in coordination with the school's larger mission? Were the players learning anything about life? If they were, what kind of lessons? Godding feared that the constant losing could actually be harming the athletes.

Learned helplessness. That's what Godding feared. It's a psychological theory that's occasionally used to explain everything from depression to why a person would stay in an abusive relationship. Godding wondered if Trinity's players were falling victim to learned helplessness through their involvement with athletics, specifically the football team.

"They say, 'Here's my situation I'm in, it doesn't matter how hard I work, I can't impact the situation,'" Godding explains. "You don't want to turn out kids who are feeling that way. That is not the life lesson you want them to learn. Fortunately, I think time has born this out, that that was not happening."

Still, Godding kept his résumé updated, pursuing other positions during his first five years in Ellendale. That changed in 1996. At a church service, a man told Godding that if he just stayed in town and tried to be comfortable with where he was at, "there will be things accomplished beyond what you think and beyond what you can imagine."

So Godding settled in. Shortly after that church service, Trinity did begin to accomplish things that went beyond what Godding could have imagined when he took over the program. Victories no longer came with the frequency of a leap year. Success, tangible success, came to the program. Three victories in 1999, three more in 2000. Finally, in 2000, five victories, matched against five losses. A .500 record, a mark that by definition signifies mediocrity, but at Trinity means much, much more. It was a season when "victory" wasn't preceded by the word "moral." Those five wins included a victory that, in retrospect, looks even more impressive: In the final game of 2000, the Lions defeated Rockford 27–20. Trinity held Rockford running back Marcus Howard to 41 yards rushing. Three years later he ran for 326 yards and five touchdowns in Rockford's 105–0 victory.

A strong 1998 recruiting class keyed Trinity's improvement, but other internal and external changes were just as important. The school added a business minor, which helped with recruiting. Also, and perhaps most important in Godding's mind, Trinity joined the UMAC in the late 1990s, giving the school a consistent schedule and giving the players something to shoot for.

"You could show them a picture of our all-conference players from the year before, and they knew they had an opportunity for recognition," he says. "You don't get that if you're an independent. It was great for those kids."

So how did Trinity go from that 27–20 victory over Rockford to a 105–0 loss, from a 5–5 mark to a three-year losing streak? Well, Godding left, taking over the football program at Southwestern Assemblies of God University in Waxahachie, Texas. The exit left some hard feelings behind, especially because of the timing of Godding's exit. Godding, though, had little control over the timing.

After spending the first few years of his Trinity tenure searching for other work, Godding had made himself comfortable in Ellendale. But in December 2001, he inquired about the opening at Southwestern, a school that had a program in disarray. Godding had a couple of interviews, spoke with the school's athletic director and vice president of academics, and then didn't hear anything else about the job. Southwestern hired a coach who was already on its campus. Then, in March 2002, on the Thursday before Good Friday, Godding left the Trinity campus early to take the rest of the afternoon off. The phone rang minutes after he sat down in his recliner with a book.

The director of student services at Southwestern was on the other end of the line, asking Godding if he still had any interest in the school's coaching position. The previous hire didn't work out. The school needed a coach. Quickly.

Godding accepted the position, becoming the school's fourth head coach in five years. The spring departure left Trinity scrambling. The school hired former player Jeff Headrick for the winless 2002 season and then hired Bentley. Trinity hasn't won a game since Godding left for Texas.

Godding still closely follows the Trinity program, just like his former coach. While Tatum attends many of the home games—and is also a presence at Trinity volleyball and basketball games—Godding follows from afar, checking each weekend for the latest score from Ellendale. He feels the team's pain. He also regrets that some people back at Trinity still resent his decision to take the Southwestern job. Considering Godding gave three years to the program as a player and ten more as a coach, it's hard to argue that he didn't pay his dues at Trinity.

"It pains me," he says about the program's current struggles. "I invested a ton of effort there, real sweat. The whole thing I saw come to fruition. I had always hoped when the day came if I stepped away, it would be at a position where it'd be stable enough where the next person could come along and continue it."

In three years at Southwestern, Godding has struggled to do what he finally accomplished at Trinity: stabilize the program. Southwestern went 1–10 in 2004, but while the record might be similar to Trinity's, Godding said there's a "night and day" difference between the programs. Southwestern's a school of just under seventeen hundred students, only thirty minutes south of Dallas. In the off-season, the football team—which has a recruiting coordinator on staff, something Godding could only dream about at Trinity—targets approximately three hundred possible recruits. Compare that with the sixty or seventy he'd look at with the Lions.

"There are probably two hundred high schools in the state of North Dakota," Godding says, "and now we probably have two hundred within a fifty-mile radius."

Godding certainly has the resources to bring the Southwestern program to the level Trinity reached in his final years there. The question
is if Trinity's program can get back to the level Godding had it at by the
2001 season. Forget, for a moment, about victories. Can the program
first get to the level where the games aren't decided by halftime? Can
the program get to the level where there are enough players on the roster to ensure that only a few, if any, have to play both ways?

Or, as Eric Slivoskey says, "There's a big difference between
going out there and losing compared to coming out and just being
shark meat for these teams. When you're losing 77–6 every week,
that's when it gets a little scary."

All of Trinity's coaches, past and present, agree that player reten-
tion is a crucial aspect for the program's survival. That 1998 recruiting class that Godding brought to Trinity stuck around, maturing for
four years, both on and off the field, and finally found success as seniors. A similarly strong class, this one in 1996, lost many of its top
players and the program struggled.

"It's going to be really difficult to continue to go out and restock
the shelves with twenty-five, thirty guys every fall," says Slivoskey,
who actually talked with Godding about coming to play at Trinity in
the mid-1990s. "To look at your roster in February and say, 'Well, we
have nine coming back for sure.' What can you do with nine? Or
twelve? It would be so nice in February or March to look at it and
say, 'Wow, we have twenty-four that are definitely coming back.' It's
nice to have a program, but it's a whole lot nicer to have a program
that has a chance to compete a little bit."

Of course, the difficulty comes in finding kids whom are likely to
stick around Trinity for four years. And that goes back to issues that
often have little to do with football. It's about finding people who can
fit into the school's social, academic and spiritual environment.

"If you think the kid's not going to fit into the situation, it's better
to leave him alone," Godding says. "It's just going to be frustrating to
him, to us, and the school. You have to tell them, 'This is who we are.
Is this who you are?' And then do they have the athletic ability? Do we
have a program that fits you? We were able to land a lot of kids that
just weren't limited to football, they were leaders on campus."

While Godding frets about Trinity's present and future from half a country away, Tatum watches the Lions' struggles up close, on the field that bears his name, with the feeling that he could, perhaps, help turn the team's fortunes if he had the opportunity. He would love to volunteer his efforts as an assistant, but the time requirements at the Oxenrider make that impossible—for now.

"I could help provide at least a trained coach in one position," he says. "It would be better than somebody that you're breaking in new every year, and the program would be better off, provided I didn't try to cause a problem. And I've never been critical of the coaches. I understand everything they're going through."

The current coach struggles with the idea of what is success at Trinity. Does winning have anything to do with success?

"I didn't get brought here to win football games," Bentley says. "I got brought here to be in the ministry. We keep talking about sharing the gospel through football. Bible colleges have to do that; we're the ones that have to do that."

Trinity, he says, is not a school for a kid who just wants to play football. Even a Christian kid. It's just a game, he says. "And I love it," he adds. "And I love to scheme it. And I love to sit there and watch professional games and know what the play's going to be the very next play. I just wish I had the same chess pieces as everybody else has to play with. In ten years, nobody is going to remember some score. Because it doesn't matter, it really doesn't matter. It matters for paychecks. It matters for the kids getting drafted. But for anybody else, who does it matter for? Honestly. Nobody else. I know if I said that to 90 percent of the people across the country that were looking to hire me, I wouldn't get the job. But if we tell them it's just a game, we have to live it that it's just a game."

Assistant Tim Rasmussen agrees. To a point. But he questions whether Bentley can fulfill any obligations at Trinity, even the ones that don't involve the scoreboard.

"I don't necessarily think the purpose of the school is to have this huge athletic program," the former Trinity player and current assistant says. "But if you're going to do it, you should to it right. As a coach at Trinity, you need to be able to treat people the right way.

You can't be one way to their face and another way behind their back. A coach is going to have to find a way to work within the limits that we have. You can't let your players feel that. Part of the reason I love Trinity so much is that it's not a place where kids come for scholarships or for money. Obviously there's other things here that draw them other than football. And a lot of kids who do come to play football play for the love of the game, the moral fiber, the belief in God. I don't ever look at that as an obstacle for us to overcome."

In other words, the challenges inherent in coaching at Trinity should be viewed as that—challenges, not excuses.

But since they do keep score at the games, what are realistic expectations for Trinity's football team? Trinity *should* be able to compete against Principia, against Crown, against Maranatha Baptist. That's what Godding says, and he only says "should" because his teams did just that. Achieving a .500 record with the Lions will always be a tremendous accomplishment, and one that probably won't ever happen on a yearly basis. Not with the geographical hurdles, not with the academic and social challenges. But maybe it can happen every few years. And those years it doesn't happen, maybe there can be more "good" losses and fewer defeats that leave the Lions feeling like, well, shark meat. Again, the key is not only finding good players, but keeping them anchored in Ellendale.

It'll be tough. Tough for Bentley, tough for anyone. So tough, Godding's not even sure he'd be able to pull it off again. Or would even want to try.

"Honestly, I don't know that I could do it now," he says. "When you're young, you're energetic; you're going to change the world. You don't realize you don't have any scholarship money. You don't have any majors to recruit to, and you're going against athletes that are way better than you and the kids you've got. But hope always springs eternal every year."

Even at Trinity.

Chapter Eleven

Rockford's Return

OCTOBER 14, 2004

Thirteen months and fourteen games ago the Trinity Bible College Lions took a bus trip to Rockford, Illinois, for a nice game of football. They came back battered, bloodied, and 105–0 losers.

Now they get another shot at Rockford.

Trinity's not afraid of its rematch. That's the good news. The coaches don't fear a repeat, and neither do the players. It helps that fewer than ten of Trinity's players were actually in uniform for that game. There's something to be said for only welcoming back a handful of players from the previous season: fewer guys are burdened with bad memories.

But maybe Trinity should be a bit worried, because Rockford is better this year. Yes, so is Trinity. But for the 2004 Lions improvement means Haskell defeated them by fifty-seven points, instead of sixty. Improvement means Crown defeated the Lions by fifty-four points, instead of sixty-one. Rockford, on the other hand, has only lost twice, including once in overtime. While it's sometimes pointless to compare scores of common opponents, it's hard to ignore Rockford's 73–14 victory over Principia, or its 33–12 triumph over Crown, two teams that defeated Trinity.

This year's game will at least be on Trinity's home field.

Common sense dictates there won't be a recurrence. Given the flak Rockford coach Mike Hoskins took in some quarters—deserved or not—after the historic game, you get the feeling that he'll do everything but tackle his own players to keep the game from getting so out of hand again. Hoskins told reporters after that game that he wasn't going to tell his quarterback to take a knee just to keep the score under 100. This could be a tougher call to make if history starts to repeat itself.

"If I was a betting man," Bentley said two days before the game, "I'd bet neither team would want the same thing to happen. Coach Hoskins has taken a lot of heat, but none of it from me. Still to this day I haven't said anything negative, and I won't."

From Trinity's perspective, the timing of this game couldn't be worse. Coming off four consecutive routs, the players' confidence is at a low point.

So is their luck.

At Thursday's practice, lineman Michael Moss watched the team conclude its workout while sitting on the grass, nursing an injured knee. Moss hurt it earlier in practice, as the team played what was supposed to be a carefree game of touch football. The team was short on numbers at the start of practice, and the game should have been a chance for a bit of fun. It was, until Moss went down.

"I started walking around, next thing I know, whoa, that hurts a lot," Moss says. "It started swelling up. I was like, 'Coach Slivo, can you come look at this?'"

"We have to be the only team in the nation to play touch football and lose a starting lineman," Bentley laments.

Back in his office after practice, Bentley slides a tape into his VCR to show a visitor Trinity's latest television appearance. This one's much more positive than the blurbs the Lions received over the air after the 105–0 defeat. The Fox affiliate out of Fargo shot some tape of one of Trinity's recent games and runs a report that basically provides an update on the health of the program. The station interviewed Bentley, whose face is now up on the screen, explaining Trinity's philosophy and outlook. He might not have movie-star looks, but the man is a natural on TV; his ability to weave a tale proves a perfect fit in front of the cameras.

Bentley doesn't mind the attention. Likes it, actually. The spotlight usually doesn't shine on teams that haven't won in three years. But it has found Trinity. Trace it all back to the 105–0 game, the game that first alerted many people nationwide that Trinity existed and had a football team. After that game, Bentley was forced to deal with the publicity, whether he wanted to or not. He could have rejected the interview requests, but what would that have accomplished? He wasn't ashamed and didn't feel he had any reason to climb into a self-induced isolation.

But some players wonder if the coach doesn't enjoy the attention a bit too much.

"It's almost like he enjoys losing," Andy Brower says. "To me it seemed like he feels like he gets more recognition if he loses than if he wins. This way he keeps getting publicity."

OCTOBER 15, 2004
The kids are with a baby-sitter.

Tonight the Bentleys are, again, just a two-member crew. Sage and Rusty are on the road, headed to Aberdeen for dinner and a movie. A viewing of the recently released *Friday Night Lights* is on the agenda. Rusty can't get to Aberdeen fast enough. He can't wait to see a movie about an old love of his: Texas high school football.

Bentley sits in the driver's seat of the couple's white Suburban while Sage relaxes next to him. They're comfortable, the conversation light. They need a trip out of town. These nights are rare enough—when the fifth child comes in two months, they'll be even scarcer. Rusty and Sage wouldn't have it any other way, though there's been plenty of heartache and upheaval in their nine-year relationship.

In late 1997, eight months after the two married, Sage miscarried the couple's first child. She gave birth to Trey—so named because he's the third Russell Bentley—in November 1998. In the six years since, there have been three more births and another on the way. The couple has moved six times, Rusty is on job number four, and each has gone through a master's program.

"Our stress level should be off the charts," Rusty notes.

Should be tonight, too, one day away from a return engagement with Rockford. No coach ever had a debut like Bentley's. That 105–0 game will follow him for as long as he prowls the sidelines. It's a shadow. It defines him. It would almost be a scarlet letter if Bentley didn't wear it with a touch of pride. Maybe that can change in a few years, if he turns the program around. But with each week bringing another lopsided defeat, his first college game seems increasingly as if it's going to serve as the most memorable of his coaching career.

Tomorrow he gets to face that team again. No problem, he says.

"We have to perform for our own self. It's wonderful. What kind of pressure is that? None at all. I have no fear at all."

Sage remembers the call Rusty made to her in the moments after last year's Rockford game. The assistant coaches' wives were over at the house with Sage when she heard the score.

"I was trying to figure out how to be there for him," she says. "Part of me wanted to go out with like shaving cream and decorate all the guys' cars, just to let them know we still supported them. But then I thought, no. I didn't know. I had no idea what to do."

By the time the Bentleys finish dinner and make their way to the Aberdeen theater, the cineplex is crowded with Friday night fans. Sage and Rusty find aisle seats, but twenty minutes into the movie Rusty begins squirming in his chair.

Hollywood has added a little spice to H. G. Bissinger's original tale, in the form of some rather mundane PG-13esque adult situations. In the book racism and convoluted educational values at Permian High School in Odessa are two of the most unsettling issues. Pleasures of the flesh cause unrest in the screen version—at least for Bentley. In one scene, starting quarterback Mike Winchell, the reluctant leader of the team, accepts the advances of a blonde Permian groupie.

Nothing's really acted out in the bedroom, simply implied. The camera shows the pair putting their pants back on, followed by a brief peek at the girl's floral panties, a good-bye smooch, and a forlorn gaze into the mirror by Winchell, who looks like he just ran over his dog. Seconds later, another scene, this one featuring singer Tim McGraw's redneck screen character Charlie Billingsley, watching his son, a Permian running back, make out with a gal who's obviously a big fan. It's meant to be an uncomfortable scene, providing a glimpse into the troubled relationship between the Billingsley men. It succeeds, even if the scene wasn't in Bissinger's original telling, and the most shocking aspect of it all is the appearance of McGraw's heretofore unseen chest hair. The first twenty minutes of the movie, which introduce the characters and set the atmosphere surrounding the football program, surprise Bentley. Eventually, he turns from his chair and, with a touch of exasperation, asks, "Is this stuff in the book?"

The implied and interrupted sex scenes eventually end. From there the film follows the more standard sports movie formula Bentley was expecting, albeit with the featured team actually losing the big game. But the movie wins him over, in a big way. And not just because of the intense football scenes or the emotionally wrenching heartbreak experienced by many of the key characters. The setting reigns.

"I'm homesick now," Rusty says as he exits the theater with Sage on his arm. "This is the most I've missed Texas in two years. It all came back, the sounds, the voices. Everything. I miss it."

Following the flick the Bentleys swing by Wal-Mart, which is still brimming with shoppers at 9:30 p.m. Rusty needs handwarmers. Not just gloves—handwarmers. Forecasts for Saturday's game call for raw temperatures, barely in the forties, with stiff winds approaching twenty miles per hour. On Trinity's exposed field, it promises to be a chilly affair.

While Sage stocks up on some groceries, Rusty wanders around the hunting section, unable to locate the warmers.

"This is date night for the Bentleys," he says.

An employee ends Bentley's search, telling him the warmers have sold out. Looks like everyone's stocking up for the first cold spell of the season.

Bentley faces bigger problems. The onions he had with his dinner aren't settling well; the indigestion brings about a series of pained grunts.

"I need some Rolaids, babe," he tells Sage.

Fortunately, Wal-Mart's stock of Rolaids hasn't been raided.

His stomach settled, and the groceries purchased, the Bentleys head back for home, this time with Sage in the driver's seat.

In between a short prayer for the ride home—"Lord, please don't let us hit a deer,"—and a short discussion about the TV sports report that recently aired on the team, Bentley ruminates on the upcoming game. Knowing victory on the scoreboard is a long shot, if not an impossibility, what constitutes victory?

"Getting through the game without any injuries would be the first victory," he says. "If we score, that would be victory number two. If we can keep them at fifty or less, that'd be victory number three. The whole world would just think we won the ballgame if we kept them at fifty or less."

Discussion shifts to *Friday Night Lights*. Rusty particularly appreciated Billy Bob Thornton's character, Permian coach Gary Gaines, who spends much of his time fighting off Permian boosters. Bentley found the swearing in the movie a bit tougher to take, calling it "harsh."

"I say harsh," he says. "It was just different because we don't ever hear it. You know, old Billy Bob didn't say a swear word the whole time."

"He said one," Sage says.

"Did he? What'd it start with?"

"An 'a.'"

The Bentleys go through this same dance every Friday. Rusty speculates about the game, Sage listens, occasionally throwing in her thoughts. As the Suburban crosses back inside Ellendale's city limits and winds through the lonely streets, Rusty lets out a sigh, asking, "What are we gonna *do* tomorrow?"

"Clean house," Sage replies.

"I hope we clean house. Oh, you're not talking about the football game, are ya? All I gotta do to be a winner tomorrow is pull into Char's Grocery Store and pick up four packages of Reese's Peanut Butter Cups. I bring them home, now I'm a winner. Ain't that right, babe?"

That might be the only victory of the day.

OCTOBER 16, 2004

Around the UMAC, Rockford has something of a reputation for being the league bully. Two league coaches specifically compared the difference between playing Rockford and Northwestern, another strong conference team. Northwestern, they said, "doesn't want to beat you up," something they didn't say about Rockford.

The 105–0 game did nothing to help alleviate that view. Coach Mike Hoskins acknowledges the existence of that sentiment, but he believes it's misguided.

"I think our kids take a bad rap," he says. "Our kids are physical and we play hard. Some teams in the league think we're cheapshot artists, and we're not."

And to think, people hold those views about a school that originally began as a female seminary back in 1847. The school is located in Rockford, Illinois, a city of 150,000 about eighty-five miles northwest of Chicago. Renowned turn-of-the-twentieth-century social reformer Jane Addams, who won the Nobel Prize for Peace in 1931, is the school's most famous graduate. The school's Web site also claims, with a touch of pride, that former FBI director J. Edgar Hoover once called Addams "the most dangerous woman in America," because of the activist's peace efforts.

Although the school's heritage stretches back nearly 160 years, football's a new venture. The school only added the sport in 2000.

Rockford can sympathize with Trinity in some regards—the football team knows what it's like to be downtrodden, though its time at the bottom of the standings was short.

The Regents finished 1–9 their first season, which included that 27–20 loss against Trinity. The program quickly established a level of consistency, winning five games in 2001 and four more in 2002 before improving to 7–3 in 2003. The Regents enter the Trinity game with a record of 4–2.

The forty-five-year-old Hoskins, who manages to meld a persona that's amiable yet gruff, patiently waited for his turn to lead a college program, spending ten years as a college assistant and twelve years in the high school ranks before ascending to the top spot at Rockford. Like Bentley, Hoskins experienced a coaching debut unlike any other, only he was on the right side of the 105–0 finale. In some ways, though, Hoskins lost by winning, receiving criticism from many quarters. He shrugs off the complaints, confident he didn't run up the score in that 2003 game. While the gripes don't seem to bother him, Hoskins does worry that the victory tarred the players, just like the accusations of being "cheap-shot artists." But overall Hoskins and his charges seem fine with their lot in life, content that the team is earning victories, if not many friends.

Trinity does have Rockford beat in one area: mascots. The name "Lions" may be shared by hundreds of schools, but it does project a strong image. But Regents? It's hard to think of a nickname that would be less threatening than the image of a group of impassive, well-dressed regents sitting around a boardroom debating tuition hikes.

Fortunately for Rockford, the team is much tougher than the nickname.

On the field, the Regents are now a solid contender each year for the conference title. Philosophically, however, Hoskins says Rockford doesn't quite fit in with the rest of the conference's schools, with their strong emphasis on religion. It's not that the other teams' ways are bad and Rockford's are good, he says. They're just different. Always will be.

"We say 'shit' or 'damn,' and everyone looks at us like we're renegades."

An hour before kickoff, Trinity is just looking at Rockford with a bit of envy.

Eric Slivoskey and Tim Rasmussen sit in the outer coaches' office while Bentley visits with Hoskins outside the locker room. When he comes back in, Bentley tells the others, "They only brought sixty," referring to players.

"What would it be like to say that?" Slivoskey wonders.

As the players enter the locker room, the ghosts of a past lost are there to greet them. A long, white banner with large letters hangs on the wall. The words read, "What will the headlines say today?" Beneath it are about a dozen computer printouts: postings from Internet chat rooms, college football Web sites and newspaper stories, all of which cropped up after the 105–0 defeat. There's one from the

NetShrine discussion forum, where someone posts an e-mail purportedly from Rockford President Paul Pribbenow: "Unbelievable—actually, a bit embarrassing . . . Trinity shouldn't be playing football (the coach was quoted as saying that 'they were there first and foremost to testify.' Yikes!)"

John Walters's article from CNN/SI.com is up. So is a column by Chuck Offenburger, who runs the site offenburger.com. That story quotes an e-mail from Rockford's SID, Dave Beyer. "Yup, it was an *ugly* truth!" Beyer also told Offenburger he "felt so bad for the TBC coaches in the press box, that I broke with my usual rule of 'media/staff only' in the actual working area and fed them some pizza and pop at halftime."

Some posts poke fun at Trinity, some express pity. They all catch the eye of the players, who pore over each story. A few players chuckle, others just grunt and shake their heads. The stories undoubtedly fire up a few, even the players who didn't play in the game. Bulletin board material doesn't come much better than this. Who posted them? Who knows? Bentley says he didn't do it. Rasmussen says he didn't do it. Brandon Strong's work? It remains a mystery.

Lee Odell is one player who doesn't need any extra motivation. Last year's game means little to him—he was at Kansas State at the time—and he's not intimidated by the Regents. But he is upset by the comments of a teammate, who said the Lions should just be hoping to hold Rockford under seventy points. Could be a realistic goal, especially for the players who experienced last year's debacle. When Odell hears the words, though, he seethes.

"I was like, how are you saying that? It's football and you don't know what's going to happen. If you've got better technique, you can beat somebody, even if they are stronger. Some guys just get so scared during the game and they're freaking out in the huddle and it's like, calm down, he's a man, just like you are."

Well, most of Rockford's players are men.

Michael Moss, whose touch football injury will sideline him, stands in the office with the coaches. Moss, decked out in a camouflage jacket that makes him look like he's ready to shoot some pheasants, looks over the Rockford roster, which takes up two sides of paper and has eighty-six names on it. Moss zeroes in on No. 99—placekicker Julie Harshbarger. He looks up, his face contorted. Julie? A girl? This is too much for Moss. Now teams aren't even using men against the Lions?

"Has she played all year?" he asks. "Or are they just using her against us?"

No, Harshbarger is not on the roster to mock the Lions—she's a legitimate part of the team. The 5-foot, 10-inch freshman was an all-conference high school kicker in northern Illinois, and is also a stand-out soccer player for the Regents (on the women's team). Rockford is in her blood; her mother, grandmother, grandfather, and uncle all graduated from the school. She's also done her family proud on the field. In September, she kicked three extra points in a victory over Principia, becoming the first female to score a point in a UMAC game. But Moss's concern is moot. Though Harshbarger is on the roster, she won't appear in today's game.

The conversation in the office bounces around as players pop in and out in various states of dress; one can't find his game pants, another needs some athletic tape.

"Find Brandon Strong," they're told.

A handful of players seem loose, others have the nervous mannerisms of a pimply-faced sixteen-year-old boy preparing for a prom date with the homecoming queen. Talk turns to college football, specifically the University of Nebraska's embarrassing 70–10 loss against Texas Tech a week earlier.

"So much for the West Coast offense," a player says of Nebraska coach Bill Callahan's newly installed offense.

"I'm running the Midwest Offense," Slivoskey retorts. "I'm just trying to figure out exactly what it is."

Overall the mood's fairly light, though Slivoskey and Rasmussen make it clear that they expect a substantial improvement from last year's game. Not just improvement in the score—it's seemingly impossible for the game not to be closer—but in Trinity's execution and cohesion. Four weeks after the team's narrow loss against Principia, which seemed to indicate 2004 would be much different than the struggles of 2003, the Lions have suffered four straight blowout losses. Though they avoid saying the actual "m" word, it's clear the coaches would take some moral victories today.

Slivoskey just wants to see "a fire in the belly," and, he hopes, a decent first quarter. First-quarter blues have plagued the Lions. Then again, so have second-, third-, and fourth-quarter blues.

"I came across a quote and I read it to the guys," he says. "It goes, 'I get knocked down seven times, but I get up eight.' If you do that, you're still winning the battle. As long as you keep getting up, there's honor in that."

The game marks the return of Dusty Hess, though not as a quarterback. The broken right wrist he suffered against Blackburn kept him out of nearly four full games, and it's still far from healed. He sports a giant plaster club on his right arm. It would make a great weapon in a street fight, but is ill suited for catching a football. Nonetheless, he's expected to see time in the defensive backfield, where perhaps he can use the cast to bat the ball down. Though the new accessory on his arm has diminished his physical skills, Trinity will benefit from his football experience.

Taped to Trinity's locker room door, the last thing the players read before exiting, is a piece of paper with a Lion emblazoned in the background. It reads, "I am a Lion. I play for my savior. I am unstoppable. My team is my pride. My teammates are my brothers. Together victory is ours."

The teams take the field on a sunny but cold day, with the thermometer struggling to crack forty degrees. Bentley definitely could have used those handwarmers.

"Welcome to the frozen tundra," a Rockford player says before warm-ups.

"Yeah, but I'd much rather be at Lambeau Field," replies a teammate.

A short, hyper Rockford assistant leads the team in calisthenics; his military-like commands produce jumping jacks that would make an elementary physical education teacher beam. "Everybody's going to get a shot today, so let's go!" he exhorts, trying to fire up the players for a game they know they're not going to lose.

With about ten minutes left before kickoff, Rockford's players become temporarily discombobulated when the Trinity choir starts belting out the "Star Spangled Banner." Quickly, the Regents take off their helmets and respectfully stand at attention, bringing laughs from the singers and the crowd. False alarm—the choir was simply warming up. Unfortunately for the Lions, it's pretty much the last time they'll fool the Regents.

Rockford scores five minutes into the game. Then two minutes later, then three minutes later, then four minutes later. After one quarter the Regents are actually on pace to break their scoring record of 105. They lead 28–0. As Bentley watches the first-quarter clock tick down, he says, "We've gotta get out of this quarter without giving up another score."

The Lions do, only to see Rockford's John Feehan break off a fifty-five-yard touchdown run on the first play of the second quarter to put Rockford up 35–0. The Trinity players are quiet on the sideline. With Rockford putting up five touchdowns in the span of sixteen minutes, it's hard to imagine the players—at least the ones who played last year—aren't thinking, "Is it really happening again?"

Frustration shows for Trinity with some chippy play in the second quarter. Nothing serious, just a few bumps after the whistle. They don't get flagged for any wrongdoing, but a few Rockford players voice their complaints. Freshman lineman Reggie Patrick declines to join in, telling a teammate, "I can't get mad at 'em. I used to play for a piss poor high school team. I know how they feel."

Trinity's fortunes temporarily change for the better a few minutes later when Rex Causey—a fine 6-foot, 4-inch, 215-pound athlete who also plays on the school basketball team—sacks Rockford quarterback Travis Stocker and forces a fumble. Trinity recovers at the Rockford seventeen-yard line. Two plays later, on a smart call wonderfully executed, Tony Snyder finds Stephen Poyser open in the end zone for a touchdown, the first time in three years Trinity has scored against the Regents. Trinity's fans give the offense a standing ovation, remaining on their feet as the offense runs off the field. To this point, their loudest cheers came when cornerback Michael Guyton deflected a Rockford pass in the end zone, temporarily keeping the Regents from scoring.

Poyser's touchdown means the Lions will accomplish one of Bentley's goals for the game—a score. Keeping Rockford under fifty points was another goal, one that will not be accomplished. Following Snyder's scoring pass to Poyser, Rockford ends the first half with two more touchdowns, including a sixty-eight-yard sprint by Joseph Mariani, that give the Regents a 49–6 lead at the break.

Bentley's final goal, not to get any players injured, also falls by the wayside. Early in the third quarter, a horde of Rockford defenders pummel Sannon Norick, injuring his neck. Trinity's bullish fullback—who was limited to two yards on eight carries before the injury—sits on the bench, unable to move his neck left or right. Pastor Brady sits next to Norick and says a short prayer with the glum sophomore, who can only look straight ahead, a grimace glued to his face. Brady's young grandson, Austin, follows his grandpa throughout the game—a water boy apprentice and perhaps the most excited person at the game, other than Rockford's backups.

The third quarter provides little relief for Trinity's defense. Stocker throws a pair of touchdown passes while Mariani scores on a seventy-two-yard run. In the fourth quarter backup running back Tim Kiddoo gets into the act with a forty-eight-yard touchdown, Rockford's fourth scoring run of longer than forty yards.

Rockford could have used Julie Harshbarger. Not to win the game or anything, but to save starting kicker George Anderson's leg. Anderson's eleventh extra point of the game gives the Regents a 77–6 lead, prompting one of the officials to say, "Eleven touchdowns, eleven extra points. She's a blowout."

But not as bad as last year's game.

One member of the Trinity family still believes in the team.

"Come on blue," Pastor Brady shouts as the fourth quarter begins, "this is our quarter."

In a way, it is. Andy Brower, enjoying the best game of his season with three catches, turns his fourth reception into the most exciting play of the game, breaking tackles and sprinting down the field in front of the Rockford sideline for a seventy-nine-yard touchdown. One of Brower's catches earlier in the game elicited grumbling from Rockford's players, who lectured teammates that they "were giving up way too many yards." Those players really won't like this development.

The game ends 77–12, a sixty-five-point defeat for the Lions, but a forty-point upgrade from the previous year. Rockford scored seventy points through three quarters, but only added one more TD in the fourth, just the way Coach Hoskins wanted.

"I mandated no more scores after it got in the mid-70s," he says after the game. "I didn't want it to go to 80. We were almost in the position today where we were going to have to start taking a knee. I didn't want to do that. I think it's demoralizing to their kids, plus our kids get goosey."

Like the 2003 meeting, Rockford's numbers are again eye opening. The Regents rewrite their five-year-old record book, racking up their most total yards in a game (647) and most rushing yards in a game (547).

Mariani does the most damage with 276 yards on a mere fourteen carries. Feehan's totals look pedestrian by comparison—154 yards on eleven carries.

On the other side of the ball, the Regents hold the Lions to minus-nineteen yards on the ground. Worse, they batter Trinity's stable of running backs. In addition to Norick's neck injury, Poyser leaves the game with a possible concussion.

"I literally had no running backs left by the end of the game," Slivoskey says back in the safety of the coaches' office.

He says it in a matter-of-fact fashion, without self-pity, like a guy ordering a club sandwich at a diner. But the statement highlights the battles Trinity faces every week. Lose a couple of players at the same position and the replacements are going to be players who have rarely, if ever, practiced at those spots. No amount of imaginative play calling can make up for that kind of inexperience. Imagination can be tossed out as well—coaches have to stick to the basics with guys who haven't been trained in those basics. As much as anything, Trinity's lack of depth is a big reason many of its games can get out of hand in a hurry.

"It starts getting tricky with what to call," Slivoskey says. "We're just not experienced enough to get into some of the more advanced techniques. You just don't have time to explain things to everybody right before a play. I was putting people in that third quarter that basically had no idea what to do in certain situations. There's times I'm just trying to keep certain people from getting hurt."

Compared with Trinity's perennial personnel difficulties, Hoskins's problems are about as troublesome as a hangnail. He still manages to bristle at the crumbs his staunch defense allowed the Lions, particularly Brower's long touchdown reception.

"It's a hard way to coach," he says of the effort to toe the line between giving his starters playing time and not wanting to rub Trinity's face in it. "You really get a catch-22 there. Number one, we're in the top five in the defense in the country, and we give up a seventy-yard pass play you know you wouldn't give up. That's a little frustrating."

Hoskins was grateful for the week his team had leading up to the Trinity game. Keeping the players interested in the game proved challenging, but Rockford used the week of practice to heal its injuries. The Regents took it easy during the week. Practices ended at 5:00 p.m., instead of 5:45. Coaches mixed in preparations for next week's game against Blackburn. And as for the saying that anything can happen in any given game? Hoskins didn't try to fool his players.

"You basically tell them, 'Hey, who you kidding?' We're a lot better football team. We gotta go out and take care of business. You can't mess around. That's how you get kids hurt."

But no Rockford player finished the game in the shape Norick was in: stuck on the bench, hunched over, unable to look sideways unless he swiveled his entire upper body. The injury was diagnosed as a neck strain, which induced muscle spasms. In a way, Norick's own strength is partly to blame for the pounding he takes each game. His body would be better off if Norick was more of a weakling.

"He's the type of runner, when you hit him, he won't go down with the first hit," Slivoskey says. "He gets gang tackled. By the time the third or fourth guy gets there, he's in a position where he's not protecting himself."

"If I can get one-on-one, I can usually beat the guy," Norick adds, "but I can't beat four-on-one."

Trinity's coaches decompress in the office—Strong at the computer, Rasmussen on the couch and Slivoskey on a chair. Bentley retires to his office to look up scores from other conference games, contests the team's brain trust discuss for several minutes. Talking about the other UMAC games is a welcome diversion for the coaches, providing a few minutes of respite from the typical postgame postmortem, which usually involves counting up the injured bodies and searching for some positive aspect to pull from the defeat.

They compliment Brower's performance, especially his efforts after catching the ball. "He really ran hard," Slivoskey says, a fact that was evident on the long touchdown, when the freshman broke tackles to turn a short reception into a long TD. He finished with 118 receiving yards, the highest total for a Trinity player in two seasons. On the defensive side, Josh Thompson seemingly recorded every stop for the Lions, finishing with fourteen tackles. Brower and Thompson: two bright spots in another mentally exhausting game, whose effects are evident in the body language of Slivoskey and Rasmussen. They're each slumped in their respective seats, as if they'd taken part in a boxing match with hands tied behind their backs.

Martin Luther, probably the best team in the conference this year, comes to Ellendale next week, Trinity's third straight home game against a tough opponent. Slivoskey wonders what sort of lineup the Lions will send out onto the field. Norick is probably out next week; Poyser could be, too. The battered offensive line, already down Michael Moss, lost his replacement, Lester Williams, to a concussion. Another lineman, Matt Johanson, has shown Gehrig-like durability in the past few weeks (he played virtually every snap at offensive guard and linebacker against Rockford), but his body has to be wearing down. The rematch with Principia, the game Trinity has been looking forward to pretty much from the moment Hess's quarterback sneak came up short, is in two weeks. The coaches want the team to be as healthy as possible. It's probably the only contest left on the schedule that's winnable. They have thirteen days to piece everyone back together. But they have to get through the Martin Luther game first.

"We're one or two injuries away from really being in trouble," Slivoskey says. "If we were to lose our center now, or our quarterback, I don't really know what we'd do."

Bentley picks up a stat sheet and reads aloud some of the numbers that stand out. Numbers might lie sometimes, but it's hard to accuse these statistics of dishonesty: one Trinity rusher finished with positive yardage and that was Norick with two yards; Rockford rolled up more than six hundred yards; Trinity was two-for-sixteen on third downs. "Two-for-sixteen!" Bentley shouts a second time.

"It was 35–7 at one point, though," he adds.

"I think they were pretty ticked when we scored off their first team defense," Slivoskey says, and he's right.

The coaches say their good-byes and head home. Bentley can pick up those Reese's Pieces from Char's for his kids; Slivoskey has to do some classwork preparation and get the house prepared for Essy's return from Baltimore, where she attended her brother's wedding.

"Well, coaches," Rasmussen says as he rises from the couch, "I will see you all on Monday."

When they get to do this all over again.

Chapter Twelve

Dog's Ear

The door is closed to Brandon Strong's first-floor dorm room. It's a quiet Tuesday evening on campus, a rare silent night for Strong.

In the Kesler Hall lounge, a few students gather to watch Game 6 of the American League Championship Series between the Yankees and the Red Sox, better known as the game in which Curt Schilling became a national idol for the heroic act of bleeding into a sock.

Even though he's a big baseball fan (a long-suffering Detroit Tigers fan, in fact), Strong's not in front of the TV. Instead he's unwinding, holed up for a bit in his room. Finally, he's got a few minutes to relax. Finally, he has time to breathe, to not think about football or the romantic problems of the guys living on his floor. A nice, stress-free night. Until a knock comes at the door.

"Come in," he calls.

In walks one perturbed young man, nearly frothing at the mouth with anger and disbelief. He's a Trinity student, though not a resident of Strong's floor. The kid just finished up his job cleaning the school's gymnasium and field house. Perhaps not surprisingly, his washing and waxing efforts brought a chorus of ribbing from a few students who were passing by, students he recognized from Kesler. School custodians have endured wise-ass remarks forever, but these barbs struck a nerve, probably because they came from the kid's schoolmates. The rant starts right when Strong opens the door. The aggrieved student demands to talk to Nate Gideon, a resident hall director at Kesler. Now.

Strong gives Gideon a ring, puts the phone down, and tells the visitor he'll be right over.

"You all right?" Strong asks.

The student, sounding like a cross between a schoolmarm and Rodney Dangerfield, unleashes a long list of grievances.

"Yeah, I'm all right," he says, though he's not. "People just need to respect me when I'm cleaning that field house, and if they can't do that I'm going to end up locking up that *whooooole* building, and I won't let anybody in it until I'm done. So your boys here in your hall, they need to respect me when I'm cleaning over there and don't, don't, don't lip off. If the door's locked, walk around. It's not that hard. People don't respect me over there when I'm cleaning it. A lot of people do and there's people that don't. Those people that don't, if they can't respect me when I'm over there I will lock up that whole place so I can get my work done."

"Uh-huh," Strong responds, sympathetic to the student's plight, but slightly surprised by the serious, world-is-ending tone of the message.

"And I wanted to slap the guy that was walking by. Actually, there was three of them. I bit my tongue. I bit my tongue pretty hard."

Gideon arrives, grinning and helpful. He cheerfully asks, "What's up?" Strong's happy to cede jurisdiction on this situation. As Strong shuts the door, the kid's voice, now slightly muffled by the barrier, still resonates, this time telling Nate, "People need to respect me when I'm over there cleaning and don't bang on the door like a moron . . ."

Ah, the glamorous life of an RA.

Strong settles in his chair, lets out a sigh, smiles, and slowly shakes his head. But this is what he signed up for when he joined the student life staff. You expect to deal with grievances, both petty and serious. It's his other school duties that are proving more draining, physically and emotionally. With his myriad jobs and responsibilities taking up much of his time and energy, Strong's grades have been suffering, something that's never happened to him before. Eric Slivoskey's classes are the toughest; Bentley's the easiest. He's grateful for those challenges from Slivoskey in the classroom—he doesn't want to breeze through. Well, maybe sometimes he does. It'd make life a lot less stressful. As the football team's season kicked off with slightly higher expectations, only to descend to depths similar to the 2003 season, Strong bore the brunt of many of the players' frustrations. Not because they blamed him for the situation, but because he was so close by as a resident advisor. The football players on his floor trudged into the room night after night, often until one or two in the morning, venting to the guy responsible for bringing many of them to Trinity. Strong feels a tinge of regret because he recruited many of the first-year players. He doesn't think they're bad for the program, but he wonders if the program is bad for them. He convinced them to leave their homes for a program that appears to be in disarray. The players, though, tell him not to worry about that; they probably would have come even if they did know the full extent of the team's struggles.

For an escape from the campus pressures Strong occasionally goes off-campus.

He keeps an apartment—one of the $25 units in the same complex the Odells live in—which he uses for storage and as a sanctuary where he can crash for a short time. There's also a new face in his life, fellow Trinity student Samantha Moon. The two started dating in late September. Only a month into the relationship, Strong is already asking the big questions. Well, he hasn't asked Samantha the BIG one yet, but he's thinking about it.

"I told her, I'm not going to date just so I can date," he says. "I'm dating for a purpose, for a reason. That is to have a wife. I'd say she was in the same kind of mindset."

Strong doesn't want a long engagement, no more than six months he says, and, "come this spring, if I think things are right, I'm going to go to the jeweler."

That's why he's looking forward to the next few days, when Trinity takes its fall break. School recesses after classes on Wednesday and students aren't back for six days. He's traveling with Samantha to her home in northern Minnesota. It's time to meet the parents. He'll return Friday and will be at the team's game on Saturday.

He's ready for a break from football, even if it's just for a few days. The losing, the tension, the job load—he's not going to miss any of it. He also wonders how much longer he can maintain his current pace in the current environment.

"I hope ten to fifteen years down the road I can say, 'Ah, now I see. Now I understand.' But right now, Lord, I hope you know what you're doing."

The week of the Martin Luther game starts off on a frightening note for one Trinity player. Lester Williams suffered a concussion during the Rockford game, which is bad enough, but for Williams it's, by his count, and this might be an underestimation, the seventh concussion of his life. He's now in Steve Young/Troy Aikman territory, star NFL players whose careers ended prematurely because of numerous concussions. Williams thought he'd be OK, despite the most recent brain jarring. But he kept having headaches in the two days after the game. Eventually he started throwing up. Still, he kept the information to himself, not wanting to alarm anyone. Finally, his roommate, Kevin Kloefkorn, told the RA, and it's obvious a doctor needs to check him out.

Williams is an old hand when it comes to dealing with concussions, an area you don't want to be overly experienced in. He recites the time and location of each injury like a war veteran showing off battle scars at a school assembly. When he was a kid, Williams's friend accidentally drilled him on the side of the head with a bat while the two were swinging away at a tennis ball. Another mini-calamity occurred when his head hit a urinal. The urinal won. In high school, a severe car crash led to another concussion, and he also endured them on the football field. They've followed him to Trinity, first during the loss against Morris, and now against Rockford. This doctor's trip is probably overdue.

Trinity watches film on Mondays. The team gathers in a classroom in the administration building for a look at their most recent game and the upcoming opponent. Before the session, Slivoskey ducks into Bentley's office, telling him that Williams needs to be taken to Aberdeen and he's driving him down. Slivoskey often chauffeurs Trinity's wounded down to South Dakota. It's a role that's not in his job description, but one he does willingly and eagerly, his previously stated desire for a trainer on staff looking more urgent by the day. Halfway through the season, the injuries are taking their toll on the already thin roster. Sometimes Slivoskey takes an even more active role in caring for the athletes; during the baseball season he'd drive to the grocery store to get ice for his pitchers' shoulders. With potentially serious injuries like this one, he's not taking any chances, forfeiting film work to take Williams in.

Bentley agrees with Slivoskey. First, though, he wants Williams in the office for some prayer time. With Williams standing in front of Bentley's desk, the coach takes him by the hand and recites a short prayer, asking Jesus to "look over Lester and help him in this scary time." It looks like Williams might not even know who Jesus is; his dazed look and half-open eyes suggest he just woke up. Or is suffering from his seventh concussion.

Williams and Slivoskey head for the coach's truck while Bentley walks to the classroom to start the film. As the players slowly trickle into the building—many of them are still feeling each tackle and hit from the Rockford game—Bentley buys several of them hot chocolates to sip during the upcoming show. No more than twenty players sit in the classroom as he fiddles with the screen and projector. Before hitting play, Bentley asks the players to say a prayer for Williams.

He also wants their input on the upcoming practice schedule.

In a week and a half, the Lions will travel to Minneapolis for the UMAC's Dome Day festivities, an all-day football gala that takes place in the cavernous Metrodome. Trinity will get another shot at Principia, in a rematch from the second game of the season, the game Trinity felt the officials took from them. But it won't be a showdown at high noon. Instead the teams will trudge onto the field at the inhumane time of 8:00 a.m., an hour when the players are usually struggling to stay awake in class or still sleeping. It's the price each team must pay for being at the bottom of the conference's North and South Divisions. Four other games follow Trinity's clash with Principia, the last one kicking off at 8:00 p.m. between each division's respective champions.

Bentley tosses out the idea that the team should acclimate themselves to the early kickoff by practicing in the early morning hours. All season the coaches have lamented the team's slow starts to games—how slow will they begin at 0800 hours? His plan is to practice early—six-thirty or seven in the morning—on Thursday and Friday before the Martin Luther game. They'd follow the same routine the following week before the Principia contest.

A few players grudgingly give their approval. Others aren't so sure, wondering if a few days of early wakeup calls will really matter.

"If you go fishing," Brower says, "you don't get up at four in the morning the week before just to get used to being up early."

"This ain't fishing," Bentley says. "This is playing a football game."

Bentley calls for a vote, despite the relatively small sampling of players who will decide the sleeping fate for everyone.

"Those that aren't here aren't going to get to vote."

It's been a problem all year for the Lions, trying to get all of the players to practice. It's still a losing battle. A dozen of them are missing in action today, and other than Williams, Bentley's not sure of the reasons behind any of the absences. In a school setting, this would be a good class size, giving the teacher a better opportunity to give individual attention to each student. In a football setting, Bentley's depressed by the spectacle—another reminder of his struggle to bring the players to heel. Or, in Bentley's view, the players' inability to make their teammates accountable.

"I know you're tired of losing," he says. "I know you're tired of getting beat up. I know you're tired of giving 100 percent when your brother's not. But I am not in the business of rounding guys up. Everyone has to pull their weight or the whole project is an F or a D or a C. It's a group grade, not an individual grade. You have every right to check them on it. You have every right to challenge them."

The players share the same feeling about their coach.

Bentley takes a head count. Eighteen in attendance. Before conducting the vote, the team debates a bit more on the motion before the floor. Since it's still dark at six-thirty or seven in the morning, the practices would be in the gymnasium. No, it won't work to light up the field with car lights. Sannon Norick expresses concern about developing shin splints from practicing on the wooden floor after a season spent on natural turf. There are other considerations. Lee Odell works in the campus cafeteria in the morning and wouldn't be able to make the practices. This halting moment of democracy finally comes to a head when Bentley asks for a show of hands. Only six go up in support of the predawn practices. Ten players are against it. Two apparently abstain.

That task completed, the team first watches the Rockford film. Darkness descends on the room as a player switches the light off. Unfortunately, the screen's also dark. The tape's difficult to watch, the camera too far away, the details of the game action only a rumor. Eventually, after some tinkering with the brightness and contrast of the picture, the action becomes clearer. There aren't a lot of good highlights to be had; the game speeds by as Bentley fast forwards through Rockford's touchdowns and subsequent kickoffs, finally stopping to watch Trinity's first touchdown of the game. The players chatter throughout the film while Bentley mostly watches, muted, occasionally asking the guys to quiet down.

After Bentley fast forwards through another Trinity punt, Brower, who's relaxed as can be, with his legs stretched out on a chair and his University of Texas baseball cap on backwards, suggests a video-game strategy, "We should just play like PS2, go for it on fourth down every time."

A handful of players concentrate on the screen, but many are more immersed in the conversations, fairly oblivious to the matinee in front of them. Someone makes a request, asking for a replay of a Trinity player being laid out after a Rockford interception. The group groans—partly out of compassion for their teammate, partly out of admiration for the Rockford player—as the hit is played again, and then again.

Eventually the attention turns to Martin Luther, a strong team that Trinity has never beaten or come close to beating.

"On first down, look for 'em to run," Bentley tells them. "On second down, you might want to think about maybe a run or a run.

On third down, anticipate a run. On fourth down, anticipate a run. Anticipate discipline. They do pass, but it's a halfback option pass."

On the tape the Martin Luther offense is an exercise in efficiency against Morris, crisply eating up yardage on the ground, executing whatever play they want, whenever they want. It's a jolting difference between this tape and Trinity's game against Rockford, like watching a movie in color after a black-and-white film. The basic differences between Trinity and its opponent are all up there on the screen. The Knights have speed on both sides of the ball and their offensive linemen are a cohesive unit, firing low off the ground; it looks like the Lions are in for a long day. Martin Luther's also rounding into shape, having won five straight games after dropping the first two of the season.

Bentley delivers a director's commentary during the film, telling the team, "We've got a very, very big task ahead of us. Last year when we played Martin Luther, our goal was to score once. We were going to hold them to fifty-two points last year [they scored sixty-three]. What kind of goal was that? Those were realistic goals."

Realistic, perhaps. But it's still maddening to some of the players, who have never been in a situation where the white flag is thrown up even before the battle begins. Even after seven losses to start the season—with only one of them being close—Odell still feels the team should prepare as if it's entering the game with a chance at victory. Moral victories are one thing—complete capitulation is another. It upset him before the Rockford game when it came from a teammate. It upsets him even more coming from his leader.

"I just get frustrated when he's telling us we're trying to get some respect or he says we're trying to get that dog ear," Odell says. "If you go coon hunting and the coon bites on the dog's ear and gets killed, but bit the dog's ear, that's what we're trying to do, he says. That's frustrating."

The primary goal for this year's game against the Knights is not to get any players hurt. The Lions want a full deck for the Principia rematch in two weeks. Norick, bothered by the neck injury he suffered against Rockford, is among the players who will sit out the Martin Luther game for precautionary reasons. Williams will also miss the game. Fortunately, doctors did not find any major damage, and he could be back for the dome game. If his brain feels up to it.

Minus Norick, Williams, and a host of other injured players, it's going to be much tougher for Trinity to bite that dog's ear.

During chapel service Monday morning, students listened to a talk from missionary Peyton Harris, who has spent substantial time working overseas in Kazakhstan. He's the kind of speaker the school loves to parade in front of the students, a world traveler with Jesus in his heart. The student musicians play a couple of songs before Harris's speech, the lyrics superimposed on the large screen at the front of the chapel. Harris falls on his hands and knees during the songs, just one of many chapel attendees moved to such a display.

Once front and center, Harris proved to be a vibrant speaker—passionate, engaging, and plenty loud, even before his microphone was properly tuned. He seeks to rouse the students to action, get them fired up about the possibilities of serving abroad. In many ways he's preaching to the converted, since many students have taken or will take mission trips. Several Trinity players have already done it, including Dustin Harper and Michael Moss. Harper spent time in Sri Lanka, Moss in Belize.

Moss grew up in south-central Arkansas, ten miles from the Louisiana border. When he left for Belize, he figured he knew what would happen.

"I was expecting to see all these things and it's just going to break me."

He didn't break. There was no, as he calls it, "Mother Teresa style" work. Instead the simple things changed him: seeing the joy villagers took from having their pictures taken, seeing a kid his own age work on a coloring sheet, "just so innocent and so pure."

"It's not the big, grand things that save people," Moss says. "It's just being there for people that changes people's lives." And those people don't have to be on another continent. Moss says it can be the person walking down the street.

It's the same type of message Dan Kuno preaches, both in chapel and his classrooms. Kuno talks about "felt needs," helping people in everyday life. Help, Trinity hopes, that's part of a larger message. It's part of the lesson Trinity learned from its missteps when first arriving in Ellendale, when their message, or at least its delivery, turned off people. Shoveling someone's sidewalk would meet a felt need. It could mean feeding someone that's hungry, "learning to touch them where they hurt," Kuno says. "Before their heart is filled, their belly needs to be filled. I think that's really where Christianity is lived out, in the everyday part of life."

Even Harris's worldly message includes words about home, about "finding Christ where you live."

"Where you live," he tells the packed chapel, "is where you have your problems, but it's also where you have your victories."

The Lions know all about the former. They just hope they get to experience the latter before the season is over.

OCTOBER 21, 2004

With Norick on the shelf this week, the Lions need a new running back. And maybe they've found him. He's built like a fullback, loves to hit, and is showing off some deceptive quickness.

"I hope they call my play," Lee Odell says.

The play is unofficially known as the "Odell special," and there's nothing tricky about the wishbone formation or the execution. On it, Odell receives a furlough from the offensive line and sets up as fullback. The play's a simple dive up the middle, the Lions hoping Odell's power can pick up a few yards. Ever since Refrigerator Perry gained fame by plowing over defenders on his way to the end zone, linemen have occasionally been used as blockers or rushers in short-yardage situations. Offensive linemen might say their dream play involves a pancake block on a defender, but it's a lie. They fantasize of one day being in the end zone with their mitts on the ball, whether on a fluke fumble recovery or as a substitute running back.

But Odell's not just going to be used near the end zone as a short-yardage specialist. In practice he breaks free from the line of scrimmage and scampers into the open with nothing but green grass in front of him. The only problem with putting Odell in the backfield is finding a replacement on the line. Odell is the starter, backup, and third-stringer; there really is no full-time backup. For these plays, though, Josh Thompson, a scrawny, tough 190-pounder who leads the team in tackles from his linebacker position, fills in at center. Odell likes his new position, maybe too much.

"Look at him," Hess says with a smile. "Thinks he's a running back now. You still gotta snap the ball, son."

Slivoskey expects to break out the Odell special. He'll have to be creative, a week after nearly having all of his running backs wiped out. Since the season started, Slivoskey has seen his starting quarterback break a wrist, forcing him to the defensive secondary; his number-one wide receiver has moved to quarterback; and his number-one running back is out with a neck injury. But it's tough to get too creative with guys who have to concentrate on simply learning their positions.

While focused on Martin Luther, Slivoskey's also thinking ahead, to the team's second shot at Principia. With a short week before that game—the UMAC's dome day takes place on a Friday—Trinity will squeeze as much as possible into the remaining practices. Commentators often compare coaching strategies to chess. Against Principia, Slivoskey feels the Lions actually have an opportunity to be something other than a pawn. In a way, he's going against the old mantra of take 'em one game at a time, but he wants that first victory. The realist in him knows the odds the Lions face against Martin Luther.

"This is one week where I'm allowing myself to look ahead," he says on the practice field. "Whether that's right, I don't really know. It's more realistic. We just played the third or fourth best team in the conference this week and they hammered us. We play the number one team in the conference this week. They're a step up in competition."

But thinking about the Principia game provides plenty of motivation. Now all the Lions have to do is survive against Martin Luther intact.

"Martin Luther thinks that they can walk up and you're going to lie down and roll over for 'em," Bentley tells the team after Friday's practice. "They'll be groggy, they'll be sleepy, and they're already cocky. They wanna know why they have to play Trinity, and that's the truth, guys. That is the absolute truth. Y'all need to show 'em tomorrow."

OCTOBER 23, 2004

Tomorrow's here. The Knights don't look all that cocky or, for that matter, groggy. Relaxed, yes.

Trinity, meanwhile, suits up twenty-three players while a third that many stand in jeans, sweatshirts, baseball caps, and stocking caps on the sidelines, serving as cheerleaders or assistants to Pastor Brady on the water crew. Even before the game starts, Strong receives bad news: the computer used to keep statistics is dying and there's little hope for resuscitation. Strong always knew this could happen. He'd even been warned about it, not that he could have done anything differently.

"At our SID meeting, they talked about having a backup computer for games," he says. "We have like three computers on campus."

Bentley's whoopin' it up during drills, "We're playing college football this afternoon!" he shouts. "What is it you'd rather be doing?"

They'd rather not be vomiting, which is what one offensive lineman does after a set of pregame drills, not exactly the most strenuous of activities. He staggers off the field, falls to all fours, and deposits his breakfast on the unluckiest patch of grass in Dickey County.

"Puke later," Rasmussen says. "That's what happens when you don't come to practice."

Trinity's grand plan of not getting anyone hurt this week lasts one play, when two-way performer Rex Causey limps off. Causey returns, but each play brings new fear that another player will be dinged.

Martin Luther left a handful of its top players back in Minnesota, including the starting quarterback, a starting wingback, and a defensive lineman, deciding they wouldn't be needed today. It gives several second- and third-stringers the opportunity to shine. Of the Knights' five straight wins, two were by three points and another by a point, which means that the starters played the entirety. For the backups, today's their biggest game.

Martin Luther wastes no time in taking control, scoring on a touchdown run with its first possession and returning an interception fifty-two yards for a score on Trinity's next drive.

It's the start of a long day.

Offensively the Lions drop pass after pass. Snyder will finish the game six-for-twenty-six, but there are probably six drops by the receivers.

Another mangled pass off the hands of a receiver, which would have given Trinity a first down, finally sets Slivoskey off.

"I'm sick of these gloves!" he says to no one, and everyone, while slapping his play sheet. "Sick of them."

Slivoskey regards receivers who wear gloves in the same light as dentists view patients who don't floss. He loathes gloves—they're his personal peeve. He didn't wear any during his playing days, and he wishes he could ban them for the Lions. Maybe the school could rewrite the dress code to disallow them. This isn't the rant of some codger, unwilling to accept something new—it's a practical argument. Slivoskey simply thinks the players catch better without the gloves, that they get a better feel for the ball.

Proof exists that supports his opinion of gloves. At a practice earlier in the year, Brower, who struggled early in the season with dropped passes, ditched the fashion accessory after some persistent badgering by Slivoskey. Brower has since emerged as Trinity's top receiving threat, a solid target over the middle with big-play ability. Brower's higher confidence level, more than the *au natural* look, is the likely cause of his increased production, but on the play following Slivoskey's rant, Brower makes a diving catch across the middle for a first down, providing a bit of vindication for the offensive coordinator.

The Lions pick up only five first downs in the game. Even these defensive transgressions upset the Knights on the sideline, who shake their heads whenever the Lions manage to move the chains.

The Martin Luther players talk to each other about the effort. One of them comments, "We play better against good teams. We're playing down. This is ridiculous." The 28–0 halftime lead, achieved with ease, apparently isn't good enough. The Knights keep it simple throughout the game, running the ball forty-eight times compared with ten passes. One of the passes, though, is a halfback pass back to the quarterback, the play Bentley warned the Lions about on Monday.

Bentley appears at a loss at halftime, struggling for words of encouragement or words about a change of strategy. As the players nibble on Teddy Grahams and other snacks provided by Brady, he tells the team, "Guys, on defense, is there anything I can tell ya?" followed by, "There's no adjustments we can make."

The players sit on the grass, quiet.

The second half does offer up the Odell special. Odell acquits himself nicely, picking up six yards on a carry and finishing with eight yards on three attempts. Eight yards ain't much. Those eight yards, though, lead Trinity in the game. Odell should frame the box score. For the first time, possibly ever, a starting center leads his team in rushing. Without Norick, the rushing game runs on empty. Martin Luther limits Trinity to minus-eleven yards on twenty-seven attempts.

The Lions do escape without any other major injuries, if not scares. In the fourth quarter a pair of Martin Luther defenders hammer Brower after a catch, leaving him flat on the ground, writhing. It's hard to tell what's hurting him most: his knee or shoulder. Wincing, he returns to the game with the Lions trailing 48–0. He's not the only one playing through pain. Isaac Smith, still hurting from an injured left shoulder, battles opposing linemen with one arm. The wounded limb looks like it's taped to his torso.

The Lions give this effort all season. No matter the score, no matter the deficit, those in uniform were always eager to get back into the game or stay in it, provided they could walk. Usually their return simply brings on more pain. If they can't play, the replacement is usually someone who has just shuffled over from another position, a player battling his own injuries. From Dustin Harper's bruised ribs to Andy Brower's dislodged jaw to Lester Williams's concussions to Lee Odell's back spasms to Dusty Hess's broken wrist, not a single Lion escaped the season unscathed.

Of course, football's different from other sports. One of its main purposes is to inflict pain. You can get embarrassed on the basketball court, but aside from a bit of fatigue, there's no physical punishment. You can get embarrassed on the baseball diamond without any physical pain. Swimming, tennis, volleyball: it's all the same. In football, though, you don't just get beat—you get beat up. It's much easier to withstand that punishment when winning by fifty. Maybe this will all help with the carving, as Dan Kuno said. Maybe the players will look back in fifteen years, remember the injuries, remember the losses, and believe they can overcome anything in their lives. Or maybe they'll just remember the pain.

But how much longer can the players last this season? And what keeps them going?

"You know all your teammates are in pain, and you don't want to let them down," Harper says. "You just have to lay it all out there."

The game concludes with one bit of misplaced trash talking. Late in the fourth quarter, a Martin Luther defender drops a potential interception, which would have given the Knights a chance at a third defensive touchdown.

"Nice hands," taunts Heavy Nichols from the sideline.

Gotta get your verbal shots in whenever possible, Nichols says. The defender is kind enough to not point at the scoreboard, which reads: Guest 55, Lions 0.

After the game Martin Luther coach Charles Hussman lingers on the field to accept congratulations from players' parents. Relaxed, chipper, and barely sweating, Hussman looks like he just finished nine holes of mini-golf. That he's even in Ellendale today is a rather odd occurrence.

Veteran coach Dennis Gorsline retired just a few weeks before Martin Luther opened the season, creating a bit of panic for the program, which has been a pillar of consistency in the conference for some time.

Gorsline was the reigning UMAC coach of the year. Hussman had been the school's track and cross-country coach for several years, but retired a year earlier. He did have football experience, having spent more than thirty years as a high school coach in Illinois. Still, it had been nearly ten years since he'd been on the sidelines. Martin Luther thought he was the best man to pinch-hit for Gorsline. All the school had to do was track him down. It was like trying to find the Unabomber's shack.

Hussman spends a lot of his time at a cabin in northern Minnesota, near the Canadian border, free from modern technology, free from the outside world. He didn't have any electricity or a phone; he was cut off from society and loving it. Athletic director James Unke made the hike from New Ulm, Minnesota, in the southern part of the state, and convinced him to take the job. Hussman might have regretted his decision after a rocky start. The Knights lost their first two games of the season before recovering. The victory over Trinity was their sixth in a row, including two games that they won by three points and another by one point. Though Hussman says the Lions "have a couple of hitters," overall, today's game was a nice little breather.

"I knew coming in that we were not going to score seventy points," Hussman says. "Now, you can't tell the guys that have not played not to score, and they were sitting over there saying, 'Coach, you're not going to tell us to take a knee are ya?' And I said no, but we're just trying to make it a legitimate deal."

Despite what the scoreboard reads, the Knights did have some challenges in this game. When playing a team down on numbers and talent, an opposing coach faces a testy balancing act. He first wants to get the victory, but he has to be concerned about running up the score and the perception that he's insulting the opposing team. When do you stop passing? When do the starters come out? How much should the defense attack? When the backups are in, do they have to be happy with simply running dive plays up the gut the rest of the game?

Finally, the coach holds his breath each time a top player goes down, not wanting to lose a star performer in a game the team could win without him. With Martin Luther's biggest game of the season lurking next week, that was particularly concerning to the grizzled Hussman. One player got his head banged, and another had to be taken to Aberdeen for stitches. Overall, though, the game was a success—in all facets.

As champions of the UMAC's North division, the Knights will face Westminster from the South in the conference's marquee matchup during the upcoming dome day.

Hussman looks forward to that game, the last of his career. Really. No more coaching. He's enjoyed his return, but this will only be a one-year stint. He gets to go out on top. He also has a plan for avoiding any future pleas from the school.

"Well, they knew where the cabin was at so now I think what I'm going to have to do is find a cabin that's a little deeper in the woods."

Bentley talks to Sage on the field after the game as Annie runs around, playing on the Lions' bench. Two weeks left in the season. Other than Annie, the whole Bentley family looks ready for it to be over.

Trinity's locker room quickly clears out. With fall break here, many of the players are headed out of town to catch a few days of relaxation. Others are just headed to everyone's favorite destination, a movie in Aberdeen.

Slivoskey talks to some of the players, offering words of encouragement. He often struggles to find those words. When he played, the assistant coaches would walk through the locker room after games, reliving plays, asking the players how the game went, what they did well, what they could do better.

"I've come to dread that time at Trinity," he says. "Where it's postgame. I just try to encourage, let them know that if they can look themselves in the mirror, and know they gave everything they had, you really can't give anything more than that. That's pride, if you keep picking yourself up."

Strong sits in the coaches' office, exhausted, his head resting on his left hand. He picked up one victory this week: the trip to Samantha's parents went off without any major disasters; he even bonded by hitting some golf balls out in the yard with her father. The trip did nothing to stop him from thinking about that possible trip to a jeweler.

If only this game could have gone that well. Another loss—that's no different from every other game he's experienced at Trinity, as a player and as a coach. The computer failure provided a new wrinkle, but it's the atmosphere around the program that discourages him. Thankfully, dome day is coming next week, the game that gives the Lions a chance to play in a 65,000-seat stadium and provides them their best chance at breaking a three-year losing streak.

But Strong won't be watching that game from the sidelines.

Chapter Thirteen

Dome Day

Rusty Bentley might be out of Texas now, but he'll never be too far removed from his former home. Bentley was born and bred in the Lone Star State. Eventually, it seems inevitable he'll wind up back there, even if his current home is on the other end of the country. Much of his identity is wrapped up in hailing from Texas. From his adoration of the Dallas Cowboys, to his love of the state's high school football, to his devotion to his former governor and current president, George W. Bush, to his distinct voice, he's definitely a product of his environment.

As such, it's a requirement that he know how to make and brag about his own brand of Texas chili.

Sunday night, the day after the Martin Luther game and five days before the team faces Principia, Rusty invites the whole team over to his house for a chili feed, where he dishes up his own brand of the meat and bean concoction. Though many players have left Ellendale for the weekend, about fifteen players and several other Trinity students fill the Bentleys' kitchen and living room, enjoying Rusty's handiwork and watching some NFL football. Few college kids are going to pass up an opportunity to eat a free meal.

"It's not as spicy as I usually make it," Bentley says, but the guests quickly devour the offerings.

At the same time, Sage, nearly eight months pregnant and battling a cold, and Jacqui Odell try to feed and entertain the Bentleys' four children. Essy Slivoskey is there, too, toting around Kodie and Kamryn, but Eric arrives later. The kids eat hot dogs together at the kitchen table, the processed meat temporarily providing a much-needed distraction.

After eating, little Ty—the linebacker of the family—goes on a rampage. The giggling, three-foot, diaper-clad pinball bounces off anything with two legs; all the while he runs laps around the main level of the house.

"He runs like coach," one player observes.

"Yeah, but I think he's faster," says another.

The group gathers in the living room, where they're watching the ancient Emmitt Smith and the Arizona Cardinals knock off the Seattle Seahawks. Bentley gets a kick out of seeing old Emmitt shine one more time—he reminds Bentley of Dallas's glory years. Earlier, Bentley watched Green Bay dismantle the porous Cowboys. If he can't watch his favorite NFL team win, he'll settle for watching one of their former stars excel.

Strong sits on the floor, Samantha next to him. For several minutes he entertains Annie Bentley. Annie jumps on Strong's lap a few times. She hops off, gets a running start and jumps back on. The frivolity ends when the four-year old leaps on an unsuspecting Strong and lands . . . well, on a *very* sensitive area of the male anatomy. It gets huge laughs from the room. Of course it does. For thousands of years the sight of a man taking a groin shot has brought joy to all. Except, of course, to the unfortunate victim. If a video camera had been rolling, the tape could have been sent to *America's Funniest Home Videos* and might have had a chance at the $10,000 grand prize. It's not quite as humorous for Strong, who doubles over and lets out a low moan. He puts on a brave face, but only recovers after taking a few deep breaths. Though she provides a sympathetic pat on the back, even his girlfriend sports a small smile.

When the NFL game ends, Bentley inserts the Principia game tape in the VCR. If the chili hasn't caused any upset stomachs, this will. The tape's put on fast forward until the crucial moment—Hess's sneak on the final play of the game. Bentley rewinds the play five times. The result never changes. Judging by the dismayed reaction of the players, who do everything but fling Saltines at the TV, neither does the team's certainty that Hess scored.

"It makes me sick watching this," Slivoskey says from the entry-way, where he stands and watches, slowly shaking his head each time the referee waves his arms.

Lee Odell slides next to Slivoskey. He good-naturedly lobbies for more carries as a fullback—he's had a little taste of the limelight and would like some more. Besides, didn't he prove himself last game as the leading rusher?

"I'll see what I can do," Slivoskey finally promises and that satisfies Odell. Not only is he going to get more action as a fullback, but it's also going to happen in the Metrodome.

"Bowl week," as the players are calling it, has started off on a good note. At least for the starting center.

OCTOBER 26, 2004

Strong thought about the idea for several weeks. Having a partner come along for the ride just makes it a little easier. Strong and his friend Neil Huenefeld want to return to the field. Back to the field that produced more pain than pleasure a year before.

Trinity's injuries keep mounting, and the team could use a couple of more bodies. With Huenefeld, though, the Lions will get much more than that. They'll get a player who was the team's best player in 2003; the team's leading tackler, a strong leader and fierce competitor. His shoulder problems kept him out for most of the season. When Huenefeld initially told Bentley he wasn't going to play football this year, the coach's reaction surprised him—he says Bentley became more distant, there was a cooling in the relationship.

"It bothered me that football Neil and non-football playing Neil were treated in different ways."

Those concerns don't keep him from going forward with the plan.

Strong's parents didn't want him playing any more football. They're not going to be happy to learn this news—when they learn the news. He hasn't told them yet, and says he might not tell them until Thanksgiving, when maybe he can break the news while asking for a second helping of pumpkin pie. He hopes they don't receive any calls before then telling them their son is in the hospital for more knee surgery. Samantha Moon doesn't like the comeback, either.

But Coach Bentley's comfortable with the idea—he's more than happy to welcome back football-playing Neil. And after Dean Kuno gives his approval, there's only one more group to ask: the players.

It's not a simple issue, even if at first glance it appears to be. Why wouldn't a team with fewer than thirty players want to add two more to the roster? Especially one with Huenefeld's credentials?

But several players are leery, though not because they have anything against either Strong or Huenefeld. To a man they appreciate their desire to help the team.

But . . .

"I'd rather lose with guys who have busted their butts all season," Josh McGillvrey says.

That's the rub. Sure, the players say, we might have lost every game this season, but we've lost with the guys who have been here all season. Why change now, this late in the year?

This calls for a vote. Bentley puts the issue to the team at the Tuesday practice, three days before the Principia game. The practice didn't get off to the best start as Slivoskey, Tim Rasmussen, and others searched for the missing footballs, finally discovering them in Jerry Rush's concession trailer. Slivoskey joked about going home to get his son's Nerf ball, but the situation just leaves him shaking his head, slightly bewildered. Bentley arrives at the practice field five minutes later, calling the assistants and team captains to a huddle. Huenefeld and Strong are still back in the locker room, waiting to hear if the Lions want them as teammates.

Bentley explains the situation to McGillvrey, Norick, Tony Snyder, and Dustin Harper. Cornerback Michael Guyton, a shy freshman from New Jersey, hovers near the circle like a bee at a picnic, trying to hear what's going on. Rasmussen asks him to step away for a few minutes. When Guyton wanders back toward the circle, Rasmussen again shoos him away. Nothing to see here, folks.

The captains see both sides of the issue. They understand what Strong and Huenefeld must be going through—two players who would have been with the team the whole year if their bodies hadn't broken down last season. They can't fault them for wanting to suit up again, for wanting to help the team in the game that could produce the program's first victory in three years. But if they do play, they'll take time away from guys who have been on the team all season? Is that fair?

Both players have said they want to simply help out wherever they're needed, whether it's defense, offense, or just special teams. The captains like the idea of having them play special teams and having them on the sideline to help out in case of injury or fatigue.

Bentley calls the whole team together. With the wind fiercely whipping across the practice field, the players remove their helmets to listen to Bentley's assessment.

"The captains have decided, let's use them on special teams and use them in situations when we need them. They decided, if it's fourth-and-three and we're up by five and Principia has the ball and it's the last play of the game, and we got a man that had 129 tackles on the sideline—they said don't put him in. Let's lose with the eleven we have or win with the eleven that we have. So, gentlemen, give me an opinion, a quick one."

Odell speaks up, specifically asking about Huenefeld.

"Everybody on the campus probably wants to come out and play in the dome, but I think we should go with the guys who have been here. It's great he wants to play against Principia, but if he wants to play, why didn't he want to play against Rockford?"

"He's coming in for the right reasons," McGillvrey interjects.

Another player wonders if just playing special teams will satisfy the two, especially Huenefeld, Trinity's best player a year ago.

"That's exactly what he told me," Bentley replies. "Bottom line, though, guys. Somebody goes down, I throw Neil in there; I'm the head coach. I'm giving you your chance to say your piece now. I want to be questioned now—I don't want to be questioned then. You put your faith in me to make the right decision."

Another player chimes in, "We play for God and we play to win. We don't play for pride," but it's unclear if this means he's for or against the addition.

Finally, with a few players getting antsy about how long the discussion's taking, Bentley tells the players to take a knee and bow their heads. It's time for another vote.

"Everybody shut your eyes. If you open your eyes, then your vote don't count. You wanna let them play, raise your hand."

"Under the stipulations we talked about?" a player asks.

"I make all the decisions," Bentley says. "So whatever I told ya, I'm not going to be held to."

This proclamation causes a few players to look up in surprise. What's the point in asking for their opinions, they wonder, if they're just going to be disregarded? Why not just make the decision as the coach and not even ask for a vote? That'd be easier to take than giving the players a voice and then ignoring it. A majority of the players still vote to have Strong and Huenefeld join the team. With that, Bentley sends a player off to the locker room to tell the two newest Lions to join the practice. The team can begin preparations for Principia.

But Slivoskey wonders if it's now a divided team. Do the benefits of adding two players outweigh the rift it could cause with some of the players? He doesn't know. His admiration for both players makes the situation even tougher.

"I love both of those guys," he says. "If you had a son, and they turned out like those guys, you'd be happy. But if I'm going to go down on a ship, I'd rather almost go down with the people that were there with me. Not to criticize their desire to come out. I'm frustrated on Saturdays when I look around and I don't know who to put in because we're so banged up. So from that perspective it's great because maybe it keeps somebody else from getting hurt. I don't know what the right answer is."

A few weeks ago, Slivoskey adds, the decision would have been more of a no-brainer: with the number of injuries on the team, the addition of two more players would have almost been necessary "for the survival of the program." But the dome game will see the return of Norick, Lester Williams, Michael Moss, and others. The

Lions will be as deep as they've been all year. Slivoskey hopes Trinity won't experience subtraction by addition with Huenefeld and Strong's return.

The two jog onto the practice field and ease their way into the action. Though both are leaders in many other aspects of their lives, they stay in the background at practice, blending in as just two more players trying to get the team that long sought victory.

The short week of practice leaves little time to dawdle. Slivoskey's grinding. He's got little patience for wasted time or mental screw-ups as he tries to implement a couple of new plays, knowing the players only have two full practices to absorb the information.

Rasmussen works with the offensive linemen, barely speaking to Bentley throughout the practice. On Monday, the two had a confrontation over, well, Rasmussen is not quite sure. Rasmussen had been discussing some defensive sets with his brother Dave. A few of the players saw the suggestions, and thought they looked like good ideas. Tim Rasmussen took the ideas to Bentley on Monday, figuring it was a simple act of an assistant going to his head coach.

"He called me the devil," Rasmussen says, flummoxed. "He's like, 'You took this to the players.' He told me I was allowing the devil to cause divisions. He's responsible for what goes on, but I feel I have the right to make suggestions as an assistant. He thought I was plotting against him."

Maybe Bentley is paranoid. He's not sure himself. If not paranoid, then insecure. Mostly it stems from inexperience, and certainly the two-year quest for a victory hasn't helped. Bentley can tell himself he believes in what he's doing, in his methods, but when the losses pile up that feeling of certainty will take a hit. Three years ago Bentley sought another job in the UMAC, but now he says he's thankful he didn't land that job—he wasn't ready to run a college program. He still harbors some doubts.

"I look at these kids looking at me for answers," he says. "I'm coaching kids that are way better athletes than I've ever been, as an athlete, performance wise. And they're looking to me for answers, and you don't have 'em. I don't have the answers for them, I don't."

It's one reason this dome game is so important. A victory could provide at least a bit of validation. One win probably won't change the view of the players, who feel their head coach is in over his head. They don't look at just the wins and losses when making that assessment. It's the practices, the film sessions, the organization, the game decisions. It's the whole package.

"He doesn't have the experience, and he doesn't know how to run a team," Andy Brower says. "Which is not any slam against him. It's just, you know, some people are golfers, some people are fishermen—stick to what you know how to do. He knows how to be a dad. Be a dad. Some people aren't football coaches."

No, a victory against Principia won't alter those feelings.

Bentley hears the rumblings, can see the frustration in his players. He says he has a plan—he just needs to stick with it. But he admits it's tough when people are wondering if he's up for the job.

"The Bible talks about being as wise as a serpent and harmless as a dove," he says. "And I need to do that. I need to be a little bit tougher to my criticism. Is that insecurity? I don't know. Does insecurity make me listen to everything that everybody says? Is that paranoia?"

While Trinity's busy adding two players to its roster who haven't seen any action this year, Principia will be welcoming back two wayward sons.

Following its controversial victory over the Lions in the second week of the season, Principia endured numerous blowouts, but one more sensational victory. Three weeks before meeting Trinity, the Panthers defeated Crown 36–35 in overtime and finished with a school-record 533 yards of offense, including 451 through the air, delighting pass-happy coach Mike Barthelmess. The victory capped a Principia comeback from a 28–12 fourth-quarter deficit. The game showed that Principia might be at a different level than Trinity, the teams' first meeting notwithstanding. Crown defeated the Lions earlier in the year 74–20.

But a pair of lopsided defeats followed the victory over Crown. Blackburn defeated Principia 53–7 and Westminster drilled the Panthers 74–0. Principia played that game with only twenty-three players, two less than normal. The reason those players didn't play highlights a key difference between the Panthers and Trinity. Barthelmess suspended two starters for the Westminster game for failing to show up for mandatory weightlifting. They'll be back for the Trinity game; but it's the type of decisive action many Trinity players have practically been begging Bentley to take. They see players miss practice without any consequences. That situation's much more divisive than adding two new players to the mix. And it's been happening since the first day of practice.

Barthelmess, on the other hand, had no problem slicing his already thin roster.

"Life lessons, that's what we're trying to teach here," he says. "They learned their lessons."

OCTOBER 27, 2004

It's two days before dome day, Trinity's "bowl game." Bentley can hardly walk, doesn't know exactly when the leg injury occurred or what it is. He hobbles from his office to the practice field. "I wrestled with the Lord last night, and he bruised my thigh."

As the offense works against the scout defense, Heavy Nichols, a sucrose peddling Good Samaritan, stands behind the action, passing out some lollipops to teammates. A severe knee injury robbed Nichols of the opportunity to play this season. Nichols is a wisecracking, twenty-eight-year-old who's unafraid of speaking his mind, whether speaking to a coach, a teammate, or an official. Well, he's usually unafraid.

With the presidential election six days away, Nichols gets talking about politics, loudly expressing his views on various candidates and issues. At the end of the conversation, he lowers his voice for his final admission.

"I liked Bill Clinton," he says, "but you don't want to say that too loudly on this campus. People won't like that."

They like lollipops, though. Coach Rasmussen wants to know why he doesn't get one. Nichols, a 250-pounder who disdains being called by his birth name, Dustin, obliges, forking one over. It's his last one.

"For a fat guy to give up his last sucker, that's love," he says.

Later in the practice, members of the starting offensive line take a break. Odell stands with Michael Moss, whose touch football injury should finally be healed enough this week to allow him to return to contact football. In addition to battling his ever-present back spasms, Odell is bothered by a big bump on his arm, courtesy of a blow he took while working out as a fullback. Who knew those little guys went through so much?

"Man, I have a new respect for running backs," he says, gently rubbing the wound. "They do take punishment."

Eventually the talk turns to more critical matters, like cartoons from yesteryear, when cartoons were really good. Moss fondly remembers shows like *Flying House* and *Bear Tales*, admissions that bring raised eyebrows from Odell, but also take him back to his own childhood and recollections of his favorite animated shows.

"When I was in kindergarten," he says, "I'd go home every day and watch *G.I. Joe*. Then they came out with *G.I. Joe: The Movie*, and Duke dies. I couldn't believe it."

"That had to be the first *G.I. Joe* casualty ever," Moss replies. "Because no one ever died on *G.I. Joe*. Five hundred guys unloading on each other and nobody dies. You never think about that as a kid."

At the end of practice Bentley tells the team they'll be practicing the next morning at 6:15. A week earlier the team shot down the idea of working out at that time the entire week, but Bentley's insisting on it now, primarily because the team is leaving Ellendale for Minneapolis early the next day.

"Here's the one thing," he says. "The Bible says in Philippians 2:14, 'Do all things without arguing and complaining.' It's about the chain of command. I'm handing it down to you through the chain of command. We're going at 6:15, and if you're late tomorrow, then you tell yourself if you're prepared to play on Friday or not."

Odell shares those thoughts, though for different reasons. Despite his outwardly loose nature during the practice, he's worried that the Lions are going to be taught a lesson against Principia.

Despite the three-year losing streak, despite the current winless campaign, Odell fears some of the Lions are actually overconfident about defeating Principia. They're so certain Trinity won the first meeting between the teams, they have no doubt the dome matchup will show their superiority. Odell's not one of those players. That's a little surprising since he has been attempting all season to help the team fight through what he sees as a defeatist attitude, believing they're beaten even before kickoff. All year he has preached the idea that a superior team can be beaten through technique, through execution. The little things can lead to a big upset. This week, however, he's dealing with the opposite problem. In both cases he believes the team's inexperience is to blame. Guys who haven't played much in the past have been intimidated playing against some of the better teams in the conference—such as Rockford and Northwestern. Now they feel like Principia is not only an equal, but actually inferior to the Lions. Odell thinks the Lions could be in for a rude awakening at the dome, and not just because of the eight a.m. kickoff.

"They beat Crown, and we got beat pretty badly by Crown, but guys don't seem to think about that," he says. "We can't go into a game thinking we're just going to run over them."

For Odell it comes down to respect, whether Trinity's facing a top conference team or a fellow bottom dweller. Respect the good teams, but don't fear them. And respect the less-talented teams—don't overlook them. Do those things and the Lions will be the ones earning the respect.

It's official: Huenefeld and Strong will be in uniform in the dome. The two take their physicals at Aberdeen from a female doctor—"that was sort of different," Strong says—and they both receive passing marks, though Strong just barely. His knees are still in bad shape; really, they probably always will be, a fact he accepts without much thought or outward concern. He also has a heart murmur that doctors will have to check every couple of years. For the two weeks it's needed, though, his body should be OK.

"I really didn't want to do it, just because I didn't want to risk baseball," he says. "But at the same time, deep down inside, being part of a football team is so different, so unique. Once you're part of it, you kind of crave it a little bit more, a little bit more, no matter if you're winning every game or losing every game."

Being part of a team, helping a team. That's really what Strong and Huenefeld's return was about, not personal glory or a desire to take time away from wide receivers or defensive backs. Of course, no one's playing for personal glory at Trinity—the only personal recognition any of the players are really aiming for is the all-conference team. For that they get their names posted on the league Web site. Media coverage consists of the short articles Steve Tvedt submits to the *Dickey County Leader*. No, the possibility of fame doesn't bring any players to the Trinity program. Strong kept in the mix throughout the season due to his coaching duties and SID responsibilities. But being around the team isn't the same as being *on* the team.

OCTOBER 29, 2004

The majesty of playing in the Metrodome is tempered by the cold, wet weather that greets Trinity on a dark Friday morning. Football's not meant to be played this early. Ninety minutes before the 7:45 sunrise, the Lions pull into the dome parking lot, having spent the night at the Hospitality Inn & Suites in nearby Bloomington.

The UMAC's been operating a dome day for five years. To most Minnesotans, the Metrodome is about as popular as April blizzards or Republican presidential candidates. The stadium, which opened in 1982 and houses the Minnesota Vikings and Twins, along with the University of Minnesota football team, is considered well below average as a baseball stadium, though fans are a little more forgiving when outside temperatures are barely breaking thirty-two degrees. The giant inflated bubble covering the structure puffs out like an oversized parachute, taunting baseball purists who long to see an outdoor stadium for the Twins. The dome did play a vital role in two World Series titles for the Twins, championships that likely wouldn't have been won without the stadium's turf quirks, bad lighting, and the sound generated by 55,000 rabid fans confined in an indoor structure. Thanks to those championships, Minnesotans will always have at least a shred of goodwill directed toward the dome.

The facility proves more acceptable as a football joint, providing the Vikings a distinct home-field advantage when the fans are excited and drunk enough to cause the opposition problems. Unfortunately for those fans, the most memorable Vikings game in the Metrodome was probably a loss, in January 1999, when the heavily favored home team lost the NFC Championship to the Atlanta Falcons.

Trinity has no such ambivalence toward the dome. The coaches and players savor the opportunity, as do the entire league's teams. To a man, this game is the highlight of the season for Trinity's players and coaches.

Trinity's last victory came in the Metrodome—a 27–19 triumph over Crown in 2001. The Lions fully expect a similar result this year.

Once suited up, the team huddles in the tunnel leading to the field. Dustin Harper guides the team in a short prayer, concluding with, "Lord, help us get our first win, and help us knock some people on their butts."

Amen.

Big Tom Chaplin, the lone senior, gets the honor of leading the team onto the field.

When the players reach the turf they let out several loud shouts, sounding like ancient gladiators emerging from the bowels of the Roman Coliseum. They'll know in three hours if the dome will be the site of their greatest triumph or just another gridiron sacrifice.

Bentley, meanwhile, watches the drills while bordering on exhaustion. All the Bentley children are sick. Cold, cough, misery. The whole crew was awake in the hotel room until the early morning hours, unsuccessfully trying to get healthy and some sleep. They pretty much failed on both counts. In the hotel room next door, the whooping and crying penetrated the thin walls, limiting the sleep of several players. Fortunately, adrenaline should make up for any lack of rest.

For Vikings games, the Metrodome holds approximately 65,000 fans. But as the 8:00 a.m. kickoff approaches, there are more players on the field than fans in the stands. Roughly fifty fans sit in the blue seats behind the Trinity sideline, all of them corralled in the same section of the Metrodome, save for one man on the opposite side of the field, who looks like a drifter lost in a blue sea.

The small number of fans is inconsequential to the Lions—really, it's not much different than their home games—because it's the venue that matters. The Vikings play here. The Vikings! Daunte Culpepper plays here. Randy Moss plays here (when he feels like it). The NFL's stars play here. The 697th-ranked team in college football shares turf with the pros. Josh McGillvrey, a big Vikings fan, spends the pregame practicing his, well, Lambeau Leap into the stands (he can't help that the hated Green Bay Packers have practically copyrighted a phrase for jumping into the crowd). He also tests the stadium's acoustics.

"I yelled a word I probably shouldn't have," he says, "and it echoed like eight times."

A good portion of the people in the stands are there to watch McGillvrey—his aunt, grandma, and several cousins are all seeing him in a college game for the first time. They'll be seeing a lot of him because McGillvrey will get many snaps at fullback in addition to his full-time duties in the defensive backfield.

The two newest Lions walk to the field together, separate from the rest of the team. Strong puts his pads and jersey on for the first time in a year. But before he could get into a player's mindset and head to the field, he had to tape his teammates. He may have stepped off the sidelines, but he hasn't escaped his season-long duties. Huenefeld is emotionally psyched up as well, looking like he's ready to hammer someone the minute his helmet's strapped on.

Despite the early hour, the dome staff has opened up the concession stands. Not that a hot dog is the most appealing of breakfasts. Still, it's the best choice available—the bun will provide some type of breadlike substance.

The minuscule crowd size doesn't prevent field security from doing its job with the vigor of the Secret Service. A septuagenarian attendant prevents a man toting a hot dog and soda from stepping onto the field, the worker apparently oblivious to the fact that anyone desperate enough to fork over $3.00 for a Dome Dog at 8:00 a.m. *will not* be stymied by half-hearted security efforts.

On the sideline, Pastor Brady is impossibly cheerful as he prepares the team's water jugs, his 4:30 a.m. wakeup call not affecting him at all. Dome day's not just an event for the players and coaches; everyone associated with the team basks under the huge Metrodome lights, enjoying the payoff of a long, hard season.

Matt Hill's enjoying the day, too. The UMAC commissioner, who's also the athletic director at Northwestern, will be at the stadium for the whole day—from Trinity's 8:00 a.m. kickoff, to the 8:00 p.m. game between Martin Luther and Westminster. Five games, a kickoff every three hours. It was pitch dark outside when Trinity pulled into the Metrodome parking lot before 6:30 a.m., and it will be pitch dark outside when that last game finally concludes.

On the field, Hill points up toward the press box area. Several of the Principia assistants are up in the nearby booths, headsets at the ready. Game statistics will be available, Hill says, in the space next to where the Trinity assistants will sit. After noticing the three Lions coaches on the field and none up in the sky, Hill adds, "Well, where they would be."

It's a special occasion for Lee Odell, who turned twenty-three at the stroke of midnight. He's crisp during workouts, eager to hit someone on his birthday. To hear him talk, though, it might as well be his eighty-third birthday.

"I feel old, that stinks," he says. "Twenty-three—that's old. I just got used to the fact I was twenty-two."

It's hard to imagine a better gift for Odell. Here he is, a year after thinking he'd never play football again, suiting up in front of 65,000 seats, if not that many fans. Trinity's counting on Old Man Odell to key the offense—and not as a fill-in fullback. The line has to produce today to give the Lions any hope of staying close.

Earlier in the week Slivoskey said the team needed at least 100 yards rushing. Trinity must keep the ball away from Principia, especially in the dome, where the Panthers' strengths are accentuated. While the teams are similar in roster size, the Panthers have proven their ability to light up the scoreboard, something the Lions have struggled to do.

"Playing on turf, all of a sudden, if you're an offensive football team, it makes you better," he says. "It's the best place in the world for them to play. That's what scares me about them because they're more precise than we are, they're more athletic, and in the dome they'll be even more athletic."

Moments after kickoff, Principia immediately displays some of that athleticism. After forcing Trinity to punt on its first possession,

Principia takes over on its own forty-yard line. Quarterback Kyle Gillum, who was held in check in the teams' first meeting, finishing eleven-for-twenty-eight with two interceptions, finds Owen Jarrette for a thirty-six-yard gain. The game's first crucial moment comes three plays later.

The Lions force Principia into a fourth-and-two play from the sixteen. Gillum gets the call, picking up the first down by no more than six inches, a spot the Trinity coaches take umbrage with.

A few minutes later, Trinity again holds Principia the first three snaps, this time setting up a fourth-and-six play. Trinity's players and coaches are buzzing on the sideline—a stop here could provide the type of momentum and confidence that a winless team craves. Unfortunately for the Lions, the fourth-and-long play turns into a fourth-and-inches play when a defensive lineman jumps offsides on a hard count by Gillum. The Principia quarterback gets the first down and six points when he runs in for a four-yard TD on the next snap.

The heat on the field quickly saps the players. It's hard to imagine what sort of oven the place would be if it had more than a few dozen fans.

The early kickoff time didn't help. Those who ate breakfast are still digesting it. Those who didn't are playing on an empty stomach, having not eaten since the previous night. But it's the heat that's causing the most damage. Pastor Brady and Trinity student Jerry Rush—who's helping out as assistant water boy—do their best, handing water to anyone coming off the field. It doesn't seem to help.

Linebacker Josh Thompson, who's again all over the field, spends several minutes with his head buried in a garbage can along the sideline, heaving in front of the stands. McGillvrey walks off, takes a knee, and breathes deeply. Principia's passing game keeps him running around on defense, and he's platooning in the offensive backfield. "It's tough to go both ways in this place," he says, and his day has just begun.

Despite the score, and the fatigue, the standout safety continues to vex the Panthers. McGillvrey, who had two interceptions back in September, adds another in the dome. Otherwise the Lions are offering little resistance on defense. Six minutes into the second quarter, Gillum hits Ben Stevens for a five-yard touchdown, Principia's third score of the game.

Trailing 19–0, the Lions keep the ball on the ground, not wanting to abandon their game plan this early. Their drive consists of six runs, one twenty-yard gain by McGillvrey—who displays the same tenacity with the ball as he does on the defensive side—and five carries by Norick. The dome's turf makes all the players faster, but Norick's carries have little to do with speed—he's simply running through people. He has back-to-back runs of eight yards, then one for nine, then for five before, finally, breaking up the middle for a fifteen-yard touchdown. It's his first touchdown in a Trinity uniform. He only had to go through seventeen games, a sprained ankle, a concussion, and a neck injury to get it.

Stephen Poyser's two-point conversion brings Trinity within eleven, the surge in confidence obvious on the Lions' sideline. This is what they've been expecting all along.

The Lions actually get too caught up in the moment; the excitement leads to a holdup in getting the kicking team onto the field. The resulting delay of game penalty on the kickoff—"Not something you see very often," says one of the officials—puts the ball back five yards and takes some energy from the Lions. Principia quickly responds to Norick's score, marching sixty-two yards for its fourth TD of the half. The drive concludes with Gillum finding Tucker Savoye for a twenty-four-yard score.

On the ensuing kickoff, Andy Brower breaks a couple of tackles and returns the ball thirty yards, carrying defenders the final few feet. But inches before his knee hits the ground, Principia strips him of the ball. The Panthers recover, skipping off the field with the ball and all the momentum. Brower slaps the turf in frustration. What happens next feels inevitable. Principia runs into the end zone four plays after the fumble, seizing a 32–8 advantage over the stunned Lions.

At halftime the Lions adjourn to their assigned locker room. They might be getting the chance to play on the same field as the Vikings, but the locker room bears a striking similarity to the one back in Ellendale. Small and a bit dingy, the quarters still easily hold the thirty-man squad. The exhausted players feed off bananas, orange juice, Gatorade, and cookies provided by Brady. For some it's the first meal of the day.

The team's subdued, but not despondent, despite the large deficit. Somehow the twenty-four-point margin doesn't seem like too much to overcome, even though the Lions have only scored fifty-three points in eight and a half games. They're moving the ball, especially on the ground. In both meetings between the teams, Trinity's running game has given Principia fits. The Lions' own mistakes are killing them, specifically illegal procedures on offense and offsides on defense. All told the Lions jumped six times in the first thirty minutes. The defense seems to be falling for every hard count Gillum gives while the offense struggles to remember the snap count.

"These are things that can be corrected," Bentley tells them. "Make something happen this half. We are going to win this football game. Do you wanna win this football game? Do you wanna win this football game?"

"Yes!" they shout in unison.

"If they can score thirty-two in a half, then we can score thirty-two in a half," Slivoskey adds. "All we need is the momentum, fellas. Get one score early. You know how the momentum works."

So does Principia. It takes the Panthers two minutes to seize the momentum for good. Gillum connects with Jarrette for a forty-three-yard score four plays into the third quarter.

Gillum is playing like Barthelmess's former pupil, Andre Ware, circa 1989.

McGillvrey stalks off the field. "I'm covering two-thirds of the damn field because they won't throw near me."

The remainder of the second half holds little drama as far as the final outcome. Trinity scores two touchdowns in the fourth quarter, but Principia's first-half eruption and early second-half TD sealed the victory long ago.

One Trinity player does manage to put on a show.

Norick was a high school star back in Chester the last time he experienced a game like this. Whether it's the big-time setting or just the sight of Principia—his previous best games have come against the Panthers—Norick's bordering on the unstoppable.

Throughout the game Norick backs up one of his previous statements—when he gets a defender one-on-one, he usually wins the battle. And thanks to the line's efforts—which plays its best game of the year and probably the best game for a Trinity line in three years—Norick consistently gets those matchups. On several carries he falls only when three or four Panthers are wrapped around him, one with an arm, one with a leg, one with a shoulder.

By the time the game ends 46-22 in Principia's favor, Norick has run for 150 yards, doubling his previous career best mark.

Norick staggers alone up the long tunnel to the locker room. With his head down, helmet in hand, each step looks like it might be the last before he collapses. He finally does crumple, but only after reaching the cramped locker room. Stripped of his game jersey and shoulder pads, he lies on his back as teammates swarm over him with water. A few players fan his torso, trying to cool him down. Trinity summons the trainer on-site, but he won't be needed. Norick's going to be all right. Leaving everything on the dome field left him with nothing back in the locker room.

"The adrenaline just left me, and I was like, 'Aw, crap, I'm going down,'" he says later.

Norick's only regret is that his dad couldn't be in the dome to watch his performance. Shawn Norick is Sannon's biggest fan, but he never saw his son play this year. He thought about driving to North Dakota for the Martin Luther game, but all he would have seen that day was Sannon on the sidelines with an injured neck. Against Principia, he would have seen the player who starred at Chester High School, not the one who spent many games buried under an avalanche of defenders.

"To him I'm the best football player in college," Norick says. "I wish he would have been in the dome, but other than that I'm kind of glad he's not here watching me. But he knows if I get that fifty-yard game, I earned those fifty yards. That makes him just as happy."

Birthday boy Odell's presents didn't include a victory. They did nearly include a touchdown. Odell got his shot at end zone glory in the third quarter. After gaining four yards on his first carry of the game, Trinity called his number from the two-yard line. The play went south from the snap and Snyder's handoff to Odell was awkward. Principia bottled up the Lions' newest offensive threat, forcing Trinity to turn the ball over on downs.

"I saw nothing but goal line," Odell says. "I got it at my knees and in my mind I was thinking, '*Nooooo.*' It was all I could do not to fumble."

While the Lions' running game was thriving, the passing game again struggled. The early thirty-two-point blitz by Principia forced Trinity to throw more than planned. If the game had been close, Norick and Poyser might have been good enough to carry the Lions to the win. Instead the Panthers were able to tee off on Snyder, who threw a pair of touchdowns but finished just nine-for-twenty-nine with a pair of picks. When Snyder stepped in for Dusty Hess in the third game of the season, he found himself in an unenviable position. Not only did he have to take snaps behind an inexperienced offensive line—the majority of Trinity pass plays end with Snyder scrambling, searching for freedom and a receiver—but he had to do it without access to the team's top receiver: Tony Snyder.

It was a bittersweet game for Andy Brower, who caught a fifteen-yard TD pass from Snyder, but lost the fumble on the second-quarter kickoff return. The touchdown, though, was his third of the year, one more than the entire Trinity team had in 2003. Over the last half of the season, he's proven to be one of the more potent receiving threats in the league—when he's able to get the ball. He stopped dropping passes and showed a knack for catching it over the middle, no matter the physical consequences. After a slow start, he now has nineteen catches for more than 300 yards, a sixteen-yard per catch average.

"You don't really catch Andy missing many routes," Slivoskey says. "He really became a go-to guy for us, and he's a great young guy to build on."

For the two newest Lions, the dome game was like 2003 all over again. Huenefeld looked like he had last played twelve days ago, not twelve months. He leads the team with seven tackles. Strong, meanwhile, plays primarily on special teams, the role he envisioned when thinking about his return.

In the Trinity locker room, the coaches take turns speaking while the players slowly shed their sweat-caked uniforms.

"Sannon Norick, unbelievable today," Bentley says as the players applaud the starting fullback, who is finally able to sit up on his own.

More applause follows when Rasmussen singles out Lester Williams, whose inspired play on the offensive line is even more remarkable given his concussion scare from the previous week.

"Guys," Rasmussen says, "you can't expect to just win on Saturdays. You've gotta be disciplined every single day of your life and that's in football and in your home."

"Our job is to make men out of you," Bentley adds. "We get one more chance to get that win this year. It's not over."

Mike Barthelmess, meanwhile, couldn't be happier with the result. This victory doesn't change anything about the first win over Trinity—the lopsided margin of victory doesn't mean Trinity's effort in the first game was a fluke. But after feeling "dirty" following that September victory, this win provides a satisfying finish to a tumultuous season.

"We were pretty dominant, and I'm proud of the guys because I think it shows how much they improved," he says of his twenty-five-man squad.

The lessons Barthelmess taught the previous week also appear to have worked. One of the players suspended for the Westminster game—linebacker Joel Fox—leads the team with eleven tackles, including seven solo stops.

While Trinity still has one game left in the season—the Lions will host Maranatha Baptist in the finale—Principia's ends with a 3–6 mark. Simply surviving the season would have been a victory for the Panthers—winning three games is a testament to Barthelmess and his two dozen players. After a short break, Barthelmess will be back on the recruiting path, doing everything he can to reel in some of those thirty-five recruits.

"The administration's stated that football will be here as long as we have enough players to support it," he says. "We've got great facilities, dynamite equipment, it's just a matter of having enough players and enough players that can play and feel like we can compete. And they're leaving that up to me."

Which means the school should be just fine.

The UMAC's day in the dome will end twelve hours later, though by the time Westminster defeats Martin Luther 35–28 for the overall conference title, Trinity is back in North Dakota. It's an eventful trip home. The team bus, which has faithfully hauled the players to Kansas, Illinois, and the Twin Cities, breaks down in Alexandria, Minnesota, stranding the team for a couple of hours.

Several members of the football team stay back in Minneapolis for the weekend. Bentley and Slivoskey stick around for conference meetings and the Vikings' game against the New York Giants on Sunday, using the tickets Bentley won on eBay the week before. Strong and Huenefeld stay for student life meetings.

All of the Lions leave the dome disappointed in the result—given the last-second loss earlier in the year that proved Trinity could play with Principia. When compared with last year's dome game against the Panthers—a 55–0 loss—46–22 actually shows substantial improvement for the Lions. Basically it proves what many of the players have been saying—the team has improved from 2003, "hands down better," Norick says—but it seems to be getting worse as the 2004 season winds down.

For all of them, though, one week still remains in the season. One more chance to salvage a victory. One more game to survive.

Chapter Fourteen

The End

If Rusty Bentley knew then what he knew now Trinity's season would have ended on the turf of the Metrodome, under the giant lights, with an early-morning loss against Principia. The season would have ended with a loss, yes, but it would have ended with the Lions scoring the most points (twenty-two) in three years, and it would have ended when the players were ready for the season to be over.

But the Lions have one game remaining, a home game against Maranatha Baptist Bible College out of Wisconsin, the final contest in a ten-game season. Ten games. That's the number of games Bentley was used to playing in a season, before taking over at Trinity in 2003. In his first season the Lions only played nine times, and early in the 2003 season, before he had any feel for the college game or his situation, Bentley pushed athletic director Tim Grant to add a tenth game in 2004 to the team's schedule. Ten games. That's how many they have in Texas; that's how many he wanted for his Lions.

"I was stupid for pushing that game," he says, days after the Principia defeat. "I couldn't fathom being done in October with football. I didn't realize that the season peaks with that dome game."

Peaks for the players, peaks for the coaches. The team enjoys its home games, but returning to Bob Tatum Field, near the fields of

North Dakota, one week after playing in the Metrodome is in-
evitably a letdown. No one will take to Trinity's field and "roll
around, giggling like an idiot," like Matt Johanson said he did on
the dome's turf before the game. Now Bentley and the coaches have
to motivate a group of thirty players who invested most of their
emotions in that Principia defeat. Maybe thirty players, that is. Bentley predicted the team could lose up to ten players if the Lions lost
against Principia. All season Bentley has simultaneously pleaded
with and threatened those who don't attend practice. If he had
wanted, Bentley could have used the Metrodome game as bait: Don't
come to practice, and you won't play in the dome. Now that the
dome game has come and gone, he's not sure how many will show
up or what he could even do to get all of the players to attend the
final five practices of a long, long season.

For the players, the letdown's a little—just a little—like that of
NFL players who have to play in the Pro Bowl a week after the Super
Bowl. Players are mostly disinterested and simply want to avoid injury. Of course, the Lions won't receive a check for $30,000 if they
win, and the game will be played in North Dakota in November, instead of Honolulu, Hawaii.

Sannon Norick will definitely be in uniform for Trinity's final
game, provided he can get out of bed and walk to the field. Days after
his valiant 150-yard performance in the Metrodome, Norick struggles to walk, bothered by a sore back and the lingering effects of a
neck injury. He slept until noon over the weekend, resting his aching
torso as much as possible. He refuses to see a doctor about his back
pain, which is concentrated in the middle of his back, figuring it's just
the price he'll pay for the best game of his college career. Besides, "I
don't like doctors. They tell you the obvious, that there's something
wrong with you, and that you shouldn't play."

He'll play. Norick has already survived eighteen games in a Trinity uniform. Eighteen losses, all of which were by at least twenty-four
points, with the exception of the Lions' first meeting against Principia, which they lost by twenty-four inches.

As one of the four captains on the team, Norick is privy to the
frustration felt by the entire squad, feelings that have festered with

each practice, with each defeat. They direct the frustration at Bentley and wonder if there is anything that can be done, even at this stage of the season.

"I like Coach Bentley, he's a great guy off the field," Norick says. "But coaching is a different thing. Love the man, can't stand the coach, which is kind of sad because what happens is the coach kind of takes the brunt of the frustration."

A few players even asked Norick if the team could "pull a *Varsity Blues.*" In that movie, which like *Friday Night Lights* focused on a Texas high school football team (only in more ludicrous ways), the players rebel against the head coach at halftime of a key game. They take to the field by themselves, leaving their leader behind. Good in movies, bad in real life.

"It's come up several times," he says. "It's like, guys, we can't do that. Inside I'm screaming, 'Let's go.' But this is not the time or the place for that. It wouldn't say very much for our college if we're starting a mutiny against the coach."

No, the team will finish the season. And Norick will play. Who knows how many teammates will be there with him? A more important question for the future of the program might be how many players will be there next year?

Only a handful of players say they will play football next year if Bentley returns as coach. Some won't even return to the school (good-bye, $15,000 for each one that doesn't return). They'd love to have Slivoskey take over the head position, but that might be impossible. Andy Brower is one of those players unsure of his playing future. From what Brower has heard, the only guy who has given a definitive answer of *yes* to returning is Lee Odell, "because he loves football so much," Brower says.

Brower discussed the coaching situation with his father, Stan, a devoutly religious man whom Brower says wanted to "make sure it was all Biblical" if the team voiced its complaints about its coach.

"First you go talk to the person that you have strife with because that's the way it's set out in the Bible," Andy Brower says.

Brower asked Brandon Strong and others if they had discussed their concerns with Bentley.

"They're like, 'Yeah, we talked to him. He just doesn't want to change,'" Brower says. "So that was out of the way. Then you say you bring in counsel before him. After that then you take it to somebody in higher authority. He just wanted to make sure that it wasn't unbiblical or behind his back or cheap. At least tell him what he's doing wrong so he can try to fix it."

Bentley knows the players are grumbling. If he doesn't hear it, he senses it. But if players don't come back to the team or the school, he does not see it as an indictment of his efforts.

"We don't just lose kids because they don't like my coaching," he says. "We lose kids because they don't wanna go to a Bible college. Or they don't wanna lose. Or it costs too much money. Or just a non-committed thing."

Slivoskey, on the other hand, hears the grumbling because he's been listening to it nearly all season. He wonders. Is the future of the program in question? He questions whether the program could survive losing a majority of the players and having to recruit nearly an entire new team for next season. Again. He also realizes he would be in the position of having to recruit many of those players, despite his part-time status. Part-time status, full-time stress. He knows the players' grievances run deep, but he also questions whether a bit of time could heal at least some of the wounds.

He sees the potential in the team. Sees it in a small core of talented players whom the Lions could build on. If they stick around, and if talent is added around them. Players like Norick, Brower, Odell, and Josh Thompson. Players with ability, and "good character." If they stick around, Trinity could build.

"There's some kids I look at and think, wow, if we could surround you with a little more coaching, a little more support, a little better care, if we could give you a little bit more, I know you could do so much more with it," he says.

When Slivoskey talks about time healing wounds for the players, he knows the concept firsthand. That might be what would bring him back to Trinity: time. Because at the end of the season, he is emotionally drained, and the nine losses are just a small part of the fatigue.

There's the tension with Bentley. There are the financial considerations that come with being part-time. He's thinking of taking an overnight forklift driving job when the season ends to help pay the bills. But most important, he sees the stress on his wife, Essy, and his two kids. He comes home exhausted, and wonders if it's worth it. Maybe only time can refresh him.

"I wanna be here, but sometimes I don't know that I'll belong here in the future," he says. "I feel like the players are a big reason why I am here because I really like working with these guys."

For many Trinity players, working with Slivoskey has been the only reason they've enjoyed the season.

OCTOBER 31, 2004

Victory in the Metrodome would have been the best birthday present possible for Lee Odell. But the consolation prize wasn't bad, a PlayStation 2, courtesy of Jacqui. Now Lee can enter the twenty-first century of video game technology, meaning he could finally put his old Nintendo game system in storage. He doesn't want to do that, though. Using his eBay account, Odell is close to winning the auction for the Nintendo classic *Contra*, his "all-time favorite game." Odell lost an earlier auction for the game, bowing out when it hit $25, but this one might not be as pricey; his bid of $5.50 is holding strong so far. The Odells have found other cheap treasures on the Web site, including a pair of cleats Lee used in practice. He paid ninety-nine cents for them.

But the PlayStation 2 does give Odell the opportunity to exist in an alternate reality, a world where up is down, left is right, and the Trinity Bible College Lions can be kings of the college football world.

One of his new games, *NCAA Football 2005*, gives players the opportunity to create their own teams. You can create any type of team you want, giving them the strengths and weaknesses you want. Odell plans to make a team of his home-state favorites, Kansas State. But he could also patch together a computer version of the Lions.

"Other guys have done it," he says. "You can make yourself good so maybe I should."

NOVEMBER 1, 2004

Trinity's favorite statue did not escape Halloween unscathed. Pranksters spray-painted red the Lion statue on the football field, defacing some of its face and back. No one knows for sure who did it, but Josh McGillvrey has his suspects: high school kids from town. To McGillvrey, it's just the latest example of the "disrespect" directed toward Trinity's football team by the local high school. McGillvrey heard, through the rumor mill, that a few of Ellendale's high school players had told some Trinity players that the prep kids could take the college team on the field. That idea baffled and angered McGillvrey. The hard-hitting safety knows his team's limitations—his analysis of the team's shortcomings are as pointed and spot on as anyone's—but he's not interested in listening to some high schoolers denigrate the team. Talk blossomed of a possible showdown. It wouldn't involve fisticuffs or anything, but would take place on the field. A football game between Ellendale's high school players and the college players, which might have been the oddest game put together since the guards and inmates clashed in *The Longest Yard*. Not surprisingly, it did not happen. The game might have been impossible to pull off anyway, given insurance concerns and the probability administrators at each institution likely would have stepped in before the teams would get close to kickoff.

But McGillvrey can dream.

"You don't want to hear some cocky little high school kids saying that," he says. "That's just a disgrace, a big slap in the face. They would have had to have a couple of ambulances ready. I'd love to see them tackle Sannon coming up through the middle."

Order, order, order in the classroom. Quiet, please. Bentley's commands finally do bring calm to the classroom, where the players have come for the season's final Monday afternoon film session. The week before, Bentley speculated that only half of the players would be at practices if the Lions lost against Principia. There are many missing, but twenty players do sit in the room. Any unspoken fears Bentley had about barely having enough players to field a team for the finale appear unfounded.

Bentley tells the team about the plans for game day, which will include a "fellowship breakfast," with Trinity's opponent, Maranatha, the morning of the matchup. Veteran Maranatha coach Terry Price suggested the idea to Bentley, resurrecting a meal the schools previously engaged in before battles.

"Are you asking us if we want to do the breakfast?" a player inquires.

"I don't wanna know the guy that's going to be knocking me out," Brower quips.

"We're going to do it regardless if you want to do it," Bentley responds. "A lot of times, I'll give you a vote on something, a lot of times I won't. That's just life."

The coaches won't be around for this film session—Bentley wants to meet with Slivoskey and Rasmussen in his office while the players go through Maranatha tapes. Bentley puts McGillvrey in charge of the remote.

Before exiting, Bentley tells the team, "Guys, you're all tired. You have one more week. Let's get through it. And then we can rest up. I get down and I think, 'How come this isn't happening?' I guarantee you if we follow the Biblical principles, the Lord will get us through."

"We'll be back in fifteen, twenty minutes," Bentley says as the door shuts behind him.

The players watch a previous Maranatha contest, mostly tossing in wisecracks with an occasional comment about the happenings on the screen.

When the tape ends, the players look at the clock; it's nearly 4:00 p.m. Bentley said the coaches would return in fifteen or twenty minutes, but it's been more like thirty-five minutes. Are we supposed to wait, a few wonder. Are the coaches coming back? Were we supposed to just watch the film and then leave? They all have questions, but no one has any answers. Five minutes later, the players reach a consensus: film time is finished, practice is over. One by one they rise from their chairs and walk out of the room. A few exit quickly while others look around a bit and check the door for the coaches' return, like a kid sneaking out of the principal's office. There's no anger, no bitterness in the walkout. Nobody makes any disparaging comments, just curious inquiries about what happened to their coaches. It's not a mutiny—this isn't the walkout some players discussed with Norick. The players really believe practice is over and that it's time to leave. The coaches must have forgotten about us, they figure, or maybe they're just not very concerned with what Bentley intended. All they know is fifteen to twenty minutes came and went with no sign of the coaching staff. The players file out with a bounce in their step, as if they'd just seen a matinee and need to get home in time for dinner.

Two minutes after the first players walked out, the classroom is empty. Practice is over.

Only it wasn't supposed to be. Not five minutes later, the three coaches emerge from their meeting. Imagine their surprise when they walked back into the classroom and found only desks, chairs, and a podium. No sign of human life—not in the room, not in the halls, not outside the administration building.

Several minutes later Bentley, Rasmussen, and Slivoskey are still wandering the campus, searching for their lost team, like a posse on the lookout for the James Gang.

They encounter lineman Kevin Libby, who happens to be walking near the administration building as the coaching trio passes through. Libby, not enjoying any luck this day, gets to be the sole voice providing an explanation for the players' walkout, an action he didn't even know was wrong. When told, no, practice wasn't over and that the team was supposed to wait for the coaches to return, all Libby can really do is shrug his shoulders a few times while sporting a goofy grin, indicating, "Well, sorry." He says the team waited twenty minutes, didn't see any coaches, and just went on its way. No harm intended.

Libby scurries away as the coaches return to Bentley's office, still dumbfounded, wondering if they really just saw what they think they saw. Or didn't see. Even in a season marked by moments just like this one, the film walkout seems to take the coaches by surprise. Sort of.

"I have never seen anything like this," Rasmussen says on the small couch in Bentley's office.

Uneasiness settles in the compact office, punctuated by some heavy sighs. Slivoskey finally breaks the silence in the room.

"I'm not surprised it happened," he says, "because we haven't always been consistent with time. I think it's a natural by-product of that type of situation. Where, if we had more consistency, with our times and our schedules, the kids would take it more to heart, too. They'd honor it more. And a kid would come over here and say, 'Hey, are we done? Anything else?' It's kind of like they follow what we've done. Like a kid following a parent."

Slivoskey's remarks call to mind an observation Odell made previously: "When you play for Trinity, you learn that all times are tentative. The game usually starts on time, but that's about it."

Bentley nods his head as Slivoskey talks, but his opinion differs. "In some ways, I don't completely agree with you," he says.

"Well, it's like you told them," Slivoskey says. "We'll be back in fifteen, twenty minutes. Well, thirty-five, forty minutes go by. There you go."

"I wouldn't have left. They should have watched the second film."

Bentley did not mention a second film, however, only the first one. Maybe he intended to tell them, but the players were under the impression there was only one game tape to watch. Not that it excuses their actions.

Slivoskey says they should have watched the second film, "as long as it was clearly communicated. I'm not sticking up for them. There's more the mentality around here of, 'How can I circumvent the rules?' than 'How do I cooperate with the rules?'"

"That's it," Bentley counters, his voice rising. "More than us just being inconsistent on times. Because we're going to get behind on stuff. We're going to."

"I agree."

"I'm not yelling at you. I'm just saying it out loud. If [VP of Academic Affairs Michael Dusing] said, 'I'm going to be right back,' regardless of consistency, I'm waiting until he comes back. Period."

The two fall quiet, a lull finally broken when Rasmussen asks how the Vikings game was the day before, which Bentley and Slivoskey attended together. It's the proverbial, "Hey, how about that weather?" question, a forced effort designed to turn the attention to something besides the current topic at hand. It works, but a few minutes later,

Bentley returns to the subject of the walkout. Shaking his head, he says, "These guys wanna read menus before they go into restaurants. I'm used to going in and getting a menu. My wife tells me I'm about twenty years behind where I'm supposed to be. Just do what you're told, that's what I learned."

That night Bentley sits in his home, surrounded by children who are having trouble breathing. All four Bentley children remain ill, unable to shake their sicknesses. Rylee and Ty have it the worst; the two youngest kids are both struggling to breathe. Rylee has a history of pneumonia, and Ty is hooked up to a portable breathing apparatus that he enjoys about as much as vegetables. Their dad isn't feeling much better, only his pain is an internal one caused by the day's events. A big bowl of Cap'n Crunch makes him feel a little better, but not much. Sage brings him a soda, but it has ice.

"Icky," he says. Sage rectifies the situation, but as payment she wants Rusty to rub her aching feet while she rests her eight-months-pregnant body on the couch next to him.

Four hours after he walked in and saw an empty room, Bentley struggles to figure out what happened in the film room.

"When I look in a room and nobody's in there, I say to myself: poor leadership. Or they would have stayed. But that can't be necessarily true. Poor leadership would have meant them badmouthing me, making fun of me."

NOVEMBER 2, 2004
Odell is as light as a ballerina following Tuesday's practice, still floating over the news he had been named to the UMAC's North Division all-conference squad as the second-team center. Well, Odell's pretty sure that's him on the UMAC's Web site, though his name is spelled as "Lee O'Dell," which could be a long-lost Irish brother.

"Everybody wants to spell it with an apostrophe or they want to spell it with one l," he says. "They had it wrong for our roster at Trinity. At Independence they misspelled it. When I get a new job and sign all the paperwork they make out a timecard and misspell it. It's been happening my whole life; I guess it'll probably keep happening."

Maybe at his jobs it will. But two or three more appearances on the all-conference squad should guarantee that the UMAC will know all about Lee Odell. That's O-d-e-l-l.

The honor even gets him thinking about a man that he often tries thinking about as little as possible.

"I'm considering writing my dad a letter, telling him about me getting all-conference," he says of his father, Phillip, who has about a year and a half left on his prison sentence. "But it's hard because when he's out I hear nothing from him, and when he goes back in I do."

Odell's not the lone all-conference selection for the Lions. McGillvrey makes the first team. Andy Brower and Josh Thompson join Odell on the second team. Sannon Norick, Dustin Harper, and Matt Johanson are all honorable mention selections. Johanson, in fact, twice receives honorable mention notice: once as an offensive lineman, another as a linebacker, a fine tribute for a two-way player who had never before played on the line and rarely missed a snap, usually ending games in a state of exhaustion. He also didn't begin playing linebacker until the third game of the season, meaning he had only six games to impress the league's coaches.

Slivoskey plans on rewarding Johanson for his season-long efforts. A running back in high school, Johanson has not seen any time in the Trinity backfield. Slivoskey will change that in the final game, when he expects to put Johanson at running back and hand him the ball several times. In his mind, it's the least he can do for those guys who have come to every practice, without complaint, while playing completely out of position. Since the players aren't likely to be rewarded with a victory, why not give them a small moment of glory?

"Guys like Matt, they've sacrificed a lot this season," Slivoskey says. "They deserve to have their moment in the sun."

On a divided team, players and coaches can find one issue they agree on almost across the board: the presidential election. While people across the country contentiously argue about choosing either George W. Bush or John Kerry to lead the country, debate at Trinity seems to focus on a different type of choice: which is the bigger issue to get worked up about, gay marriage or abortion? War in Iraq? Not as important. As in many other states across the country, North Dakotans will vote on a marriage amendment forbidding same-sex marriages. Electing the next president almost seems like a secondary issue for Trinity people eager to hit the polls.

"I vote on two issues," Bentley said in his office the day of the election. "Abortion and, you know, the other one. Homosexual issues."

It's not so concrete for Slivoskey, who watches ABC's Tuesday night election coverage, closely following the early returns, but observing the newscast in a reserved manner. He's not overly concerned with the two issues that will rally many to vote Republican. Although he's an admitted conservative who says he does have some "morality issues" with the question of same-sex marriage, Slivoskey's experiences color his political thoughts, making him less likely to regard politics in general, and the presidential race specifically, as a two-issue race. The fervor of some people on campus leaves him taken aback. To his way of thinking, there are issues out there that are much more pressing than worrying about whom people decide to marry.

"In the grand scheme of things, it just doesn't bother me that much. The fact that ten marines will probably die tomorrow in Iraq causes a lot more stress in my mind and in my life," says the Army veteran. "The fact ten families are going to be without a son or a daddy bothers me a lot more. I'm not saying the other issues don't bother me, but is it something that I just absolutely put at the top of my list. No."

Bush's eventual victory brought joy to current Trinity employees and former ones, most notably the first coach in the football program's history. So did the passage of North Dakota's ban on same-sex marriages. One day after the election, Bob Tatum sat in the living room of the Oxenrider Motel, receiving phone calls from his children, congratulating him on the Republican victory in the White House and various other national races. Locally, many of the candidates Tatum supported, such as U.S. Senate candidate Mike Liffrig, lost. But those results do not lessen his jubilation.

"It's a great day for America," Tatum says, smiling and watching Fox News, moments after viewing Kerry's concession speech. "Praise God."

Bush easily carried North Dakota. In Dickey County he won 67 percent of the vote, compared with 31 percent for Kerry, numbers that did not surprise Bentley. When you see God in every aspect of life, big and small, it seems inevitable that an event as monumental as a presidential election will be viewed in religious terms. And that is how Bentley views the reelection of George Bush.

"The Bible says in Romans, chapter thirteen, verse one, it says all authority is placed by God, period," he says two days after the election. "So yeah, I think God wanted George Bush to be elected."

NOVEMBER 3, 2004
Wednesday night Pastor Brady visits Bentley at his home. Brady's visit has nothing to do with the struggles of the football team, at least not directly. Rylee Bentley has been taken to the hospital with pneumonia. She's been there before with the same affliction. The other Bentley children have been stricken with strep throat and various other illnesses for weeks on end, but Rylee's condition is the most serious.

"Gonna go try and cheer up coach," Brady says as he climbs into his minivan.

Brady stops at Char's grocery store. It's a little after 8:00 p.m. and the store is mostly empty, save for a handful of employees and about five customers. Every one that sees Brady strikes up a conversation with him, or engages in one after Brady says hello. If he had all night he might never get out of the store. But he has a mission.

He grabs some orange soda and root beer, a box of popsicles, and a gallon of ice cream. When he arrives at Bentley's house, the coach invites him inside. Brady tells him he has brought over some goodies that should soothe the kids' throats: popsicles and the necessary ingredients for some killer ice cream floats.

For maybe the first time in three days, Bentley smiles wide. Sage is in Aberdeen with Rylee, and it's a lonely night. Ice cream always makes things better, doesn't it? More important, Brady's visit boosts

Bentley's spirit. Just a bit, but enough. At least for this night. He wonders about his future as head coach. Wonders about his own leadership. Wonders what will happen in the final game of the season.

Before he leaves, Brady says a prayer with Bentley in the kitchen.
Brady prays for the health of Bentley's children, not for a victory on
Saturday. The pastor stays only five minutes, just long enough to
drop off the supplies and say the prayer. After saying good-bye, Bentley leads him out the door and says good night.

He returns to his house. Alone.

NOVEMBER 5, 2004

After the final practice of the season, Bentley gathers the team in a
huddle for the last time.

"I just wanna thank you guys for the hard work you put in this
year. It gets real thin towards the second half of the season when you
start losing, and nobody likes losing. We play to win, but we also
play to have a good testimony. I appreciate your guys' attitudes.
There was times when we all get tired, we all get frustrated, that's just
part of family. That's part of the maturation process. There's a big future here at Trinity Bible College football."

The Lions still have a few tricks in their bag. Well, one. It might not
even be legal, but they're going to give it a shot.

One night before the final game of the season, Strong, Brower,
and Neil Huenefeld congregate in the school gymnasium to work on
a play Slivoskey drew up. It's sort of a variation on the old hidden
ball trick in baseball.

The design: Brower fields the kickoff and runs forward about ten
yards. Strong and Huenefeld will be there waiting for him, ready to
form a wedge and block for Brower, just like always. But this time
there's a twist. While pretending to block, Strong will slyly lift his jersey in the back, just a few inches. When Brower gets up to Strong, he
slides the ball under his teammate's shirt. Brower continues running
with his hands over his stomach, giving the impression to the opponents that he still has the ball. While the kickoff team converges on
Brower—in theory—Strong sprints straight ahead, undetected, the

oblong football lodged under his uniform. By the time anyone realizes what has happened, Strong will be alone in the open field and on his way to a touchdown. Again, in theory. The players hope to maybe use it on the opening kickoff of the game, perhaps provide a jumpstart to a team that could sure use one. Or perhaps they can break it out after Maranatha's first score. Regardless, they want it to come early, when the Lions are still in the game, when their remaining confidence hasn't yet been taken away.

On first explanation, the play sounds rather absurd. And, more problematical, impossible to pull off. Impeccable timing, and a bit of luck, will be required—two elements that have been in short supply for the Lions.

Slivoskey's also in the gym, profusely sweating after playing a game of one-on-one basketball against receiver Kevin Kloefkorn. The offensive coordinator, a decade removed from his playing days, showed he hasn't lost his athletic skills, relying on the wily moves of a veteran to knock off the youngster, 10–5. On the court, Brower takes his position near the wall, pretending to be in position for a kickoff return. Strong, who has slipped into his shoulder pads and game jersey to see if any equipment malfunctions will hinder the stunt, stands in front of him while Slivoskey heaves a football in the air, simulating a kickoff. Brower catches it and sprints forward while Strong jogs slightly ahead. Brower attempts to transfer the ball to Strong, but it falls harmlessly to the ground. They try it again. And again. And again. Improbably, they start to pull it off. Brower seamlessly slides the ball under Strong's shirt in one fluid motion. By the time they've practiced the routine a half dozen times, Strong's receiving the football without looking with the grace and efficiency of Carl Lewis grabbing the baton on the anchor leg of a 400-meter relay. They keep practicing it, and it keeps improving. Maybe it was the late hour—three hours before midnight. Maybe everyone was suffering a bit of delusion at the conclusion of a long season. But each time Brower slipped that ball to Strong, a growing sense of, hey, this thing could actually work in the game, started to overtake the players and Slivoskey. Lombardi's Packers didn't run the power sweep as well as Brower and Strong operate this bit of chicanery. Visions of a surprise touchdown against a shocked Maranatha team dance in their heads.

"If we could score on that, that'd be pretty big," Slivoskey says, with a slight shake of his head in wonderment. "We have to try something. If we play anyone in our league conventionally, we can't win."

But there are more questions than whether Brower and Strong can safely make the pigskin exchange.

"I guess I'd have two questions," Slivoskey says. "Is it legal, and is it ethical?"

Ethical? Here are some ethical dilemmas worth pondering: Should animals be used for laboratory experiments? Should you turn in a shoplifter at a grocery store, a shoplifter you know to be poor and needy? Compared with those types of ethical questions, the players aren't struggling with concerns about a trick play in the final game of the season.

"It's ethical," Strong says almost immediately, with nods of agreement from the other players.

As for the legality of the play? No one knows. No one has a rulebook handy. And there is a good chance the rulebook might not even cover something like this. Norick, who dropped by the gym for a few minutes—his response to seeing the play: a chuckle, and a "Wow"—says it's legal. He saw it used back in Montana. Just to make sure, Slivoskey says he will check with the officials before kickoff. If the men in stripes give the go-ahead, the Lions will be eager to show off their newest play.

Slivoskey, Strong, and Brower rest on the gymnasium floor, reflecting on the season and talking about the final game. Tim Rasmussen pops in a few minutes later and joins them on a chair. He's all for the trick play, "What do we have to lose?" he asks.

Brower and Strong stand up and toss around a football. Each player jogs a few feet while the other hits him with a strike, a harmless game of catch, just like in the backyard. Their game of catch continues for a few minutes, right up until the moment Brower crumples to the ground at the midcourt line of the basketball court. No one speaks for about thirty seconds. This has to be a joke; Brower's just pulling a fast one on everyone, an attempt at levity at the end of the season. He's not making any sounds, just lying in a heap. No one moves, waiting for him to pop up, smile, and say, "Gotcha." Or at least pop up and tell them it's just a harmless twisted ankle.

Instead he lies on his back, his hands up to his face.

"Please get up, Andy," Slivoskey pleads, softly, thirty feet away from the fallen receiver. "Please get up."

Strong and Slivoskey walk over to the freshman, now holding his right ankle. He wasn't joking, and it's not just a harmless twist. The ankle is already swelling, leaving no doubt that Brower just suffered a sprained ankle. It happened while he did nothing but jump a few inches off the ground to haul in a catch, something he's done hundreds, if not thousands of times in his life.

"I should have went to bed an hour ago," he says while on the floor.

Strong retrieves some ice and applies it to the ankle, gently telling Brower, "You're playing tomorrow, Andy."

"We should probably get him back to his room," Slivoskey says.

They help Brower outside to Slivoskey's truck, where the receiver gingerly climbs into the passenger's seat for the one-minute drive over to Kesler Hall.

The pain in his ankle intensifies.

"I feel like I'm going to puke," he says while shutting the truck door. He's probably not the only one.

NOVEMBER 6, 2004

Earlier in the week Bentley professed hope the weather would turn sour on Saturday, that a snowstorm would sock Ellendale and simultaneously sully and even the playing field. Was it really too much to ask for the final game of the season?

Game day arrives sunny and warm, with temperatures near sixty, the kind of day people outside of North Dakota think only hits the state in June, July, or August. Not even Mother Nature will give the Lions a break.

Brower won't play. If the season wasn't ending today, he'd probably be out a couple of more weeks as well. It's a severely sprained right ankle; the pain lingered and got worse throughout the night. As Trinity warms up for its final game of the season, Brower arrives on the sideline, sporting crutches. All he can do is shake his head at the situation and the baffling misfortune that will keep him out of the final game of his freshman campaign.

Of all the injuries Brower suffered this year—starting with the displaced jaw in the Blackburn game, when his mouth literally came unhinged, and continuing with a painful shoulder injury of recent weeks—it seems impossible to believe his season ended on a simple game of catch.

In addition, he won't get to run his trick play. But Slivoskey hasn't run out of tricks to try.

On its second play from scrimmage, Trinity surprises Maranatha with a twenty-five-yard pass from Dusty Hess to Tony Snyder, the first time in seven weeks the two have hooked up for a completion. Only this time Hess threw the ball while operating as a running back, finding his replacement at quarterback for a halfback pass that moves the ball from Trinity's six-yard line to the thirty-one. Hess's broken wrist may have cost him his quarterback job, but his connection to Snyder proved he didn't lose his touch. Slivoskey called the play one snap after giving the ball to Hess on a pitch, a play that set the stage for the toss to Snyder. A night earlier, Slivoskey said the Lions couldn't play Maranatha—or any team in the conference—conventionally and hope to win. Brower's injury might prevent Trinity from breaking out the ball-under-the-shirt routine, but that doesn't mean the Lions won't search for points in some offbeat ways.

Norick and Stephen Poyser followed Snyder's reception with runs of seven and fourteen yards, accounting for another Trinity first down. The momentum ends when Strong drops a pass that would have given Trinity its third first down.

These initial first downs prove to be the final highlights of the game. From the ten-minute mark of the first quarter to the final second of the fourth quarter, the Lions accumulated more penalties for personal fouls and unsportsmanlike conduct than first downs.

Trinity's fifth fifteen-yard penalty of the first half—two face masks, two standard personal fouls, and one unsportsmanlike conduct—sets off Steve Tvedt. The Trinity administrator, so mild-mannered in the office, shoots photos from the sideline for each home game. Now he looks like he would rather just shoot someone. He tells the coaches to get the team under control, adding it's the worst game he's ever seen. By worst he meant the personal fouls, not the score or performance. But that's not how Poyser interpreted the remark, instead believing Tvedt had just called the Lions the worst team he'd seen. Poyser loudly disagrees with Tvedt, who proceeds to engage in a bit of back-and-forth with the starting running back. Finally Tvedt puts his arm around Poyser and tells him the two need to talk in his office the following week.

Following a Maranatha touchdown that made the score 14–0, James Castillo received the kickoff for the Lions. Castillo ran for about ten yards when, shockingly, he shoved the ball up Strong's jersey, just like Brower had practiced doing the evening before. Strong nets another five yards. The execution was stilted and fails to generate the big play the team dreamed about. It was a fun play to see, though. Strong pops up with the ball protruding from his back, looking like a blue-clad turtle. The play barely sends a ripple through the players or fans; it happened so fast and was so unexpected no one even really seemed aware of what had happened. It'll also be the play's final appearance on this playing field. With a smile, an official scolds the Lions, telling them, "Don't do that again." Slivoskey had broached the subject to the officials before the game, but the referee says he didn't think Trinity was talking about that type of play. Hard to know what part of "can we sneak a ball under a player's jersey?" the crew didn't understand, but the Lions shelve the play.

Trinity's final game contained elements of its previous nine losses: too little offense, a powerless defense, and a head injury for Lester Williams. The oft-injured lineman gets knocked senseless for the third time this season and lies face first on the ground. Tim Grant, Slivoskey, Rasmussen, and a member of the Ellendale ambulance crew gather around him. Williams eventually rises and walks off the field on his own power, but his season is finished.

Slivoskey did keep his promise and put Johanson in the backfield, feeding the starting lineman three carries, which the freshman totes for fifteen yards. Johanson savors every one of those fifteen yards, a satisfying reward for a season of sacrifice.

Late in the third quarter McGillvrey is the Lion splayed out on the field in agony, suffering from severe leg cramps. The first-team all-conference safety was popping Crusaders all over the field (maybe he pictured high school kids wearing their uniforms). McGillvrey couldn't have done much more for the Lions this season, in the lone season he'll play for Trinity. But in the end, his efforts couldn't do much to alter the final score of any of the games.

On Trinity's final offensive play of the season, the snap gets away from Snyder. He falls on it, but is sacked for a loss of eighteen yards.

Thirteen seconds later, Trinity's season ends. Maranatha 58, Lions 0.

Slivoskey lingers on the field, grabbing as many players as possible and telling them thanks for hanging in throughout the season. Trinity lost several players through the course of the season, some to injuries, some that just quit the team. He says thanks to those that survived, physically and emotionally.

Following the game, Maranatha coach Terry Price pokes his head into the coaches' office and accepts an invitation to step in. Slivoskey tells him Bentley is in his office, but Price says he wants to talk with Slivoskey. If it's happened on a football field, Price has probably seen it. Price has been a head coach for twenty-eight years. A former youth minister, Price has the paternal look of a sitcom dad from the 1950s. Now he has some words of wisdom for the Trinity coaches. Back in the 1990s, Trinity defeated Maranatha three times in a row, Price reminds them.

He tells them that his first program lost seventeen games in a row, and it took a long time to turn things around.

"You gotta get your kids who are sold on what the education is here," he says. "Because if they're coming for football, they're going to pack up."

Then Price compliments Slivoskey for some of the team's offensive plays, telling him they ran some nice things and have some better athletes than a year ago.

"The numbers have to get up," Slivoskey says. "We have to get away from situations like today. I used five, six different kids at tight end today; none of them had ever played it. Kid played left tackle today had never played in his life."

"Adversity is everywhere, it's our response to it," Bentley says as he peeks out of his office.

Slivoskey continues, "The kids' attitudes, for what they've been through, have been phenomenal. I'm not going to lie to you, the last few games, we've lost a lot of self-discipline. Just getting personal fouls, some kids take, I think, some cheap shots. That's not right, but I guarantee it's out of frustration."

"That's the toughest line you must maintain," Price says. "Because if you lose discipline, you have really lost it."

As he exits, chastising himself for "getting so excited preaching," Price tells the Trinity coaches, "God doesn't want us to be losers. But God wants us to be faithful and set a good example for these kids. So, man, listen, if there's anything I can do to help, please let me know."

"I just appreciate your support," Slivoskey says. "It's going to get turned around."

Ten minutes later Slivoskey walks out of the office.

"Right now I want to get as far away from football as possible," he says. "If there was a plane leaving Ellendale for China tonight, I'd be on it."

Instead he heads to a less exotic, but more comforting locale: home. Home to Essy. Home to Kamryn and Kodie. And away from football. At least for a while.

POSTSEASON

Odell's weekend included three celebrity sightings in, of all places, Aberdeen's Wal-Mart, where apparently you really can get everything. While Jacqui occupied herself by looking at bookshelves, Odell spotted someone he thought looked familiar.

"This guy comes to the end of the aisle, looks one way and walks the other way and I was like, I swear that was Disco Inferno."

Who? Disco Inferno, that's who, a professional wrestler whose career peaked in the 1990s, but is still on the grappling circuit, working small towns like Aberdeen. He wasn't alone. Odell followed Disco through the aisles and saw fellow pro wrestlers Norman Smiley and Lenny Lane, two other ring veterans the Trinity center grew up idolizing. This was big for Odell, who enjoyed watching wrestling as a kid but hadn't watched the, well, sports entertainment in years. Now he was face to face with three of his heroes. In Aberdeen, South Dakota, a town whose most recognizable face is Northern State football coach Ken Heupel, best known as being the dad of former Oklahoma quarterback and national title winner Josh Heupel.

Odell "kind of blurted out a hello" to the three, but "they were acting like they were in a hurry. They were asking a guy about a CD. The guy that was helping them with the CD was like, 'Are you the real Disco?' And he's like, 'Yeah,' like it's no big deal. I was starstruck to say the least."

It's been a pretty good two weeks for Odell: an appearance in the Metrodome, an All-conference selection, PlayStation 2, brush with celebrities. The only negative has been continued pain in his back, courtesy of the spasms that have bothered him throughout the season. Perhaps some rest after the season will help. No more practices, no more games. Odell has found a home. The Odells have found a home. He wishes the team could have won at least one game, though he remains certain the Lions did win in the second week of the season against Principia. Overall, though, Odell says he can't complain about much. Well, other than the bumbling Kansas City Chiefs, who are going to miss the NFL playoffs after a disastrous season. But he definitely can't complain about his own playing situation.

He earned respect from his teammates, coaches, and opponents. He plans on throwing himself into the recruiting process for Trinity, calling as many players as possible. He sees potential for success, but knows it will take time and talent. For now, he's content to look back on his season with pride, appreciative of the opportunity he had to resurrect a career he thought might be finished. He's come a long way from that ejection in his first college game.

"The way I look at it is, I love football, and I thought I'd never get to play again," he says, one day after the end of the season. "But God gave me the chance to play again. I'm getting to do something that I love. How many people wish they could play college football, and don't get to? I'm getting that chance. So I'm not going to whine too much about winning and losing. At least I'm getting a chance to win."

Strong is still kicking himself for dropping a pass on Trinity's first possession against Maranatha, a reception that would have given the team a first down, but would have had as much impact as the coin flip on the final result. He has already watched the film, rewinding it and playing it again, rewinding it and playing it again. A catch there might have extended Trinity's first drive three, four, five more plays, nothing more. Still, Strong sees that pass hitting his hands and dropping to the grass. He chastises himself. The ball-under-the-jersey gag worked a little better at least, picking up about five more yards on the kickoff and fooling everyone on the field, including teammates.

Says Strong, "[Teammate Heston Huwa's] like, 'I didn't even know what was going on. You stand up and there's a football in your back.'"

Strong avoided his dorm after the game, instead crashing at his off-campus apartment.

He slept off three months of stress. Now he's done with football. With playing, with coaching, even, for now, with recruiting. With football out of the way he can look forward to his favorite sport: baseball. Because of the unpredictable weather—unpredictable in that it's impossible to know how long the predictably bad weather will last—preseason baseball in the Upper Midwest lasts forever before teams can actually get outside. Strong remains undeterred, excited to get into the batting cage and get some swings in, even now, more than three months before Trinity's first game.

God, he loves baseball, Strong says. Always has been his favorite sport, always will. But in ten, twenty years the memories he will recall at the snap of a finger will be football memories. He'll remember the scars, and all he'll have to do is look at his knees. He'll remember the losses: eleven as a player, eight as a student assistant. He'll remember the small triumphs, such as being the only member of his high school football team to catch a pass as a college player, "even though, by far, I was definitely not the best player in high school," he says. He won't remember the victories—there weren't any.

He'll remember the struggles—those on the field, and those off the field. He'll remember those, all right, because chances are he'll use the lessons he has learned from those struggles for the rest of his life.

"I'm taking so much away this year," he says. "Sure, I'll pay fifteen grand, but I have an experience that will last forever. Not many high school coaches can say 'I played college football, I played college baseball, I helped coach, I was an SID.' It'd be so easy for me to say that I regret coming here. But in actuality you grow through adverse times. It says in the Bible, God's not going to give us any more than what we can handle. At the time you're going through it, it's like, oh my world, this is the most stressful thing in my life, and you don't know if you can handle it. Once you're past it, you're like, please, I can handle anything."

Bentley feels bad about the way the season ended, with the flurry of unsportsmanlike flags during the Maranatha game.

"This book, *Successful Coaching*, I was looking at it a while ago," he says. "They said when athletes misbehave, they're either frustrated or they think they're better than the coach. And I know it wasn't that they think they're better than the coach."

A week after the film room debacle, and two days after the season-ending flag fest against Maranatha, Bentley says he has gained a sense of calm about his future, no matter what it holds. He says he accepts the fact he may just be a "transitional man" for the college. Accepts the fact he could have coached his last game at Trinity. Accepts the fact he may have to pack up Sage and the kids for yet another move, to another job, in another destination.

"Did I run a program like most colleges?" he asks from his office chair. "No. Did I try to? Within the confines we have, yes. I can look myself in the mirror and say, 'Was it top notch?' Within the realms, it was top notch."

One week into December, the school relieved Bentley of his coaching duties. Trinity invited him to remain on as a teacher. In an e-mail, Michael Dusing, vice president of academic affairs, wrote that due to confidentiality issues, the school could not publicly provide specific reasons for the decision. But he did write that the coaching dismissal had nothing to do with the team's win-loss record, or any questions about "morals and characters," but had to do with a "variety of issues," which, when analyzed, led the administration to decide Trinity needed a new coach for 2005.

Two weeks later, on December 14, Rusty and Sage welcomed the newest addition to their family: a baby girl named Molly.

The search for Bentley's replacement lasted several months. Slivoskey applied for the position. He would have been the players' ideal choice. Though hopeful he'd land the job, he also knew his inexperience and youth would probably work against him. Athletic director Tim Grant was again looking for an older coach, just as he was before he hired Bentley in 2003.

In the end Trinity did go with experience, hiring veteran coach Jim Dotson. Dotson has coached at colleges in Virginia, Tennessee, Kansas, and England. He also spent twenty-three years as a high school head coach, winning a Virginia state championship in 1972. He lives in Florida, but will live in Ellendale during the football season. Dotson will likely only stay with the program for a couple of years, long enough to attempt to stabilize the program. After that, the school indicated Slivoskey would be the heir to the position.

Slivoskey and some others on the team got an early start on recruiting, contacting potential Lions immediately after the season, attempting to help Dotson get a jump on his new challenge.

When Dotson leads the Lions into battle in the 2005 season opener, the team will be looking to snap a thirty-game losing streak, which dates back four years. They'll be coming off two straight seasons that ended with them being ranked as the worst college football team in the country. And they'll take the field each week, believing victory will someday be theirs.

God help 'em.

Epilogue

Trinity Bible College made it back into the national sports headlines in January of 2005. Only this time it had nothing to do with anything that has happened with the football team; it had to do with what will happen with the football team.

USA Today ran a story on the odd challenge the Northwestern football team made for itself. On October 8, 2005, Northwestern will host Trinity Bible College at 1:00 p.m. in St. Paul. But Northwestern's day won't end when the football game against the Lions concludes. Instead the team will hop on a bus and make a five-mile drive across St. Paul, where Northwestern will face the Macalester football team on the Macalester campus.

Two games, one day. *USA Today* quoted Northwestern athletic director Matt Hill (also the UMAC commissioner) as saying, "We are not trying to embarrass any schools. We're just trying to get ten games in."

That may be true, but it was hard to believe Northwestern would have scheduled two games unless the Lions were somehow involved. Trinity will simply be a warm-up act.

"I think that kind of sums up how Trinity football is viewed," noted Eric Slivoskey. "They probably figure to barely break a sweat against us and then travel on down to play their next opponent."

And so it goes.

Through much of the spring, Slivoskey was still uncertain if he would be with the Lions for that game or any others in the 2005 season. He said he felt a "commitment to the players" to return; it all just depended on the teaching situation. Eventually, in April, Trinity hired Slivoskey as a full-time teacher in the physical education department. He'll teach his classes, coach baseball, and be the defensive coordinator for new football coach Jim Dotson. Following the conclusion of the 2004 season, Slivoskey led the team in informal 6:00 a.m. workouts four days a week, working on cardiovascular and agility exercises. He again committed himself to the football recruiting campaign, determined to help Dotson field a team with at least thirty-five players. He also led the Trinity baseball team to six victories. His travels continued, unabated. Over the holidays, the Slivoskeys went to Phoenix—Eric attended the Fiesta Bowl to see the University of Pittsburgh play—and the family trekked through their former stomping grounds in Utah and Montana. In May, the family planned on a three-week vacation through Europe. Eric, Essy, and the two kids will visit England, Germany, Austria, Switzerland, Italy, and the Czech Republic. The world travels won't stop anytime soon. Yet tiny, rural Ellendale, North Dakota, now has a hold on Slivoskey.

"If there wasn't a spiritual reason I was here, I'd probably have been gone long ago," he said. "To be honest, there's probably a million other places I could think of being, a billion different things I could think of doing. But the last eighteen months, I've almost felt like I'm gaining a better understanding as to why I'm supposed to be here. Maybe some of it is just to be here for the situation, for the struggles. Hopefully, by the end of the day I can say I contributed something here, that I had a positive influence on some of these kids."

Rusty Bentley, on the other hand, knew he would not be back on campus. Bentley chose not to return as a teacher for the 2005–2006 school year. Instead Rusty, Sage, and the five kids are moving back to the Fort Worth, Texas, area. Bentley hopes to continue coaching, perhaps at the sub-varsity level or at a middle school.

In the spring doctors told the Bentleys that the family's two youngest children, Ty and Rylee, have chronic asthma. Doctors determined that Rylee never had pneumonia, even on the occasions she was hospitalized.

Bentley hoped to spend the summer relaxing and taking time with his family. No matter where he ends up teaching, however, he's determined to remain on the sideline.

"I'm a coach," he said, adding that he hopes to "grow within a district, maintaining my Christian testimony as a coach, and take a head position with that same district."

Brandon Strong and Lee Odell will both be back at Trinity. Strong will be wearing an extra piece of jewelry on his left hand. He and Samantha Moon were engaged during the spring semester, and the two planned an August wedding. Strong will also be a part of Coach Jim Dotson's staff, helping out as a position coach. Throughout his time at Trinity, Strong has often wondered if he made the right decision in coming to the school and if he should stay at the college. He asked God whether he should stay at Trinity. Never got a verbal answer, just a "feeling inside." Or maybe he did get an answer.

"Had I left, I never would have met Samantha."

Odell, meanwhile, threw himself into off-season workouts, gaining strength and dropping down to 260 pounds. He planned on staying in Ellendale for most of the summer. Already, though, he's looking forward to September.

"I'm more pumped for this next season than I've been for any other season in my life," he said. "I really do, in my heart of hearts, believe this is the year we will end that losing streak."